Freedom to Serve

On the eve of America's entry into World War II, African American leaders pushed for inclusion in the war effort and, after the war, they mounted a concerted effort to integrate the armed services. Harry S. Truman's decision to issue Executive Order 9981 in 1948, which resulted in the integration of the armed forces, was an important event in twentieth century American history.

In *Freedom to Serve*, Jon E. Taylor gives an account of the presidential order as an event that forever changed the U.S. armed forces, and set a political precedent for the burgeoning civil rights movement. Including press releases, newspaper articles, presidential speeches, and biographical sidebars, *Freedom to Serve* introduces students to an under-examined event while illuminating the period in a new way.

For additional documents, images, and resources please visit the *Freedom to Serve* companion website at www.routledge.com/cw/critical moments

Jon E. Taylor is Professor of History at the University of Central Missouri.

Critical Moments in American History

Edited by William Thomas Allison, Georgia Southern University

The Battle of the Greasy Grass/Little Bighorn
Custer's Last Stand in Memory, History, and Popular Culture
Debra Buchholtz

Freedom to Serve
Truman, Civil Rights, and Executive Order 9981
Jon E. Taylor

Freedom to Serve

Truman, Civil Rights, and Executive Order 9981

Jon E. Taylor

Routledge
Taylor & Francis Group
NEW YORK AND LONDON

First published 2013
by Routledge
711 Third Avenue, New York, NY 10017

Simultaneously published in the UK
by Routledge
2 Park Square, Milton Park, Abingdon, Oxon OX14 4RN

Routledge is an imprint of the Taylor & Francis Group, an informa business

Library of Congress Cataloging in Publication Data
Taylor, Jon E., 1968–
Freedom to serve: Truman, civil rights, and Executive Order 9981/ by Jon E. Taylor.
p. cm.
Includes bibliographical references and index.
1. Truman, Harry S., 1884–1972—Political and social views. 2. United States—Armed Forces—African Americans—History—20th century. 3. United States. President's Committee on Equality of Treatment and Opportunity in the Armed Services. Freedom to serve. 4. Segregation—Law and legislation—United States—History—20th century. 5. African American soldiers—History–20th century. 6. African Americans—Segregation—History—20th century. 7. African Americans—Civil rights—History—20th century. 8. Civil rights—United States—History—20th century. I. United States. President's Committee on Civil Rights. To secure these rights. II. Title.
UB418.A47T39 2012
355.3′308996073–dc23 2012011993

ISBN: 978-0-415-89449-4 (hbk)
ISBN: 978-0-415-89448-7 (pbk)
ISBN: 978-0-203-08152-5 (ebk)

Typeset in Bembo and Helvetica Neue
by Florence Production Ltd, Stoodleigh, Devon

SUSTAINABLE FORESTRY INITIATIVE
Certified Sourcing
www.sfiprogram.org
SFI-00555
The SFI label applies to the text stock.

Printed and bound in the United States of America by Walsworth Publishing Company, Marceline, MO.

To all of those who served,
but especially for Rhonda and Braden

Contents

Series Introduction

Welcome to the Routledge *Critical Moments in American History* series. The purpose of this new series is to give students a window into the historian's craft through concise, readable books by leading scholars, who bring together the best scholarship and engaging primary sources to explore a critical moment in the American past. In discovering the principal points of the story in these books, gaining a sense of historiography, following a fresh trail of primary documents, and exploring suggested readings, students can then set out on their own journey, to debate the ideas presented, interpret primary sources, and reach their own conclusions—just like the historian.

A critical moment in history can be a range of things—a pivotal year, the pinnacle of a movement or trend, or an important event such as the passage of a piece of legislation, an election, a court decision, a battle. It can be social, cultural, political, or economic. It can be heroic or tragic. Whatever they are, such moments are by definition "game changers," momentous changes in the pattern of the American fabric, paradigm shifts in the American experience. Many of the critical moments explored in this series are familiar; some less so.

There is no ultimate list of critical moments in American history—any group of students, historians, or other scholars may come up with a different catalog of topics. These differences of view, however, are what make history itself and the study of history so important and so fascinating. Therein can be found the utility of historical inquiry—to explore, to challenge, to understand, and to realize the legacy of the past through its influence of the present. It is the hope of this series to help students realize this intrinsic value of our past and of studying our past.

William Thomas Allison
Georgia Southern University

Figures

Abbreviations

AGCT	Army General Classification Test
CHR	[United Nations] Commission on Human Rights
CIC	Commission on Interracial Cooperation
CORE	Congress of Racial Equality
CRC	Civil Rights Congress
EO 8802	Executive Order that created the Fair Employment Practices Committee
EO 9808	Executive Order that created the President's Committee on Civil Rights
EO 9980	Executive Order that prohibited discrimination in federal employment based on race, color, religion, or national origin
EO 9981	Executive Order that created the Committee on Equality of Treatment and Opportunity in Armed Services (Fahy Committee)
EO 10210	Executive Order related to non-discrimination in defense contracting for the Korean War
FEPC	Fair Employment Practices Committee/Commission
NAACP	National Association for the Advancement of Colored People
NCJC	National Committee for Justice in Columbia
NECAMV	National Emergency Committee Against Mob Violence
NNC	National Negro Congress
NUL	National Urban League
PCCR	President's Committee on Civil Rights
PWA	Public Works Administration
SCHW	Southern Conference for Human Welfare
SNYC	Southern Negro Youth Congress

SPARS	Semper Paratus—Always Ready
SWPL	Southern Women for the Prevention of Lynching
TAAF	Tuskegee Army Air Field
UN	United Nations
WAAC	Women's Army Auxiliary Corps
WAC	Women's Army Corps
WAF	Women in the Airforce
WAFS	Women's Auxiliary Ferrying Squadron
WASP	Women Airforce Service Pilots
WAVES	Women Accepted for Volunteer Emergency Services

Timeline

June 16, 1940	Harry Truman delivers campaign speeches in Sedalia, Missouri, that discuss civil rights.
July 14, 1940	HST addresses the Colored Democratic Convention in Chicago.
June, 1941	A. Philip Randolph organizes march on Washington.
June 25, 1941	FDR agrees to create the FEPC.
August 27, 1942	Creation of the Advisory Committee on Negro Troop Policies (McCloy committee).
February 29, 1944	War Department Pamphlet No 20–6 "Command Of Negro Troops" is released.
October 1944	Army Service Forces Manual M5, "Leadership And The Negro Soldier" is released.
April 12, 1945	Harry Truman becomes president after FDR's death.
October 4, 1945	First meeting of the Gillem Board.
February 1946	United Nations Commission on Civil Rights is established.
February 13, 1946	Isaac Woodard is beaten in South Carolina.
February 24–25, 1946	Mob violence in Columbia, TN.
April 27, 1946	"Utilization of Negro Manpower in the Postwar Army Policy," known as Circular 124 is released.
June 6, 1946	Harry Truman appoints Fred Vinson as Chief Justice of the Supreme Court.
June 6, 1946	National Negro Congress submits petition to U.N.
June 21, 1946	Civil rights address by Attorney General Tom Clark.
July 25, 1946	Lynchings in Monroe, Georgia.
August 6, 1946	Formation of the NECAMV.
September 19, 1946	HST meets with the NECAMV.
September 20, 1946	HST sends Tom Clark a letter instructing him to closely examine the recent lynchings.
September 23, 1946	HST meets with Paul Robeson and the American Crusade to end Lynching.
December 5, 1946	Truman issues EO 9808 that creates the President's Committee on Civil Rights.
December 20, 1946	The President's Advisory Commission on Universal Training met for the first time.
January 15, 1947	First meeting of the PCCR committee.
April 15, 1947	Jackie Robinson makes his debut at Ebbets Field in Brooklyn.

May 29, 1947	The Advisory Commission on Universal Training issues its report: *A Program for National Security.*
June 29, 1947	HST addresses the NAACP on the steps of the Lincoln Memorial.
October 10, 1947	A. Philip Randolph and Grant Reynolds organize the Committee Against Jim Crow in Military Service and Training.
October 23, 1947	NAACP submits *An Appeal to the World* to the U.N.
October 29, 1947	PCCR submits *To Secure These Rights* to HST.
November 19, 1947	Truman advisor Clark Clifford submits a memo about the campaign strategy for 1948 to HST.
November 23, 1947	National Negro Congress merges with the CRC.
December 9, 1947	HST asks Clark Clifford to draft recommendations for a comprehensive civil rights program.
February 2, 1948	HST delivers a special message to Congress on civil rights.
March 13, 1948	Seven of fifteen southern governors reject HST's civil rights program.
June 12, 1948	Women's Armed Services Integration Act becomes law.
June 26, 1948	A. Philip Randolph organized the League for Non-violent Civil Disobedience Against Military Segregation.
July 17, 1948	States' Rights Democrats or Dixiecrats meet in Birmingham, Alabama, and nominate Strom Thurmond for president.
July 22, 1948	Leon Henderson, Chair of Americans for Democratic Action, sends HST a letter urging him to issue an EO to eliminate segregation in the military.
July 26, 1948	HST issues EO 9980 that eliminates discrimination in federal employment.
July 26, 1948	HST issues EO 9981 that eliminates segregation in the U.S. armed forces and establishes a committee to oversee the implementation of the EO (Fahy Committee).
October 29, 1948	HST delivers a campaign speech in Harlem.
November 2, 1948	HST wins the close presidential election.
December 10, 1948	The U.N. General Assembly approves the International Declaration of Human Rights statement.
January 12, 1949	Fahy Committee holds its first meeting.
March 28, 1949	Louis Johnson replaces James Forrestal as Secretary of Defense.
May 11, 1949	Secretary of Defense approves the air force integration plan; rejects the plans of the army and navy.
June 20, 1949	Gordon Gray replaces Kenneth Royall as Secretary of the Army.
June 7, 1949	Secretary of Defense approves navy's plan for integration.
July 27, 1949	Fahy Committee releases interim report.
August 25, 1949	HST appoints Tom Clark to the Supreme Court.
September 15, 1949	HST appoints Sherman Minton to the Supreme Court.
September 30, 1949	Secretary of Defense approves the army's integration plan; however, the Fahy Committee had not seen the plan.
October 6, 1949	HST refers to the army's plan as "Progress Report."
October 15, 1949	HST appoints William Hastie as a judge on the Third Circuit Court of Appeals.
January 14, 1950	Fahy Committee approves the army's revision of Circular 124.

May 22, 1950	President's Committee on the Equality of Treatment and Opportunity in the Military releases its report *Freedom to Serve.*
June 25, 1950	The Korean War begins.
November 1950	CRC submits *We Charge Genocide* to the U.N.
July 13, 1951	Project Clear preliminary report is released.
November 1, 1951	Project Clear final report is released.
March 29, 1952	HST announces he will not seek re-election.
June 13, 1952	HST speaks at Howard University.
October 11, 1952	HST speaks in Harlem.
November 4, 1952	Dwight Eisenhower defeats Adlai Stevenson for the presidency.
October 30, 1954	Army announces that all units were integrated.

Introduction

On July 24, 1998, General Colin Powell traveled to Independence, Missouri, to commemorate the fiftieth anniversary of Harry Truman's decision to integrate the military with Executive Order (EO) 9981. In the speech he reviewed Truman's record on civil rights, but he also placed himself in the story. He recalled that at the time Truman issued the EO he was eleven years old and that he was living in the South Bronx section of New York City. Powell told the audience:

> He knew his country considered him to be different. He knew his country considered him a second-, third-, fourth-, or tenth-class citizen. He knew there were places he could not go, opportunities he could not have. There were dreams he dared not dream.

Powell then described how he entered the military in 1958 after he had served in the Reserve Officers Training Corps (ROTC) at the City College of New York and noted:

> The military was the only institution in all of America—because of Harry Truman—where a young black kid, now twenty-one years old, could dream the dream he dared not think about at age eleven. It was the one place where the only thing that counted was courage, where the color of your guts and the color of your blood was more important than the color of your skin.[1]

Powell also praised the army and the other services for implementing Truman's EO and argued that they too should deserve some credit for making his entry into the military a success. He observed:

> An environment had to be created, an atmosphere that was based on ability, an atmosphere that had been washed clean of discrimination and racism and all of the legal or informal barriers to performance. It was an atmosphere in which the armed services reached out through equal opportunity and affirmative action to find qualified people . . . That is what the armed forces of the United States did.[2]

Understanding the atmosphere in which Harry Truman issued EO 9981 is what this book is about. On February 2, 1948, Harry Truman delivered a special message to Congress on civil rights and asked Congress to pass legislation in ten key areas. This civil rights message was based on a report that the President's Committee on Civil Rights (PCCR) had issued in 1947 called *To Secure These Rights*. While the integration of the military was not one of those ten key areas that Harry Truman discussed in his February message, it was one of the recommendations in *To Secure These Rights* and Truman hoped that he would be able to use his executive authority to push for an integrated military. He delivered the message at a time when racial tension was high and the country seemed to be divided between black and white. It was a binary equation that resonated strongly during this period. The African American population represented 10 percent of the country's population during the 1940s and they had always supported the wars that America found itself fighting in the twentieth century, but they expected that their support for these wars would translate into less discrimination and more rights at home after hostilities ended.

The United States struggled with a number of issues relating to discrimination, civil rights, and human rights challenges. For example, several states in the south used poll taxes to deny African Americans the right to vote. In other places, racial violence was carried out against returning veterans and there was discrimination in public accommodations and also the segregated military. How could the United States seize the moral high ground in the Cold War if the nation's military was segregated? In 1950 the President's Committee on Equality of Treatment and Opportunity issued its final report, *Freedom to Serve*, that outlined how the armed services had complied with Truman's EO 9981 and the Korean War accelerated the implementation of the military's desegregation plan.

As you read this book think about several issues. How do wars focus attention on human rights and civil rights issues? What motivates individuals to act? Does Truman simply integrate the military because he wants to court the political support of African Americans or does he issue the executive order because of international concerns? Furthermore, are there moral reasons why Truman acts or is he just reading the political leaves and acting accordingly? Compare and contrast Truman's civil rights and human rights decisions with those of other presidents like Franklin Roosevelt and Lyndon Johnson. Who was more successful? Why or why not? Think about the issue of human rights and civil rights in international terms. It was clear that at this time the old adage that "What goes on in Vegas stays in Vegas" did not apply to America's quest for civil and human rights during this period. What went on in the United States was closely watched around the globe and there were international implications to the way in which America handled its civil and human rights abuses.

Think about the African American organizations that constantly pushed these issues to the front—don't forget to think about the Southerners and their reaction to these issues. Why did particular groups respond as they did? Also consider the different views black leaders had when they crafted strategies to address civil and human rights issues. How did the Cold War influence the positions they took? While the focus is on race how did human and civil rights issues during this period apply to gender—specifically to women who wanted to serve in the military and also to gays and lesbians who served their country? Did equality of treatment and opportunity apply to them?

Also consider the role of the military. What reasons did military officials give as to why they were reluctant to integrate? What arguments did others make for integration? Think about whether or not those arguments were valid within the context of the Cold War. Consider whether or not integration was inevitable or whether it happened sooner due in part to the efforts of organizations like the National Association for the Advancement of Coloured People (NAACP) or of individuals like A. Philip Randolph, who made sure this issue stayed on the radar screen of Truman administration officials.

Freedom to Serve, issued in 1950 by the President's Committee on Equality of Treatment and Opportunity in the Armed Services, and *To Secure These Rights*, issued by the PCCR in 1947, were two of the most significant documents drafted under the direction of the Executive branch in the twentieth century. As you read the following pages and examine the primary documents, assess how these two documents represented a key turning point in America's quest for civil and human rights during the 1940s and 1950s. Do not forget to analyze the objectives, goals, and recommendations that both documents outlined and to assess whether or not those objectives, goals, and recommendations were achieved within the historical context of the period. Remember that it is entirely possible to say that there were real achievements and also real failures. That is what historians do: argue about the past. You have the opportunity to do the same. Enjoy the ride and enjoy the challenge in crafting your own argument about the significance of this period and these documents to our nation's quest for civil and human rights.

CHAPTER 1

Franklin Roosevelt, African Americans, and the Coming of World War II

It is an irony of our day that three-quarters of a century after the adoption of the Amendment forever outlawing slavery under the American Flag, liberty should be under violent attack. And yet over large areas of the earth the liberties which to us mean happiness and the right to live peaceful and contented lives are challenged by brute force—a force which would return the human family to that state of slavery from which emancipation came through the Thirteenth Amendment.

President Franklin Roosevelt's comments on the seventy-fifth anniversary of the ratification of the Thirteenth Amendment, October 6, 1940

When Franklin D. Roosevelt became president on March 4, 1933, the country was in the throes of the Great Depression. African Americans, the nation's largest minority population, made up about 10 percent of the population. Over half of all African Americans who lived in the United States in 1930 lived in the South, while more than two million lived outside of the South.[1] By the end of the 1930s over 400,000 African Americans had left the South for northern cities where they hoped to find better jobs and less discrimination.

Surprisingly, African Americans in 1932 supported Herbert Hoover, despite the fact that Hoover had disbanded the black Tenth Cavalry and his refusal to be photographed with African American leaders. Franklin Roosevelt did little to appeal to African Americans in the campaign. He even refused to answer a questionnaire that the NAACP had sent to him to collect his views on issues important to them. Historian Harvard Sitkoff noted: "Although black unemployment hovered around 50 percent, over two-thirds of those Afro-Americans voting went Republican, an even higher proportion than had voted for Hoover in 1928."[2]

Politically, Roosevelt was in a tough situation to move on civil rights. He wanted Congress to pass relief and reform measures to help the country get through the Great Depression and that legislation had to have the backing of the Southern Democrats. Roosevelt knew if he pushed hard on civil rights he could alienate the Southern votes he needed to get his relief and reform measures through Congress. However, this did not stop Roosevelt from changing the Democratic tone on racial and civil rights issues.

During his presidency Roosevelt allowed himself to be photographed with African American leaders and he did openly accept African American delegations to the White House. He spoke out against lynching even though he did not support an anti-lynching law. Early in his first term, Roosevelt consented to the creation of a Black Cabinet. By 1936 this group, which was comprised of African Americans who had taken positions in Roosevelt's cabinet and New Deal agencies as well as representatives from the Urban League and NAACP, referred to themselves as the Federal Council on Negro Affairs. They usually met at the home of Mary McLeod Bethune. Bethune founded the Colored Women's Clubs and in 1934 she was appointed to the advisory Committee of the National Youth Administration by New Dealer Harry Hopkins. Sitkoff concluded: "Never before had civil rights organizations had so inside a view of a national administration. Never before had black government employees had such outside leverage at their disposal."[3]

Even though Franklin Roosevelt was slow to act on civil rights issues, his wife, Eleanor, was not. Harvard Sitkoff argued that Eleanor Roosevelt showed interest in civil rights issues for African Americans in three ways. First, she served as the "unofficial ombudsman" for African Americans. Second, she could influence her husband and the advisors that surrounded him to draft New Deal programs and policies that would be inclusive of African Americans. Finally, she did not hesitate to associate with predominately African American organizations and attend their public meetings.[4]

After the 1936 election she moved beyond just being an advocate for civil rights issues and called for laws that would abolish the poll tax and lynching. More importantly, as the New Deal created a number of new federal agencies, she encouraged the heads of those agencies to be inclusive of African Americans and many heeded her request. She encouraged Harold Ickes, Roosevelt's Secretary of the Interior, who had been the former President of the Chicago chapter of the NAACP, to include blacks in the projects his federal agency oversaw. Under the Public Works Administration (PWA) African American residents occupied one-third of the housing units constructed by the PWA.[5]

The 1936 presidential election was a turning point in the Democratic push to capture the growing black vote in the northern cities, which was a product of at least two to three decades of African American migration from the South to the North. Most African Americans in the South were prohibited from voting by a combination of literacy tests, poll taxes, and voter intimidation. However, when they came north, their votes became politically important because the southern devices used against them were not utilized in the north to restrict their votes and the Democrats and the Democratic machine leaders in the northern cities wanted to capture their votes.

At the Democratic convention of 1936 the Democrats seated thirty black delegates, which had never happened before, and this action demonstrated the party's commitment to African Americans. Roosevelt selected an African American minister to deliver the invocation which prompted Senator Ellison "Cotton Ed" Smith from South Carolina to walk out of the convention proclaiming: "By God, he's as black as melted midnight! Get outa my way. This mongrel meeting ain't no place for a white man!" The New Deal commitment to African Americans in 1936 paid off because a Gallup poll determined that 76 percent of African Americans in the North supported Roosevelt.[6]

Sitkoff noted that it was difficult to determine just exactly what prompted many African Americans to switch their party allegiance from predominately Republican in 1932 to predominately Democrat in 1936. However, he did argue that African Americans were given jobs in New Deal programs like the Civilian Conservation Corps and in the National Youth Administration, but he also noted that the Democratic Party had actively incorporated African Americans into its political apparatus by creating a Negro Division that was very active in the campaign. He also argued that throughout 1936 African American leaders focused on civil rights issues and argued that the creation of the Black Cabinet and the fact that many of Roosevelt's advisors, like Harold Ickes, supported civil rights were also reasons why African Americans supported the Democrats and Roosevelt in significant numbers in the election.[7]

While African Americans were emerging as a new constituency of the Democratic Party for the first time, the organizations that supported African Americans pushed the Roosevelt administration and Eleanor Roosevelt on civil rights issues. Some of the most prominent civil rights organizations active in the 1930s included the NAACP, the National Urban League (NUL), the National Negro Congress (NNC), the Southern

Figure 1.1 W. E. B. Du Bois: founding member of the National Association for the Advancement of Colored People. Cornelius M. Battey, photographer, LC-USZ62-16767, Library of Congress.

Conference for Human Welfare (SCHW), the Southern Women for the Prevention of Lynching (SWPL), and the Commission on Interracial Cooperation (CIC).

The NAACP was formed in 1909 by both blacks and whites that wanted to address America's challenging race relations. One of its founding members was W. E. B. Du Bois, who continued to serve the organization until his resignation in June 1934. Early on, the organization worked with the black press to expose the problem of lynching. By the 1930s W. E. B. Du Bois was still with the organization and worked with Walter White, who became the executive secretary in March of 1931; however, in 1932 the organization shifted its focus from exposing lynching to attacking segregation, especially segregation in education. One of the key individuals who assisted the NAACP in this effort was Charles Hamilton Houston.[8]

Walter White hoped that the NAACP's successful legal challenges to segregation would serve as a recruiting tool for increased membership. One of the first attempts to challenge segregated educational facilities occurred at the University of North Carolina. The University barred African Americans from attending their professional schools—training that was open to whites only. However, there were no equivalent professional schools for African Americans. The NAACP lawyers found an African American student, Thomas Hocutt, who applied to the School of Pharmacy; however, his application was denied. The NAACP sued arguing

Charles Hamilton Houston

Houston was born in 1895 in Washington, D.C. He attended the Dunbar High School in D.C., which was the most important high school for African Americans in the country, and in 1915 he graduated Phi Beta Kappa from Amherst College. On the eve of America's entry into World War I, he advocated the establishment of a training camp for black officers when he served as an instructor in English at Howard University. He became an officer in the army and his experiences greatly influenced his pursuit of legal equality.[9]

Houston served as a judge advocate in the army and he observed firsthand the inequality African Americans faced before the military's legal system. Houston described the situation: "I made up my mind . . . that if luck was with me and I got through this war I would study law and use my time fighting for men who could not strike back."[10] After the war Houston enrolled in the Harvard Law School and he graduated among the top of his class and in 1924 he began teaching at Howard University Law School. He became vice-dean of the law school in 1929 and he began supplying lawyers to the NAACP in the 1930s that would oversee the implementation of the legal challenge to segregation.[11] In 1934 he became a part-time special counsel for the NAACP. He left the NAACP in 1938 and returned to his private practice in Washington D.C. where he continued to work on civil rights cases. He died in 1950.[12]

that the state had to provide the training. The judge ruled against Hocutt, but the North Carolina state legislature did introduce a bill that would provide funding for qualified African American students admitted to professional schools. However, the students had to receive the training out of state.[13]

While the NAACP focused on challenging legal segregation during the 1930s, they also focused on making sure African Americans would not be left out of Franklin Roosevelt's New Deal programs and also revived their efforts to push for a federal anti-lynching bill. White reprised his role as the chief investigator of lynchings during this period. Prior to becoming executive secretary, one of his most significant contributions to the NAACP was the investigative work he had completed on lynchings throughout the United States.

The NAACP's Legal Committee drafted an anti-lynching bill and White convinced Senator Edward Costigan from Colorado and Senator Robert Wagner from New York to introduce the bill at the beginning of the 1933 legislative session. The bill essentially stated that the federal government "would prosecute local and state officials who participated in a lynching or proved negligent in preventing one."[14]

While the NAACP focused its efforts on addressing segregation in education and on lobbying for the passage of an anti-lynching bill, they did not focus their efforts on trying to address the problems of economic discrimination. Early in its history, the NAACP allowed the NUL to focus on economic matters. The League, founded in 1910 with support from Booker T. Washington, had as its original mission the task of helping southern blacks who migrated out of the South find work in the industrial cities of the North. During the 1930s the organization lobbied the Roosevelt administration for inclusion of African Americans in New Deal programs and cooperated with the NAACP on several initiatives in the 1940s.[15] In the mid-1930s it associated itself with a new organization, the National Negro Congress (NNC).[16]

By February of 1936 a group of African American leaders, which included members of the NAACP like Charles Houston, Ralph Bunche, and A. Philip Randolph, decided that a new organization might better advocate for African American labor and economic issues. These men met and formed the NNC. Up until this point both the NAACP and the NUL had relied upon the support of white and black middle and upper class patrons and the NNC hoped that it would be an organization that would appeal to working class African Americans and include their concerns in a broader coalition of African Americans fighting for economic justice. [17]

The founding of the NNC concerned Walter White because he thought it might draw members away from the NAACP and he rejected a plan by Roy Wilkins, from the NAACP, to allow the NNC to affiliate with the NAACP. For the most part, in the early 1930s the NNC remained an organization that was strongest in the North while the NAACP had chapters spread all over the United States. However, by the mid-1930s, communists, who had also been prominent in the founding of the organization, decided to try to expand the organization in the South. In 1937 the communists in the NNC established the Southern Negro Youth Congress (SNYC). The SNYC supported an anti-lynching law and anti-poll tax legislation, much like the NAACP, and, according to one historian, the SNYC "stirred the NAACP to greater militancy."[18]

In addition to the SNYC in the South, another southern civil rights organization, the SCHW was formed in Birmingham, Alabama, in November of 1938. The black and white individuals who gathered at the meeting did so to discuss a report that had been compiled on the economic conditions of the South. The *Report on the Economic Conditions of the South*, drafted with considerable support from the Roosevelt administration, essentially argued that the South was the country's number one economic problem. Notable attendees included Eleanor Roosevelt and Mary McLeod Bethune. The organization had, by 1939, launched a campaign to eliminate the poll tax and supported voting rights for African Americans.[19]

While African Americans had fought for civil rights through the efforts of the NAACP, the NNC, the SNYC, and the SCHW during the 1930s, the Roosevelt administration continued to work for these issues during Roosevelt's second presidential term.[20] In 1938 Roosevelt's attorney general, Frank Murphy, created the civil rights section of the Justice Department. Roosevelt courted much favor with African Americans when he appointed William Hastie, who had previously served in the NAACP, as the first black federal judge.[21] Also, in 1938, President Roosevelt announced that he wanted to see an end to the poll tax. The SCHW had drafted an anti-poll tax bill and it was introduced by Representative Geyer in 1939; however, it faced significant opposition from southern Congressional delegations because if the poll tax was repealed it could possibly mean that poor blacks and poor whites might be able to register and vote and displace the white Democratic elite from political power.[22]

By the end of the 1930s the NAACP legal initiative had scored one important victory for education in the *Gaines* case, which was argued before the Supreme Court. Lloyd Gaines, an African American, attempted to

Mary McCleod Bethune

Bethune was born in 1875 in South Carolina. She was the fifteenth of seventeen children born to her parents, who were former slaves. She founded Daytona Educational and Industrial School for Negro Girls in 1904 in Florida and the school later merged in 1923 with the Cookman Institute of Jacksonville, Florida, and eventually developed into Bethune-Cookman College. Bethune served as president of the university on two separate occasions.

While her focus was on education for African Americans, she played a prominent role in the quest for civil rights during this period. She became active in the Florida Federation of Colored Women's Clubs and served as the organization's president from 1917 to 1925 and from 1924 to 1928 she served as president of the National Association of Colored Women. In 1935 she founded the National Council of Negro Women (NCNW) and directed that organization until 1949. Under her leadership the NCNW fought to eliminate the poll tax, lynching, and segregation in the military. During Roosevelt's presidency she directed the National Youth Administration's Division of Negro Affairs from 1935 to 1943 and organized the Black Cabinet. Under President Truman, Bethune served as a member of the NAACP delegation that served as consultants to the U.S. delegation that drafted the United harter. She died in 1955.[23]

enroll in the University of Missouri Law School at Columbia. His application was rejected based on his race and Gaines declined to accept an out-of-state tuition grant that would have allowed him the opportunity to obtain his law degree. The state of Missouri did not have a law that specifically stated that blacks were prohibited from entering the Law School. Gaines took his case to the Missouri courts with the support of the NAACP and Charles Houston.

Charles Houston borrowed some of the arguments he made in the unsuccessful Hocutt case in North Carolina and argued that the Law School needed "to either admit Gaines or provide equal facilities within the state." The Missouri courts rejected this and Houston appealed the decision all the way to the United States Supreme Court. When Houston rose to speak, Justice James McReynolds, from Kentucky, turned his chair around and refused to face Houston directly. Houston argued before the court that the University admitted other minorities, but yet for some reason denied African Americans admission. Houston argued that the University was not providing its African American students with equal protection before the law, a violation of the Fourteenth Amendment. In a 6–2 decision the court agreed with Houston's argument and ruled that the state must provide a substantially equivalent law school if they did not allow Gaines to enter at Columbia and, as a result, the state of Missouri provided a Law program at Lincoln University, which was the state's traditionally African American university.[24]

By 1939 the winds of war were swirling in Europe and the war would force the civil rights organizations and President Roosevelt to renegotiate and reconsider civil rights within this context. The United States was preparing to wage a war against the fascist regimes of Germany and Italy and yet African Americans in the United States faced a reign of terror in the form of Jim Crow that had gripped them since the days of Reconstruction. Three of the most significant issues African Americans worked on included secure voting rights in the South, fighting discrimination in war industry, and finally, ending segregation in the nation's armed services.

Individuals of African descent have always served in the nation's military, usually in times of crisis and when there were critical manpower shortages. During the American Revolution about 5,000 free blacks and enslaved blacks, which represented about 2.5 percent of the forces, served. In the War of 1812 African Americans served as they did in the American Civil War because manpower shortages made their enlistment a necessity. In 1862 Congress authorized President Lincoln to enlist blacks and the First Kansas Colored Volunteers was organized a few months later; by the end of the war 186,000 blacks served in the Union army in infantry, artillery, and cavalry units. The troops were commanded by white officers and placed in segregated units, making segregation the hallmark of the army's approach to the use of black troops. It has been estimated that approximately 30,000 blacks served in an integrated Union Navy.

After the Civil War, in 1869, Congress reconfigured the army and created four black units: the Ninth and Tenth Cavalry and the Twenty-Fourth and Twenty-Fifth Infantry. Most of these black soldiers were stationed in the West as detachments to the various U.S. outposts and they interacted with Americans who came to settle the west as well as Native Americans, who were already in the West. These soldiers came to be known as the "buffalo soldiers" because to Native Americans their hair was similar to the hair of the buffalo that roamed the Great Plains.

> Native Americans were not granted citizenship until 1924, and under Franklin Roosevelt's Indian Reorganization Act of 1934 the federal government terminated its policy of forced assimilation and allowed for the development of tribal governments. By 1940 the Native American population numbered 333,969, and during World War II, 24,521 Native Americans served their country.

When the Spanish American War broke out, 3,339 black regulars were joined by 10,000 black volunteers in the army, which tripled the size of the African American fighting force in that war. The Ninth and Tenth Cavalry units fought in San Juan alongside Theodore Roosevelt's Rough Riders. African Americans continued to serve in the navy during the Spanish American War; however, after the conclusion of the war, the navy implemented a policy of segregation for the first time. Also, in 1908 Congress authorized the creation of a battalion of Puerto Rican troops because the U.S. acquired Puerto Rico in the aftermath of the Spanish American war and it became a part of the regular army and in 1920 it became the Sixty-Fifth infantry.

> In February 1901 Congress allowed Filipino scouts to serve in the regular army and in 1908 Congress authorized West Point to admit one Filipino a year to West Point. When Japan invaded the Philippines in 1941, 8,000 scouts died and the scouts remained an important ally of the United States during the war. When the U.S. granted the Philippines its independence in 1946, it also granted citizenship to 5,000 Filipino soldiers and sailors.

World War I was a watershed moment for African American enlistment in the army and 368,000 African Americans were drafted to serve in the army, which represented 13.08 percent of all draftees in World War I—eventually 404,000 African Americans served their country in World War I. In contrast, the navy, which had developed a sophisticated fleet that began to rival the navies of Europe after the turn of the century, made sure that African Americans would no longer serve in large numbers as they had during the American Civil War and the Spanish American War. In fact, by the end of World War I, African Americans only made up 2 percent of those serving in the navy and by 1932 there were only 441 blacks serving in the navy.[25]

African Americans hoped their military service and support for America's war efforts would bring them dividends back home in the form of increased equality and a decrease in discrimination. That was certainly the hope African Americans had for their service in World War I; however, those hopes were dashed when Jim Crow continued after the war and on the eve of World War II the African American press was determined that if another war broke out they were not going to have their support go unrewarded again. They wanted some fundamental changes. The *Chicago Defender* asked: "What democracy have we enjoyed since the last World War? Are our people not segregated? Are they not Jim-Crowed and lynched? Are their civil and constitutional rights respected?" The Pittsburgh *Courier* observed: "Our war is not against Hitler in Europe, but against Hitler in America."[26] The challenges were great and the stakes were high; however, the lead up to the war created enough space for African Americans to effectively mount a campaign to have some of these issues addressed.

> As the winds of war blew in Europe, the U.S. Congress, during the last six months of 1940, authorized the spending of $10.5 billion for national defense, which was a figure that was greater than the budgets drafted during the Great Depression years.

CHAPTER 2

Politics and the Quest for an Integrated Military, 1937—1945

"Holy Mother! First the dogs! Then the niggers! Now the women!"[1]
Marine Drill Instructor for the U.S. Marine Corps Women's Reserve

The War Department began thinking about how it would incorporate and manage black troops if the United States were to enter World War II. The War Department drafted some of its first thoughts on the utilization of black manpower as early as 1937. The plan the War Department drafted tried to avoid some of the mistakes made in World War I. One of the mistakes was that the World War I draft created a racially unbalanced army. War Department officials decided to correct that when they established a goal to have an army that was 9 percent African American, which reflected the overall percentage of the African American population in the United States at that time. In 1937 there were approximately 360,000 regular army and national guard forces available. Of those numbers, only 6,500 were black. The War Department officials also planned to have more officers assigned to black combat units because there was a belief that they would need more training and closer supervision. By 1940 the War Department had a policy in place that reflected the points made above but also stated that blacks "would be utilized in both arms and services and in all types of units for which they could qualify," they "would be utilized in units with all-Negro enlisted personnel," that officers for black units could either be black or white, and that blacks would receive the same training, quartering, clothing, and leadership as white troops.[2]

In the 1940 presidential election the issue of civil rights came to the forefront again. The Republicans adopted a strong civil rights plank in their platform and unequivocally supported a federal anti-lynching bill and other measures that would secure voting rights for African Americans. They also supported the elimination of discrimination in the civil service and in the armed services. Walter White pushed the Democrats to adopt some of the same measures, but the southern Democrats opposed a civil rights plank; however, the push from the Republicans and White forced the Democrats to mention for the first time the word "Negro" in the party platform. This was not good enough for two of the nation's largest African American newspapers, the *Courier* and the *Afro-American*, who endorsed the Republican candidate for president, Wendell Wilkie. Wilkie openly supported a federal anti-lynching bill and he talked about ending discrimination in the armed forces.[3]

At this point, Franklin Roosevelt's political back was against the wall. In September he instructed the War Department to address segregation in the military when he stated that the policy of the War Department would be that "colored men will have equal opportunity with white men in all departments of the Army." The War Department agreed to allow its ranks to be 10 percent African American, which reflected the overall percentage of African Americans in the American population in 1940. On September 16, 1940, Congress approved the Selective Service Act, which included two antidiscrimination clauses. According to Phillip McGuire, the first clause stated that all men between the ages of 18 and 36 were eligible to volunteer to serve in all the branches of the military. The second clause stated that individuals who volunteered would not be discriminated against because of their race or color. However, the War Department had the final say on who could serve or not.[4] A week later, the Roosevelt administration announced that African Americans would be eligible to join the Air Corps at Tuskegee. Also in September, Walter White, A. Philip Randolph, and T. Arnold Hill, who was acting head of the Urban League, met with the President and demanded the desegregation of the armed forces. The Secretary of the Navy and the Assistant Secretary of War rejected this demand. Both Secretaries argued that allowing the integration of the military would weaken morale and fighting effectiveness.[5]

Roosevelt told the three men that he would continue to look at the issue; however, out of the blue and unbeknown to the three, on October 8 Roosevelt released a policy statement that was essentially the policy the War Department had outlined in 1937. However, the last stipulation—stipulation seven—proved to be the most troubling for African American leaders. It read:

> The policy of the War Department is not to intermingle colored and white enlisted personnel in the same regimental

> organizations. This policy has been proven satisfactory over a long period of years, and to make changes now would produce situations destructive to morale and detrimental to the preparation of national defense. For similar reasons the department does not contemplate assigning colored reserve officers other than those of the Medical Corps and chaplains to existing Negro combat units of the Regular Army. These regular units are going concerns, accustomed through many years to the present system. Their morale is splendid, their rate of re-enlistment is exceptionally high, and their field training is well advanced. It is the opinion of the War Department that no experiments should be tried with the organizational set-up of these units at this critical time.[6]

The statement also said that White, Randolph, and Hill had agreed with this. Nothing was further from the truth—all three had not agreed with the statement and its release infuriated them and they shared their disdain widely with the African American press when they released a statement which read: "We are inexpressibly shocked that a President of the United States at a time of national peril should surrender so completely to enemies of democracy who would destroy national unity by advocating segregation. Official approval by the Commander-in-Chief of the army and navy is a stab in the back of democracy."[7]

With the election only days away, Roosevelt moved quickly to try to court the support of African American leaders. The President apologized to White, Randolph, and Hill by letter for the confusion the statement caused. He then directed government agencies to include African Americans in training and employment programs. He ordered the War Department to remind the public that the department had agreed to create African American combat and aviation units. Days before the November election he promoted Benjamin O. Davis, an African American solider, to the rank of Brigadier General, which was the highest rank ever held by an African American. William Hastie became the Civilian Aide to the Secretary of War and Campbell O. Johnson was appointed to serve as Negro Adviser to the Director of Selective Service. Walter White dashed off a quick letter to the President which read: "We have worked night and day during recent weeks to take personally to the people the things you did and wrote, [and] I am certain tomorrow will reveal that Negroes know the truth."[8]

Roosevelt's last minute appeal apparently worked. Despite the Republican attempt to wrest the African American vote back into the Republican column, the Democrats captured 67 percent of the black vote.[9]

In the aftermath of the election, African American organizations continued to push the Roosevelt administration on the issues of discrimination in war industry, securing voting rights, and the quest to integrate the military. By the end of the war the NAACP began to couch some of these issues within an international context that would carry over into the creation of the United Nations.

The NAACP and other African American leaders who were affiliated with the organization, like A. Philip Randolph, President of the Brotherhood of Sleeping Car Porters, were very concerned that blacks would be discriminated against in the war industry. In the fall of 1940 Walter White

A. Philip Randolph

A. Philip Randolph was born in 1889 in Crescent City, Florida, and was educated at the Cookman Institute in Jacksonville, where he graduated in 1907. Jim Crow limited his employment opportunities so, like many other African Americans, he migrated north and found himself in New York City. There he married and through his wife met Chandler Owen, and together they studied Marxism and formed their own black socialist intellectual group. The duo became active in labor issues and launched their own labor paper, *The Messenger.* During the 1920s Randolph's views softened and the paper increasingly came to be associated with the Brotherhood of Sleeping Car Porters (BSCP), a union he founded to help African American porters and maids gain better working terms and conditions in their employment.

In 1935, after the passage of the Wagner National Labor Relations Act, the BSCP became affiliated with the American Federation of Labor. Randolph is best known for organizing a march on Washington in 1941 to call attention to racial discrimination in the war industry. President Roosevelt responded by issuing Executive Order 8802 that banned discrimination in defense contracting and established the Fair Employment Practices Commission to investigate claims of racial discrimination. However, Randolph continued to work on civil rights issues during Truman's administration when in 1947 he created the Committee Against Jim Crow in Military Service and in 1948 when he established the League for Non-Violent Civil Disobedience against Military Segregation.

Randolph stood at the forefront of labor and civil rights issues well into the 1960s and 1970s. In 1960 he organized the Negro American Labor Council (NALC) which was his attempt to create one union that would embrace all black workers. He also planned, through the NALC, the famous 1963 March on Washington where Martin Luther King delivered his "I Have a Dream" speech. Unlike so many from his generation, he lived to not only see the passage of the Civil Rights Act of 1964 and the Voting Rights Act of 1965 but formed the A. Philip Randolph Institute to make sure that changes would be made. He died in 1979.[10]

toured aircraft and shipyard plants on the West Coast and witnessed firsthand the discrimination that African Americans faced in these war industries. He mobilized the branches of the NAACP to lobby their Congressional representatives to launch an investigation of defense contracting. White also enlisted the support of A. Philip Randolph and he suggested a planned march on Washington to call attention to the discrimination. The National Urban League made black inclusion in the national defense industry its top priority in 1941.[11] White enthusiastically supported Randolph's idea and on June 3, 1941, Randolph sent letters to the President and other high ranking administrative officials outlining his plan for a July 1 march on Washington and his letter invited these officials to speak to the thousands who would participate.[12]

The letter quickly grabbed the attention of the Roosevelt administration. On the eve of the war, the country, which was just beginning to prepare to fight fascism, did not want to see a protest that would call attention to America's unresolved racial issues. Eleanor Roosevelt encouraged both White and Randolph to call off the planned march. Both refused and the standoff continued. Finally, a meeting was held that included the heads of the armed services, leaders from the NUL, and the African American branch of the YMCA. After the meeting, the leaders who attended attempted to persuade both men to call off the march because Roosevelt assured them that he would remedy the situation. White and Randolph had worked with Roosevelt enough to learn that assurances were not good enough. At this point, both men told Roosevelt they would only call off the march if he issued an executive order that banned discrimination in defense jobs.[13]

On the afternoon of June 25, 1941, Franklin Roosevelt issued Executive Order (EO) 8802; this stated that defense industries that received government contracts must employ workers without regard to race, creed, color, or national origin. Furthermore, the EO created the Fair Employment Practices Committee (FEPC) that would hear workers' complaints of discrimination. Walter White observed: "there never has been issued in America an executive order affecting Negroes in this country since the Proclamation of Emancipation by Abraham Lincoln."[14] On paper the FEPC looked great; however, it lacked the ability to enforce penalties if discrimination was found. Historian Harvard Sitkoff noted that the "establishment of the FEPC, and all the promise it implied, intensified the belligerence of the black community."

At the 1940 NAACP conference in Philadelphia Thurgood Marshall, who had joined the organization in 1936 as a member of the legal team, revealed that the NAACP would mount a legal campaign against the white primary.[15] In the South, since it was dominated by the Democratic Party,

Thurgood Marshall

Thurgood Marshall was born in 1908 and grew up in Baltimore. He graduated from Lincoln University in Pennsylvania in 1930 and entered Howard University where he studied law under Charles Hamilton Houston. In 1936 he joined the NAACP legal team and worked with Houston until he left; in 1939 Marshall was tapped by NAACP officials to head the newly created NAACP Legal Defense Fund (LDF), which oversaw the organization's successful legal attack on segregation. Marshall was instrumental in challenging the use of restrictive covenants in the *Shelly v. Kraemer* case, which he argued successfully before the court in 1948. He was also instrumental in arguing the *Sweatt v. Painter* case before the court in 1950 in which the University of Texas Law School was ordered to desegregate. He is most noted for bringing the *Brown v. Board of Education* case to a successful legal outcome in 1954.

Marshall furthered his legal career in 1961 when John F. Kennedy nominated him to serve on the United States Court of Appeals for the Second Circuit. Four years later, in 1965, Lyndon B. Johnson appointed him to the solicitor general position, which is the federal government's chief legal representative before the Supreme Court. In 1968 Marshall accepted Johnson's appointment to the U.S. Supreme Court, which marked the first African American appointment to the court. He continued to serve as a justice until 1991 and he died in 1993.[16]

many elections were decided in the primaries because the Democratic candidate who won the primary faced token Republican opposition in the fall campaign. In many Southern states the Democratic Party rules prohibited African Americans from voting, thus effectively nullifying their right to vote. Texas was one state where the NAACP challenged the legality of the white primary. On November 12, 1943, Thurgood Marshall, William Hastie, and W. J. Durham came before the Supreme Court to argue the constitutionality of the Texas white primary. The lower courts had upheld the constitutionality of the law; however, a previous court case, *United States v. Classic*, which was decided in 1941, had ruled that the primaries were part of the election process and were therefore subject to federal oversight. This case was critical because the argument had been made that these elections were not subject to federal oversight. If the primaries were not subject to federal oversight then the Fifteenth Amendment, which prohibited the use of race to impair a person's right to vote, could not be invoked. However, the Supreme Court, in an 8–1 decision, in *Smith v. Allright*, decided in April, 1944, that the white primary was unconstitutional. The decision would have a significant impact on the ability of African Americans to vote in Southern elections and sent shockwaves up the political spines of the white Southern Democrats.[17]

At the 1940 NAACP convention the organization adopted the integration of the military as one of its main organizational goals. They were joined in their efforts by the Committee for the Participation of Negroes in the National Defense, which was founded in 1938 by the *Pittsburg Courier* and headed by Rayford Logan.[18] The NUL also supported an end to a segregated military at their annual meeting in 1940.[19] The NNC, at their annual meeting in April, passed a resolution that said that if the United States went to war with the Soviet Union that its members would refuse to fight. At this point, the NNC, which received support from the Communist Party, faced criticism from its own president, A. Philip Randolph. Randolph declined a third term as president and pointedly observed that "It seems to be beyond the realm of debate that the Negro people cannot afford to add to the handicap of being black, the handicap of being 'red'."[20]

One day after the bombing of Pearl Harbor on December 7, 1941, a group of black editors and publishers met with a group of army officials to discuss how the War Department was handling racial matters up to that point. Although General George Marshall promised more reforms, Colonel Eugene R. Householder, representative of the Adjutant General, delivered a speech that seemed to capture the army's policy on the use of black troops and reaffirmed the War Department's commitment to a segregated military that was first announced in October of 1940:

> The army is made up of individual citizens of the United States who have pronounced views with respect to the Negro just as they have individual ideas with respect to other matters in their daily walk of life. Military orders, fiat, or dicta, will not change their viewpoints. The Army then cannot be made the means of engendering conflict among the mass of people because of a stand with respect to Negroes which is not compatible with the position attained by the Negro in civil life. The Army is not a sociological laboratory; to be effective it must be organized and trained according to the principles which will insure success. Experiments to meet the wishes and demands of the champions of every race and creed for the solution of their problems are a danger to efficiency, discipline and morale and would result in ultimate defeat.[21]

The speech outlined a couple of points the army used to justify continued segregation. The first was this idea that the army was not a "sociological laboratory" where integration might be tried out as a way to address the nation's problem with Jim Crow. The second argument against integration was that it would impair the ability of the army to fight effectively. The other branches also embraced similar arguments as to why segregation must remain in place.

The NAACP, in response, also announced on December 8, 1941, that "We shall not abate one iota our struggle for full citizenship rights here in the United States. We will fight . . . but we demand the right to fight as equals in every branch of the military, naval, and aviation services."[22] Unfortunately, during the war, it was difficult to get the military to reconsider its policy of segregation; however, that did not stop the NAACP and other organizations from investigating complaints of discrimination and from African American soldiers discussing and fighting the injustices they experienced while in the military.

During World War II over 1 million African American men and about 4,000 African American women served in the 8 million person armed forces during the war. Approximately 800,000 blacks served in the army and 600 African Americans trained at Tuskegee Institute to become pilots

Figure 2.1 African American soldiers on patrol somewhere in Europe during World War II. U.S. Army Signal Corps, LC–USZ62–133628, Library of Congress.

During World War II Japanese Americans, the Nisei, the American born sons of Japanese immigrants, were allowed to serve in the 100th Infantry and in the 442nd segregated infantry divisions. The Japanese American soldiers distinguished themselves in battle and the 100th Infantry Battalion won the Presidential Unit Citation three times and its soldiers were awarded 1,700 Purple Hearts.

in the army air forces. (The army air forces were considered part of the army until 1947, when the U.S. air force separated from the army.) Approximately 150,000 blacks served in the navy and 20,000 served in the marines and coast guard.[23] Throughout the course of the war about 500,000 African Americans saw action abroad. When African Americans served in the war effort they did so in the midst of much discrimination and, in some cases, in spite of the threat of physical harm.

Women also played a prominent role in the military by serving in the army nurse corps. By September 2, 1945, Victory in Japan (V-J Day) there were over 57,000 nurses serving in the army nurse corps. They served all over the world and more than 1,600 received recognition for their meritorious service and performance in battle. In June of 1944 nurses were granted temporary commissions in the army of the United States by an act of Congress. The law granted the nurses "full pay and privileges of the grades from second lieutenant through colonel" for the rest of the war plus an additional six months of pay. In January of 1945 Secretary of War Stimson recommended to President Roosevelt that women be drafted into the armed forces to serve as nurses. However, the legislation was pulled when it became apparent that the war was coming to a close by mid-1945.[24]

During World War II the Puerto Rican Sixty-Fifth Infantry unit guarded the Panama Canal and in 1944 the unit saw action in Europe. Over the course of the war, more than 48,000 Puerto Ricans were drafted into service.

While most of the nurses who served were white, a total of 512 black nurses served in the army nurse corps. Lt. Della Raney was the first African American Chief Nurse who served at Tuskegee Air Field in Alabama. Although they served in segregated units, they were allowed to serve overseas in places like Liberia and Burma. Of the 512 African American nurses, nine attained the rank of captain, 115 were first lieutenants and 388 earned the rank of second lieutenant.[25]

Women also fulfilled many other roles in the military besides that of serving in the army nurse corps. In the 1920s plans were made to establish a women's army auxiliary corps (WAAC); however, the General Staff of the army at the time believed that women should only serve in menial positions like cooks, laundry workers, or seamstresses. Others believed that women should not serve at all. Brig. Gen. Campbell King thought that those pushing for a WAAC wanted to create "a powerful machine difficult to control and endowed with possibilities of hampering and embarrassing the War Department."[26]

One of the challenges for women who had served in the war, as they had done in World War I, was that they were not granted military status, which meant they could not apply for veteran's benefits after the war. This happened to female telephone operators in France during World War I. Although Congress eventually approved some claims on a case by case basis, women would come to fight this same issue on the eve of World War II.[27]

> During World War II, the army organized the Ninety-Ninth Infantry Battalion, composed of Norwegians, which trained to invade German-occupied Norway.

On September 1, 1939, the day Germany invaded Poland, General George C. Marshall was appointed army Chief of Staff and in October of 1939 planning resumed to create a WAAC; however, the plan that was drafted would not grant full military status to women. This frustrated Congresswoman Edith Nourse Rogers. Rogers had witnessed what had happened to the women who had served in World War I and it troubled her greatly. When asked why she was so concerned that women be granted full military status she observed:

> My motives? In the First World War, I was there and saw. I saw the women in France, and how they had no suitable quarters and no Army discipline. Many dietitians and physiotherapists who served then are still sick in the hospital, and I was never able to get any veterans' compensation for them, although I secured passage of one bill aiding telephone operators. I was resolved that our women would not again serve with the Army without the protection men got.[28]

Eleanor Roosevelt offered two proposals concerning the use of women in the military. The first proposal committed women to work in antiaircraft barrage. The second proposal called for the creation of the Office of Civilian Defense that would serve as a service pool for women who could serve with the army, navy, and marine corps. The women would not serve under the direct command of officials in the army, navy, and marine corps, but rather under officials in the newly created Office of Civilian Defense.[29]

On May 28, 1941, Congresswoman Rogers introduced "A Bill to establish a women's army auxiliary corps for Service with the Army of the United States." Her bill did not include a provision that would have granted full military status to women because she knew there was not enough Congressional support for the measure. The army was supportive of the measure and selected Oveta Culp Hobby to help garner support for the bill. She organized a meeting between General Marshall and twenty-one of the largest women's organizations on October 13, 1941, to solicit their support for the bill.[30]

Finally, on May 14, 1942, Congress passed a law that created the women's army auxiliary corps (WAAC) and Roosevelt signed it into law and named Oveta Culp Hobby director. Initially it seemed that the public embraced the new role women were playing as members of the WAAC; however, as historian Mattie Treadwell noted:

> by May of 1943 it was already known within the War Department that the American corps, in spite of its actual record, was not to escape the traditional fate of slanderous attack, which became familiarly known to the Department's investigators as the "Slander Campaign," sometimes also called the "Whispering Campaign" or "Rumor Campaign." The slander campaign was, as its name implied, an onslaught of gossip, jokes, slander, and obscenity about the WAAC, which swept along the Eastern seaboard in the spring of 1943, penetrated to many other sections of the country, and finally broke into the open and was recognized in June, after which the WAAC and the Army engaged it in a battle.[31]

The rumor that forced WAAC officials to respond was an article that ran in a nationally syndicated column in June of 1943. The article suggested that WAACs were issued prophylactics that they were required to take with them when they left the barracks so that they could fulfill their "morale purposes" for which the army had intended. Director Hobby immediately denied the allegations in the article as did President Roosevelt and Secretary of War Henry Stimson. General Somervell of the army service forces suggested that the rumors were spread by those who were sympathetic to the Axis powers. Eventually the columnist retracted his statement, but the damage was done.[32]

Many investigations were made of these slanderous misinformation campaigns that were carried on against the WAACs. The War Department investigated and so did the army's military intelligence and they concluded that the Axis powers were not behind these malicious attacks but rather that many of the rumors originated with men in the military branches or with local residents who expressed concern about women serving in the military. One WAAC leader concluded: "Men have for centuries used slander against morals as a weapon to keep women out of public life."[33]

In a subsequent law, signed by President Roosevelt on July 1, 1943, Congress made the WAAC part of the army of the United States and renamed it the women's army corps (WAC) and women were also granted full military status for the first time.[34] On September 1, 1943, the transition from the WAAC to the WAC was completed. Over the course of the war, 140,000 women served in the WAC working in "administration, communications, medical care, maintenance, air operations, supply, and intelligence."[35] By V-J day the women's army corps was composed of 90,779 women.[36]

Women also served in the United States army air forces. In October of 1942 Lt. General H. H. Arnold established the Women's Auxiliary Ferrying Squadron (WAFS). The WAFS flew planes across the United States on noncombat missions while the combat missions were reserved for men. In August of 1943 the WAFS were merged into the newly created Women Airforce Service Pilots (WASP). More than 33,000 women applied to be a WASP and only 1,074 women graduated from the program and went on to ferry bombers and other transport planes in non-combat flying missions.[37]

Women who served in the WAAC and later the WAC could perform work outside the United States and also after November 1, 1942, drew the same pay as their male counterparts in the army.[38] Performing work outside of the United States was not allowed for the women who served in the reserve organizations created for the navy, coast guard, and the marine corps. In July of 1942 Congress passed a law that allowed the three branches to establish "the WAVES (Women Accepted for Volunteer Emergency Service), the SPARS (from the coast guard motto, 'Semper Paratus—Always Ready'), and the Marine Corps Women's Reserve" (known as the women marines).[39]

Black and white women served in the WAAC and in the WAC; however, when the WAAC was first created, Mary McLeod Bethune opposed the appointment of Director Hobby because she was from the south; however, Hobby announced that of the first 400 officer trainees, forty would be African American. With this announcement, Bethune's National Council of Negro Women withdrew its objection to Hobby's appointment. Two black companies were established as WAAC units and they were commanded by black officers and stationed at Fort Huac
By the spring of 1943 only 2,532 African American women served i
WAACS, which represented only 5.7 percent of the total numb

women that served. Their numbers slightly increased after July 1943 when the WAC was formed, but it never reached the 6 percent mark.[40]

With regards to sexual orientation, the Armed Services, beginning with World War II, attempted to prohibit homosexuals from serving through a general psychiatric screening exam that was given when they enlisted; however, as Allan Berube has demonstrated, they served. According to his estimates, at least 650,000 and perhaps as many as 1.6 million male soldiers were homosexual.[41] Berube argued that these "new screening directives and procedures, however, though ineffective in excluding the vast majority of gay men, introduced to the military the idea that homosexuals were unfit to serve in the armed forces because they were mentally ill." Berube continued: "The psychiatrists wrote this idea into military regulations and directives, the belief that gay men and lesbians constituted a class of people who must be excluded from the armed forces became an important part of military policy."[42] In 1944 the War Department issued WD Circular No. 3 that outlined a procedure on what to do with suspected homosexuals. Instead of being imprisoned for their homosexual acts, the directive required their discharge from service.[43]

While the need for women's labor was significant, most of the military's top officials were concerned about how to incorporate African American men into the military. Some African Americans who entered the army faced segregated training facilities and almost three-fourths of blacks who entered military service trained at a facility in the South.[44] For many, the segregated base was a safe haven from the surrounding southern communities that were steeped in the practice of Jim Crow.

One key African American advisor to the War Department was William Hastie. Hastie had served as dean of the Howard University Law School prior to becoming a Civilian Aide to the Secretary of War, Henry L. Stimson, in October of 1940. Hastie thought that the military's segregation policy was counterproductive in three ways. First, he believed that it would be difficult to train a black soldier to be proud and aggressive in service to their country when they knew they were serving in a segregated military. Second, Hastie thought that segregating the military was fundamentally inefficient. Finally, he thought a segregated military was hypocritical because the United States was fighting to preserve democracy but yet it still viewed one class of citizens inferior and worthy of being segregated from the rest of America.[45]

On September 22, 1941, Hastie presented A Survey and Recommendations Concerning the Integration of the Negro Soldier into the army to the Secretary of War. According to Lee, "The basic contentions of Judge Hastie's survey were that the Army could utilize many more Negroes in many more varieties of service than it was currently doing and that Negro troops could be organized more effectively for military service."[46] Hastie outlined four specific recommendations to correct the situation and the most controversial recommendation was that "At some place in the armed services a beginning should be made in the employment of soldiers without racial separation."[47]

On December 1, 1941, the army Chief of Staff, General George Marshall, commented on Hastie's recommendations to the Secretary of War:

> The problems presented with reference to utilizing negro personnel in the Army should be faced squarely. In doing so, the following facts must be recognized; first, that the War Department cannot ignore the social relationships between negroes and whites which has been established by the American people through custom and habit; second, that either through lack of educational opportunities or other causes the level of intelligence and occupational skill of the negro population is considerably below that of the white; third, that the Army will attain its maximum strength only if its personnel is properly placed in accordance with the capabilities of individuals; and fourth, that experiments within the Army in the solution of social problems are fraught with danger to efficiency, discipline, and morale.[48]
> Again, the policy of maintaining a segregated army was clear from Marshall's memo.

Hastie continued to push for the integration of African American troops in the army and in the army air corps. Remember that in the fall of 1940 that President Roosevelt announced that blacks would be able to train for the army air corps at Tuskegee. African American leaders thought this was a significant commitment because many believed that if blacks could be trained to be effective pilots there were very few positions in the military that they would not be qualified to do; however the army, which oversaw the Air Corps, was slow to implement the training program and William Hastie saw to it that the Corps moved to implement Roosevelt's request; but what he saw alarmed him.

African Americans trained at the Tuskegee Army Air Field (TAFF) in Alabama. The army air corps intentionally created a segregated base and Hastie opposed it from the start. The Tuskegee pilots were part of the 332nd Fighter Group and were organized into the all-black 99th, 100th, 301st, and 302nd fighter squadrons. After 1943 some pilots trained for the all black 477th Medium Bombardment Group.[49] The practice of segregation at Tuskegee and the fact that the army air corps refused to send the pilots into battle so greatly troubled Hastie that on January 31, 1943, he resigned his position as Special Assistant. He remarked: "It is simply impossible to maintain racial segregation of pilots in a combat area." If there was one silver lining in Hastie's decision to resign his position it was that the army air corps did pledge to send the pilots into battle and they did serve with distinction.[50]

Hastie's dissatisfaction with his role had been building ever since he was first appointed to the role in 1940; however, he had increasingly been marginalized from the dialogue about how blacks should be utilized in the military since his call for the integration of the armed forces in 1940. This was clearly evident when the War Department on August 27, 1942, created the Advisory Committee on Negro Troop Policy and Hastie was not included as a member of the committee. Although he later advised the committee on various issues, the fact that he was not included as a member was important; however, his successor, Truman Gibson, did play an important role in helping craft policies for the military, especially the army.

The Advisory Committee on Negro Troop Policy came to be known as the McCloy committee and was named after Assistant Secretary of War John J. McCloy, who chaired the committee. The Committee was to evaluate racial incidents, armed services proposed social reforms, and respond to questions about the training and use of blacks in the armed services.[51] Over the course of its life, the committee did react to the push for civil rights that came from black organizations; however, the committee also moved to re-evaluate its policies toward African American troops during the war.

Truman Gibson, who replaced Hastie, served on the McCloy committee when it drafted important policies that would guide how the army utilized and treated African American service members. The committee launched an investigation into a number of racial incidents that involved black troops that comprised the two all-black infantry divisions the army activated in 1942—the 92nd "Buffalo Soldiers" and the 93rd "Blue Helmets." The 92nd was organized in October of 1942 and the division's insignia featured a "black border and a black buffalo on an olive drab background." In the beginning, members of the 92nd were stationed at locations in Alabama, Arkansas, Indiana, and Kentucky. In 1943 the division was consolidated at Fort Huachuca, Arizona.[52]

Fort Huachuca was established in the late 1800s during the American Indian Wars. The place was desolate and barren and was comprised of 100 square miles of desert. The U.S. government thought it was the ideal place to train African American troops for service in World War II because of its isolation and the fact that white troops, except for white commanding

Truman Gibson

Truman Gibson was born in Atlanta and grew up in Ohio and in Chicago, Illinois, where he earned a BA in political science from the University of Chicago. He later earned a law degree from the same institution in 1935. He had previously worked with William Hastie in 1940 on a case that was argued before the U.S. Supreme Court that invalidated an Illinois law that used restrictive housing covenants to prevent minorities from moving into particular areas of the state. Hastie picked Gibson to serve as his assistant after Secretary of War Stimson selected Hastie to serve as Secretary of War Stimson's civilian aide.[53]

Gibson left the War Department in December of 1945 but he was asked by President Truman to return to public service when he accepted the President's invitation to serve on the Advisory Commission on Universal Military Training in 1946. In 1947 he testified about universal training before the House Armed Services Committee and stressed the importance of including all Americans in the training. He returned to Chicago where he became a boxing promoter and his life intersected with organized crime. He served as the lawyer for heavyweight champion Joe Louis and became the secretary and later the president of the International Boxing Club. The Supreme Court later ruled that the club violated antitrust laws and dissolved in 1959. In 1962 he was charged with conspiracy and extortion in a boxing scheme along with several others and was convicted of those charges and was sentenced to five years' probation and fined. He remained in Chicago and continued to practice law until his death at the age of 93 in 2006.[54]

officers, were not stationed there. The 93rd Division was stationed first at the fort when it originally received black troops in 1941. In April 1943 the 93rd Division shipped out for further training in Louisiana and when the troops arrived in Louisiana they served on bases they shared with white troops and they were also surrounded by white communities—something they were not accustomed to while serving at Fort Huachuca.[55]

The situation produced many notable examples of racial confrontation as well as examples of race riots. One riot occurred on August 8, 1944, at Camp Claiborne, which was located near Alexandria, Louisiana. The origins of the riot were many, but these kinds of incidents were not rare and they occurred in both the north and south and they concerned the McCloy committee.[56]

The McCloy committee worked on issues in 1943 they thought might resolve the racial tension around military bases. On March 10, 1943, the War Department issued a directive that required theaters and post exchanges to remove signs that designated them either whites only or colored only. Some posts complied and others did not.[57] In addition to dealing with the outward signs of Jim Crow, the committee was convinced that the local commanders were not doing enough to recognize when racial tension was increasing at their installations and the committee wanted to remind the commanders in the field that they were responsible for the welfare of those under their command. The committee also recommended that one of the best ways to deal with the tension was to send the troops into battle. In July of 1943 General Marshall incorporated the committee's concerns in a memo he sent to the field commanders which in part, read: "Failure on the part of any commander to concern himself personally and vigorously with this problem will be considered as evidence of lack of capacity and cause for reclassification and removal from assignment." Unfortunately, Marshall did not include in his memo the committee's recommendation that black troops be placed in combat.[58]

The Committee also addressed the role of the black press in stirring racial unrest. The committee expressed concern that the black press continued to print "inaccurate and inflammatory war stories." Some commanders in the field wanted the War Department to censor specific black newspapers. Upon recommendation by Assistant Secretary McCloy, the army decided to appoint blacks to the Bureau of Public Relations, which they had previously prevented African Americans from being a part of, and the army began publishing stories that appealed to the black press. According to MacGregor: "The result was a considerable increase in constructive and accurate stories on black participation in the war, although articles and editorials [in the black press] continued to be severely critical of the Army's segregation policy."[59]

The McCloy committee continued its work and oversaw the release of a pamphlet entitled *Command of Negro Troops* on February 29, 1944. The introduction to the document read: "The purpose of this booklet is to help officers to command their troops more effectively by giving them information which will increase their understanding of their men." The introduction reiterated that the black Americans had the "right and duty to serve their country" but that the "Negro in the Army has special problems."[60]

The pamphlet outlined these special problems. The first problem included the low scores blacks received on the Army General Classification Test (AGCT) when compared to white soldiers. The army said the test was "a roughly accurate measure of what the new soldier knows, what skills he commands, and of his aptitude in solving problems. It is not a test of inborn intelligence." The test divided the aptitude of those who took the exam into five different categories with categories IV and V being considered the lowest; most of the African Americans who took the test scored in the last two categories. The pamphlet stated that those who scored in the last two categories were eligible for literacy training.[61] The low test scores seemed to be a reason why many African Americans were purposely kept out of the war and in menial positions during the war.

While the document did not result in the integration of the military, it did remind the commanding officers of black troops, who were predominately white, that they were responsible for the performance of their troops and that the goal was not to waste their manpower in wartime. The pamphlet was clear: "Upon the company commander falls the definite and heavy responsibility to know his men, to assign them where they can be most useful, to promote them on the basis of true worth." Knowing the troops meant casting off some of the racial stereotypes that African Americans had been unfairly charged with like not having a "fighting heart" or squarely casting off racial theories that stated that African Americans were inferior. Of a lack of "fighting heart," the pamphlet read "there is no scientific evidence whatever to support such a view" and on refuting racist racial theories the pamphlet was clear:

> The Germans have a theory that they are a race of supermen born to conquer all peoples of inferior blood. This is nonsense, the like of which has no place in the Army of the United States—the Army of a Nation which has become great through the common effort of all peoples.[62]

Section III of the pamphlet was unusually frank and it specifically gave advice to white commanders of black troops and made them aware of the Double Victory that African Americans hoped to attain by serving in the war:

> Most Negro civilians are as American in their pride of country, in the way they want to live, and even in their prejudices, as are most whites. At the same time, they do not like the way their status as Negroes has limited their participation in the life of the country, has restricted their jobs, housing, and recreation, and has directed the prejudices of other people against them. The wartime symbol for the two-sided line of thought is found in the response of many Negroes to the "V for victory" slogan. Among Negroes arose a "double V" campaign: one V for victory in the war and a second V for victory in improved conditions for Negroes on the home front.

The pamphlet argued that the Double V was a "conflict of ideas within the Negro group, and within the mind of many an individual Negro solider" and could threaten the efficiency of his troops and that the commanding officers would be responsible for convincing the "doubters that they are wanted in the Army, that they will be used according to their abilities, and that they will be treated with justice as men and soldiers. Actions, not words, must be used to put across this idea."[63]

The pamphlet concluded by stating:

> The War Department desires that Negro soldiers be used in the most effective manner. It intends that men of all races and national origins be encouraged and stimulated to do anything done by members of any other group in accordance with their individual abilities.[64]

According to MacGregor, the *Command of Negro Troops* was a:

> landmark publication. Its frank statement of the Army's racial problems, its scholarly and objective discussion of the disadvantages that burdened the black soldier, and its outline of black rights and responsibilities clearly revealed the committee's intention to foster racial harmony by promoting greater command responsibility. The pamphlet represented a major departure from previous practice and served as a model for later Army and Navy statements on race.[65]

In March of 1944 the McCloy committee again recommended to Secretary Stimson that black troops be sent into combat. McCloy wrote:

> There has been a tendency to allow the situation to develop where selections are made on the basis of efficiency with the result that the colored units are discarded for combat service, but little is done by way of studying new means to put them in shape for combat service. With so large a portion of our population colored, with the example of the effective use of colored troops (of a much lower order of intelligence) by other nations, and with the many imponderables that are connected with the situation, we must, I think, be more affirmative about the use of our Negro troops. If present methods do not bring them to combat efficiency, we should change those methods. That is what this resolution purports to recommend.[66] This time Stimson agreed and combat teams from the 92nd division were sent to Bougainville in Papua New Guinea in March 1944 where the troops fought against Japanese forces, and elements from the 93rd division were sent to Italy in July.

The McCloy committee continued its work and on July 8, 1944, the War Department issued an order to the field that required the desegregation of all post exchanges and theaters. In addition to these changes, all government transportation was ordered integrated and that included not only transportation on base but also transportation that operated off base regardless of local segregation customs and laws. MacGregor observed that: For the first time the War Department "made a clear distinction between Army race policy to be applied on federal military reservations and local civilian laws and customs to be observed by members of the armed forces when off post."[67]

In October of 1944 the army published a significant supplement to the *Command of Negro Troops* pamphlet that was released in February of 1944. *Leadership and the Negro Soldier*, also known as Army Service Forces Manual M5, was 105 pages long and in eight chapters outlined how black manpower could be effectively utilized in the war effort. What is ironic is that the document came out in October of 1944, near the end of the war. It discussed many of the issues raised in the *Command of Negro Troops* in greater detail and stressed the efficient use of troops in combat but the document also remained committed to the army's view that it was not a social laboratory for desegregation.

The three paragraph foreword captured the army's view of African Americans in service:

> War Department concern with the Negro is focused directly and solely on the problem of the most effective military use of colored troops. It is essential that there be a clear understanding that the Army has no authority or intention to participate in social reform as such but does view the problem as a matter of efficient troop utilization. With an imposed ceiling on the maximum strength of the Army it is the responsibility of all officers to assure the most efficient use of the manpower assigned.
>
> It is recognized that the proportions of Negro troops in some military activities will be low, because Negro education and experience have been severely limited. The fact that race prejudice does exist cannot, in the interests of efficient operation, be disregarded. Limited education and experience, however, can be offset in part by training, and the restrictive effects of race prejudice may be reduced by a properly planned informational and orientation program.
>
> The issue is not whether the Negro will be used in the war; it is how effectively he will be used. This question cannot be evaded. Furthermore, it cannot be met successfully by uniformed

> judgments on the basis of civilian associations and personal views on the subject. The problems involved are as technical as any other problem of personnel, and can be solved only with the benefit of special study, full information, and a serious interest in their resolution.

While most of the military's policies on the use of black troops came from the army and army air corps, because in 1944 those two branches of the service had approximately 750,000 African Americans serving in their ranks, there were also more than 100,000 blacks serving in the navy. The marine corps, which accepted blacks as volunteers in June of 1942, finally admitted African Americans into their ranks via the Selective Service system in February of 1943 and by 1944 had 16,000 African American marines serving in their ranks. Rounding out the services, the coast guard, by February of 1944 had 3,600 service members.[68]

In the navy, approximately 200,000 African American men and women served under Secretary of the Navy, Frank Knox. However, prior to the start of the war and during its first few years, African Americans who were a part of the navy were usually part of the Steward's Branch. In 1942 President Roosevelt ordered the Secretary of the Navy to enlist African Americans, even though they already served in the Steward's Branch. In August of 1943 the navy established a Special Programs Unit in its Planning and Control Activity division to oversee black enlistment. Lt. Comdr. Christopher S. Sargent, a white officer, was selected to oversee the unit. According to MacGregor, "Sargent waged something of a moral crusade to integrate the navy."[69]

Like army officials who served on the McCloy committee, those on Sargent's Special Programs Unit were concerned about diffusing racial tension. The Special Programs Unit wanted to get qualified African Americans away from the Steward's Branch and placed on ships at sea. In early 1944 the Bureau of Naval Personnel assigned 196 black enlisted men and 44 white officers and petty officers to the *USS Mason*. This experiment of mixing black and white personnel was successful and paved the way for the Special Programs Unit to publish the *Guide to the Command of Negro Naval Personnel* in February of 1944. It was very similar to the army's *Leadership and the Negro Soldier*.

The *Guide to the Command of Negro Naval Personnel* acknowledged that:

> The idea of compulsory racial segregation is disliked by almost all Negroes, and literally hated by many. This antagonism is in part a result of the fact that as a principle it embodies a doctrine of

> racial inferiority. It is also a result of the lesson taught the Negro by experience that in spite of the legal formula of "separate but equal" facilities, the facilities open to him under segregation are in fact usually inferior as to location or quality to those available to others. Like the army's *Leadership and the Negro Soldier*, the *Guide to the Command of Negro Naval Personnel* also rejected racial theories that put the intellectual capacity of blacks below that of whites.[70]

On April 28, 1944, Secretary of Navy, Frank Knox, suddenly died and Roosevelt replaced him with James Forrestal. Forrestal had been a member of the NUL, which had pushed for the integration of the military on the eve of the war. There was much hope that Forrestal would support the efforts of the Special Programs Unit to integrate the navy. Forrestal did oversee the inclusion of black WAVES into the naval service—a plan that had been at work since 1943 under Secretary Knox. On July 28, 1944, Forrestal recommended to Franklin D. Roosevelt that blacks be trained as WAVES on an integrated basis. The first African American WAVE officers graduated from training on December 21, 1944, and MacGregor noted that the "Special Programs Unit came to consider the WAVE program, which established a forceful precedent for the integration of male recruit training, its most important wartime breakthrough." Forrestal also continued his commitment to exploring integration in the navy when he appointed Lester Granger, Executive Secretary of the NUL, as his special advisor on racial matters.[71]

Despite the best efforts of Secretary Forrestal, there were a couple of racial incidents that demonstrated the navy had a long way to go in resolving its racial issues. On July 17, 1944, at Port Chicago in California, an explosion destroyed two ammunition ships. The explosion killed 300 people, including 250 black seamen whose responsibility it was to load these ships. The survivors of the blast discussed how dangerous their work was and they refused to go back to work; fifty were convicted of mutiny and sentenced to prison. Thurgood Marshall and Lester Granger intervened and the convictions were thrown out and the seamen returned to active duty.[72]

In December of 1944 a riot broke out on the island of Guam between black seamen and white marines. Prior to the riot, tension had been building between the two sides after a series of shootings left one black seaman and one white marine dead. After the riot forty-three blacks were arrested and sentenced to four years in prison. Several white marines were court-martialed and convicted of offenses related to their role in the riot.

Walter White, NAACP executive director, traveled to Guam to investigate and he was called to testify during the trial; he delivered testimony that detailed the discrimination that African American seamen experienced on the island. As a result of his efforts and the efforts of others, the black sailors were eventually released in 1946.[73]

Despite some successes with the integration of black seamen on ships like the *Mason* and the integration that took place in the WAVES, segregation was still prevalent in the U.S. navy. By August of 1945 there were 164,942 African Americans enlisted in the navy, which represented only 5.37 percent of those serving in the navy. In that same month and year the navy only had sixty black officers, which included six who were women (four nurses and two WAVES), and sixty-eight enlisted WAVES. As MacGregor concluded: "The integration of the navy officer corps, the WAVES, and the nurses had an immediate effect on only 128 people." Also, by war's end, there were 68,000 black men who still served as stewards and steward's mate and another 59,000 served as seamen, which meant that most of the African Americans who served in the navy did so in "large segregated labor units and base companies."[74]

The marine corps, which by law was a part of the department of the navy, had to comply with the naval regulations regarding the use of black troops; however, they applied them in a different manner. In 1942 the secretary of the navy required the enlistment of African Americans within the ranks of the marine corps because they had no black enlistees among their ranks. The commandant of the marine corps, Major General Thomas Holcomb, was left to implement the policy and he told the navy's general board that "If it were a question of having a marine corps of 5,000 whites or 250,000 Negroes, I would rather have the whites." He believed that the marine corps was too small to have separate black units; however, after 1942 when President Roosevelt instructed Secretary of Navy Knox that blacks would be utilized in the general service of the navy, Holcomb had little choice but to comply. The enlistment of black marines began on June 1, 1942, but they were placed on inactive status until they could build segregated training facilities for the enlistees at Montford Pointe, North Carolina.[75]

In December of 1942 President Roosevelt abolished the volunteer enlistments for the armed forces and established a quota for each branch of the service that required them to take black recruits. By 1946, the year when the marine corps stopped receiving black draftees, the corps had taken in over 16,000 African Americans. As MacGregor reported: "Including the 3,129 black volunteers, the number of Negroes in the marine corps during World War II totaled 19,168, approximately 4 percent of the corps' enlisted men."[76]

The fact that Roosevelt had ordered the establishment of quotas meant that 10 percent of the draftees accepted into the marine corps must be African American. The marine corps was not ready for that high volume number of black recruits. General Holcomb worked to comply with the quota system; however, he did not want black non-commissioned officers to be senior to other white soldiers in the same unit and he ordered his commanders in the field to make sure this did not happen. Holcomb's order was not rescinded until after the war and he made sure that black marines did not participate in combat divisions; however, those that served in ammunition and depot companies did see combat action. MacGregor noted that civil rights organizations complained about the racial policies of the marines "but neither protests nor the cost to military efficiency of duplicating training facilities were . . . sufficient . . . to overcome the sentiment against significant racial change."[77]

During peacetime the coast guard normally fell under the jurisdiction of the Department of Treasury; however, under a statute passed in 1915, during wartime its jurisdiction fell to the navy. From November 1, 1941, to January 1, 1946, the coast guard was under the direction of the secretary of the navy. When Roosevelt gave the order for the navy to utilize blacks in the general service in 1942 the coast guard was ready. The Guard agreed to enlist 500 blacks to serve in general service and by August of 1942, 300 had been assigned general service duties. In December of 1942 the Guard had to comply with the racial quotas for enlistment as outlined in the Selective Service Act. The number of African Americans serving in the coast guard during World War II swelled to 5,000.[78]

Approximately 2,300 blacks served in the Steward's Branch during the war while 2,400 served in the "shore establishment." Those in the "shore establishment" worked at local coast guard stations, in security and labor details, as radio operators, or on beach patrol units. There was one attempt at creating an integrated crew on the USS *Sea Cloud*, a ship that monitored weather conditions in the North Atlantic. The ship had four black officers and fifty black petty officers; however, the coast guard did not attempt to integrate other ships. Towards the end of the war, in the fall of 1944, the coast guard recruited five black women for the SPARS; unfortunately the program ended in November of 1944, but the five women were allowed to train and received positions in integrated coast guard district offices. Like the marines, MacGregor concluded that while the coast guard did make "very real progress toward equal treatment and opportunity for Negroes in the Coast Guard" that progress was "experienced by only a minuscule group."[79]

The military clearly tried to maintain separate but equal during the war and the African American organizations voiced their concerns throughout the war about the discrimination. However, organizations like the NAACP did have some success at least in the sense of making sure that blacks would be included in the military and, at crucial times, even though President Roosevelt was not the most outspoken critic on how blacks were treated in the service, he also pushed to make sure that all branches of the military, like the air force and the marines, would include blacks among their ranks. Even though blacks were included among all the branches of the military they still faced being placed in the most menial positions of service and ironically had to fight so hard just to be able to fight in combat. Towards the end of the war some progress was made as far as serving in combat; however, much work remained to be done to end segregation in the military. In fact, it has been argued that the military's practice of segregation and discrimination against its black recruits emboldened the push for civil rights after the war. During the war the membership of the NAACP increased significantly because of the discrimination and after the war the one million plus African American men and women who served would be emboldened to speak out against the abuses they faced during the war in an effort to end them in the post-World War II period. It was this emboldened civil rights movement that Harry Truman faced when he became president on April 12, 1945, after President Roosevelt's death.

CHAPTER 3

Harry Truman and Civil Rights, 1884–1945

"I also knew that Truman's own views on race were border state, not Deep Dixie: he didn't believe in social equality, but he did believe in fair play."

Roy Wilkins[1]

On April 12, 1945, Harry Truman became President after Franklin Roosevelt died of heart failure at his retreat in Warm Springs, Georgia. The nation was stunned at the loss of Roosevelt who was elected to the presidency four times. They were not sure what to expect from a former Missouri senator who at one time in his political career owed his political start to a Kansas City political machine. He presided over the end of World War II but he also had to draft a policy that would chart a course for the nation in what would become the Cold War and he committed U.S. forces to fight in its first hot war of the Cold War by sending troops to fight in integrated units in the Korean War. However, getting to an integrated military would be a struggle—a struggle that for Harry Truman began in Missouri.

Harry Truman was born in Lamar, Missouri, located about ninety miles to the south of Kansas City on May 8, 1884. His grandparents and parents had come into Missouri from Kentucky in the 1830s and 1840s. His maternal grandfather, Solomon Young, made a fortune by freighting goods under contract to the various forts that were in the west in the 1840s and 1850s. His paternal grandfather, Anderson Shipp Truman, owned as many as five slaves. When the Civil War came to Missouri, the Young farm was raided by Jim Lane's Jayhawkers from Kansas. After the war, his grandmother, Harriet Young, filed a petition with the federal government to obtain compensation for the foodstuffs that Lane had freely appropriated on his raid of the Young farm. She remained uncompensated and an unreconstructed rebel for the remainder of her life.[2]

> Margaret Truman, Harry Truman's daughter, characterized Independence as "Deep South"; however, Bess Truman, her mother, had family ties that were clearly Northern. Bess's maternal grandfather, George Porterfield Gates, was born in Vermont, and the Gates family arrived in Independence during the Civil War and shortly thereafter purchased a mill, which brought them substantial income. In contrast, Harry Truman's forebears were thoroughly Southern.

No doubt Harry Truman grew up in a household where the Civil War was etched in his historical memory and in his early vocabulary. Harry Truman's family moved to Independence, Missouri, in 1890 so he and his younger brother, Vivian, and younger sister, Mary Jane, could attend its well respected public school system. He studied Greek and Latin in the school and become fond of history prior to his graduation in 1901. Lacking the funds to be able to go to college, he worked at several jobs in Kansas City prior to being called by his father and mother, John A. and Martha Ellen Truman, to work his maternal grandmother's 600 acre farm near Grandview, Missouri.

Harry Truman penned his first views on race at the Grandview farm. Truman wrote these words to Bess Wallace, his future wife:

> I think one man is just as good as another so long as he's honest and decent and not a nigger or a Chinaman. Uncle Will says that the Lord made a white man from dust, a nigger from mud, then threw up what was left and it came down a Chinaman. He does hate Chinese and Japs. So do I. It is race prejudice I guess. But I am strongly of the opinion that negroes ought to be in Africa, yellow men in Asia, and white men in Europe and America.[3] His earliest writings on minorities and, in particular, blacks were not flattering and are difficult to read. Surprisingly, Truman acknowledges his views for what they were: "race prejudice."

Truman was a Baptist and maintained his membership in the Grandview Baptist Church; however, he did not always attend services, especially after he became president, as he was concerned that all of the attention would be directed towards him and not on the service. While his Baptist faith might have contributed to his moral upbringing, his participation in the Masonic organization should not be underestimated. It was on the farm that he joined the Belton lodge and he founded the

Figure 3.1 Harry Truman served as Captain of Battery D, which saw action in France during WWI. Truman Library.

Masonic Lodge in Grandview and served as its first presiding officer. He defined Freemasonry as "a system of morals which makes it easier to live with your fellow man, whether he understands it or not."[4] He devoted his life to the organization and became a 33rd degree Mason.

Having grown up in a Protestant household his first significant experience with non-Protestants came when he enlisted to serve in World War I and became captain of Battery D in France. Battery D was made up of primarily Irish Catholics from Kansas City. When he returned to Kansas City after the war he married Bess Wallace in June of 1919 and promptly moved into her family's home at 219 North Delaware. The couple would call 219 North Delaware home for the rest of their lives.

He went into business with Eddie Jacobson, whom he had met when he was training for service in World War I and the two opened up a haberdashery, which was a men's clothing store in downtown Kansas City. Jacobson was Jewish and initially the business thrived; however, it did not survive the short post-war recession and by 1922 Harry Truman was looking for work.

When Truman returned to Independence he was approached by one of the members of Kansas City's Pendergast machine, whom he had met during his time in the military, and he encouraged him to run for Eastern

District Judge of Jackson County. By 1922, when Truman ran, the machine had consolidated its political power in Kansas City and was looking to widen its political reach into the rural parts of the county. Truman's experience as a farmer and his veteran status would appeal to many rural voters. He was elected as Eastern District Judge for the Jackson County court and his experiences with the machine would leave an important imprint on how he came to view African Americans as active participants in the political process.

Tom Pendergast was an Irish Catholic who had settled in Kansas City by the turn of the twentieth century. What was unique about the Pendergast machine is that by the 1920s and certainly by the 1930s they recognized the importance of including African Americans. This is significant because in contrast to most places, but specifically the South, African American men and women, especially after 1900, were denied the right to vote due in part to a variety of state measures like the poll tax, grandfather clauses, and literacy tests. However, in Missouri politics, the political machines in Kansas City and St. Louis worked for their votes. There were approximately 20,000 African American voters in Kansas City and their votes could swing elections.[5] While this was important to Tom Pendergast in 1922, it would be of little consequence to Harry Truman because few African Americans lived in Independence and in rural Jackson County, which Truman represented. The 1920s also represented the zenith of the rebirth of the Ku Klux Klan and they exerted some influence in state politics and in Jackson County.

Harry ran against four other Democrats in the Democratic primary for county judge and two were supported by the Ku Klux Klan. One of his friends urged him to join. Harry refused at first, but then gave his friend $10 to cover the cost of the membership to join. However, when Truman met privately with the Klan organizer the organizer told Truman that he would not get Klan support unless he promised not to hire Catholics. Given Truman's work with the Irish Catholics in Battery D and his relationship with Pendergast, he told the organizer he could not comply with his wishes. According to one historian, the $10 membership was returned to Truman. The Klan retaliated against Truman by bringing in a speaker from Georgia who suggested that Truman's grandfather, Solomon Young, was Jewish. In 1924 he faced similar criticism from the Klan and he confronted them headlong at a daylight meeting in Lee's Summit. Unfortunately, in that election, the Democratic Party was divided in their support for Truman, which resulted in his defeat.[6]

Truman also did not receive the support of the Kansas City Chapter of the NAACP. In all fairness, as noted previously, few blacks lived in

Eastern Jackson County, so it would not be correct to argue that lack of NAACP support sunk his re-election; however, it is quite possible that it forced Truman to seriously consider the importance of the African American vote. The NAACP found his answers to a questionnaire that surveyed his views on the Dyer anti-lynching bill, the Klan, and the opening of Jackson County Home for Delinquent Negro Boys, among other issues, unacceptable. Unfortunately, Truman's actual response to the questionnaire has not been recovered; only a newspaper account from the *Kansas City Call*, Kansas City's largest black newspaper, stated that his responses were not acceptable.[7]

One historian speculated that the reason the NAACP found his responses to the questionnaire unacceptable might have centered on Truman's answer to a question about the opening of the Jackson County Home for Delinquent Negro Boys. The Democratic machine had failed to adequately support the opening of the home and Harry Truman was a member of that Democratic machine.

While Truman was out of a job after the 1924 election, he was not out of politics. In 1926 he received Tom Pendergast's blessing to run for the Presiding Judge of the Court. With the Democratic Party now united and the strength of the Klan marginalized, Truman was successful in getting himself elected as Presiding Judge for two terms and he served from January 1927 to January 1935.[8] As Presiding Judge he became aware of the needs of his African American constituents.

One of the responsibilities of the Presiding Judge was to oversee the hospitals. General Hospital No. 2, which was established for African Americans, was one of the hospitals that fell under his jurisdiction. In 1915 William J. Thompkins, a black doctor, became the superintendent of the hospital and he held that position until 1922, when Truman was first elected to the county court. In 1927, the same year that Truman was elected Presiding Judge of the Jackson County Court, Thompkins was appointed assistant health commissioner. As assistant health commissioner, Thompkins conducted a survey of tuberculosis and the housing conditions that African Americans faced in Kansas City. Due in part to the survey that Thompkins conducted but also due to the fact that there had been a fire at the hospital in 1927, Thompkins persuaded Truman to rebuild. After much wrangling over the location of the new hospital, General Hospital No. 2 was dedicated in February 1930.[9] C. A. Franklin remarked that the hospital was the "most modern public hospital in the country."[10]

Truman listened to the concerns of Thompkins and the need to address the health concerns of African Americans and he also made sure that the home for delinquent black youths was opened and properly staffed. C. A. Franklin, the Republican editor of the *Kansas City Call*, openly supported

Truman's re-election to the county court in 1930 when he praised his efforts at building roads in the county, as well as his efficient operation of both a home for aged African Americans and the home for delinquent black youths. The reason why Franklin supported Truman was because of the machine support the black community received on the issues above but also because the Republicans and anti-boss politicians supported the Klan and in other instances utilized the police force to harass and brutalize the black community.[11]

The significance of all of this is that while in other parts of the country African Americans were still firmly in the grip of the Republican Party, African Americans in Missouri, especially in Kansas City, had already shifted their allegiance to the Democratic Party in time for Franklin Roosevelt's first election in 1932. As one historian noted, "The black vote [in Kansas City] had gone from 80 percent Republican in 1922 to 70 percent Democratic in 1932."[12] Robert Sweeney, the first African American postal examiner in Kansas City, observed:

> You know, we've had less trouble here among the races. Politically we've always gotten along well. Speaking of Democratic politics, the State of Missouri was way ahead of the other states because they combined the Negro and the white man together to win political victory.[13]

This trend in Kansas City accelerated across the state to St. Louis where in 1933 Bernard Dickmann and Robert Hannegan formed a new Democratic coalition that also included African Americans among its ranks. This early transition of Missouri's African American voters to the Democratic Party caught the attention of Roosevelt's political advisors and they sought ways to continue this trend across the country.[14]

In 1934 Harry Truman received the support of the Pendergast machine to run for the United States Senate and William J. Thompkins supported his candidacy. While Pendergast was seeking to consolidate his political hold over state politics, Harry Truman tried to solidify his hold on a political position that would keep him employed. Truman easily won the Democratic nomination for Senator and he also had the support of C. A. Franklin and the *Kansas City Call*. The editorial in the *Call* read: "If ever a man deserved public confidence on the basis of the record made in the public's service, that man is Harry Truman."[15] It is instructive that at least among the African American community in Kansas City, Truman had successfully appealed to and won the support of blacks like William J. Thompkins, who had cast their lot with the Democratic Party, but also with African Americans like C. A. Franklin who supported the Republican Party.

William J. Thompkins

Another reason why African Americans in Missouri shifted to the Democratic Party was due in part to the efforts of William J. Thompkins. In 1928, Thompkins, along with a partner, founded the *Kansas City American*, a Democratic paper that came to rival the Republican *Kansas City Call*. He also organized black support for Al Smith's 1928 presidential race against Herbert Hoover. Four years later, in 1932, he supported Franklin Roosevelt and served as president of the National Colored Democratic Association. Thompkins wanted to be appointed to the governorship of the Virgin Islands; however, Roosevelt refused his appointment, but Thompkins continued to support the Democratic Party. Roosevelt nominated him to serve as the recorder of deeds on March 19, 1934, for the District of Columbia—a position that had much patronage associated with it and a position that had been held by an African American since the 1880s when Frederick Douglas served in the position.[16]

Truman made one other important contact within the African American community prior to his move to Washington. On October 1, 1923, Roy Wilkins became a news editor for C. A. Franklin's *Kansas City Call*. By 1930 Wilkins had grown concerned about his prospects for growth at the *Call* and he sent W. E. B. Du Bois, who was editor of the *Crisis*, the official paper of the NAACP, a letter to see if there might be an opening. An offer was made, but Wilkins declined and stayed in Kansas City. In 1931 Walter White, acting secretary of the NAACP, sent a letter to Wilkins in February asking him if he might be interested in an executive position with the NAACP. This time Wilkins accepted the offer and in July of 1931 he started work in New York at the headquarters of the NAACP.[17]

The time that Roy Wilkins spent working at the *Call* allowed him a firsthand opportunity to judge Harry Truman's record on the Jackson County Court. He vividly recalled:

> I had known him when he was a judge back in Kansas City, and one of the things he had done back then was to save a home for Negro boys that the white folks thought was too good for colored children . . . It was true that he had been a creature of Tom Pendergast's Democratic machine in Kansas City . . . but I also knew that Truman's own views on race were border state, not Deep Dixie: he didn't believe in social equality, but he did believe

> in fair play. No one had ever convinced him that the Bill of Rights was a document for white folks only.[18]

When Truman arrived in Washington he took his prior experiences of working with African Americans in county government with him. The key words are "working with" because many of his fellow colleagues in the Senate, particularly those from the South, had spent most of their political careers opposing measures that would have granted voting rights protections, eliminated discriminatory practices, or approved of a federal anti-lynching law from ever passing their chamber. Harry Truman was a strong supporter of Roosevelt's New Deal; however, his only drawback, at least to some of his colleagues, when he first arrived in the Senate chamber in 1935, was his affiliation with the Pendergast machine. To African Americans in Missouri, especially Kansas City, he had at least demonstrated that he was interested in matters that directly impacted their lives so the question that remained to be answered was whether or not he would continue to be interested in those issues after he became Senator.

Interestingly enough, Truman's arrival in Washington coincided with the NAACP's renewed attempt to focus on the problems of lynching, discrimination in education, and segregation in the military. Truman's first challenge on the issue of civil rights came in 1935 when the Senate decided the fate of the Costigan–Wagner anti-lynching bill. The bill, sponsored by Senators Robert F. Wagner and Edward Costigan, provided federal punishment for private citizens and state officials found to be involved with a lynching and could impose a fine of up to $10,000 on the county where the lynching occurred. The bill, supported by Truman, was eventually filibustered; however, the NAACP's support of the bill represented a renewed attempt by the organization to stop lynching. Furthermore, the reason why a federal anti-lynching bill was so important was because the state and local governments were not doing enough to stop the violence and, in some cases, state and local officials participated in the lynchings.[19]

Truman supported a similar anti-lynching bill in 1938; however, it suffered the same fate as the 1935 bill. In the debate over the Selective Service Act of 1940 he supported the amendment that prohibited discrimination.[20] Towards the end of his first term in office Truman had taken a stand in support of issues that were important to African Americans. Meanwhile, back in Missouri, the political machine that propelled Truman into the Senate was imploding due in part to its own graft and corruption, which left Truman's re-election chances in 1940 in great jeopardy.

On May 22, 1939, Thomas Pendergast, the patriarch of the Pendergast machine, pled guilty to charges of income tax evasion and was sentenced to fifteen months at Fort Leavenworth Federal Penitentiary. Pendergast's prison sentence could not have come at a worse time for Harry Truman, who was in the process of deciding whether or not he would seek re-election to the Senate. He eventually made the decision to run; however, his campaign could no longer depend upon the padded votes that Pendergast delivered in Jackson County. This necessitated a new campaign strategy—a strategy that was not just based on patronage politics but based on appealing to various interest groups. One of those key interest groups for Harry Truman was the state's African American population.[21]

To distance himself from the corruption of the machine, Truman established his state headquarters for his re-election campaign about sixty miles to the east of Kansas City in Sedalia. In June he kicked off his re-election campaign at an all-day event that included a speech at the dedication of "Sedalia's City Hospital No. 2 for Negroes". Dr. William Thompkins introduced the junior senator from Missouri and praised his record in the Senate. Unfortunately, the newspaper did not publish Truman's speech; however, in a brief article about his appearance at the dedication, the newspaper reported:

> Senator Truman did not deliver a political address, giving a most interesting dedicatory talk to the Negroes of Sedalia in which he praised highly their accomplishments in the past several years. He told of their present-day advantages in education, business, and public life, and of their present day status in public affairs.[22]

Later that evening Harry Truman delivered the official kick off campaign speech on the courthouse steps. By Missouri standards it was not your average run of the mill speech because it outlined how he was going to appeal to the various interest groups like farmers, labor, and African Americans. No other Democratic politician in the state had defined his campaign so broadly. Truman took a certain amount of political risk with speech; however, Truman knew that if he were to win the August Democratic primary he would need every vote he could possibly get and he was not hesitant to discuss the problem of race with the predominately white audience:

> The relation of colored and white people in this community and this state is one that should be given our interest and attention. We all desire to see proper and helpful relations exist between all classes of people. Certainly there should be no injustice, no

> contemptuous or unfair treatment allotted by any class to any other class. Most of all, the stronger group should not impose upon the weaker obnoxious conditions or situations. In all matters of progress and welfare, of economic opportunity and equal rights before [the] law, Negroes deserve every aid and protection.[23] In the *Sedalia Democrat* this was the only paragraph that the newspaper reprinted that dealt with the issue of race.

On July 25, 1940, Senator Lewis Schwellenbach asked that by unanimous consent a portion of Truman's speech delivered at Sedalia be placed into the *Appendix to the Congressional Record*. The *Record* described the speech as a "tribute to the Negro by the junior Senator from Missouri [Mr. Truman]. This tribute is part of an address delivered by the junior Senator from Missouri at Sedalia, Mo., on June 15, 1940." Historians have sometimes referred to the speech as the "brotherhood of man" speech because one of the most important paragraphs in the reprinted speech read:

> I believe in the brotherhood of man; not merely the brotherhood of white men, but the brotherhood of all men before law. I believe in the Constitution and the Declaration of Independence. In giving to the Negroes the rights that are theirs, we are only acting in accord with our ideals of a true democracy. If any class or race can be permanently set apart from, or pushed down below, the rest in political and civil rights, so may any other class or race when it shall incur the displeasure of its more powerful associates, and we may say farewell to the principles on which we count our safety.
>
> During the World War the need of men for an Army and for war industries brought more and more of the Negroes from rural areas to the cities. In the years past, lynching and mob violence, lack of schools, and countless other equally unfair conditions, hastened the progress of the Negro from the country to the city. In these centers the Negroes have never had much choice in regard to work or anything else. By and large, they work mainly as unskilled laborers and domestic servants. They have been forced to live in segregated slums, neglected by the authorities. Negroes have been preyed upon by all types of exploiters, from the installment salesman of clothing, pianos, and furniture to the vendors of vice. The majority of our Negro people find but cold comfort in shanties and tenements. Surely, as freemen, they are entitled to something better than this.[24]

What is interesting about the reprinted speech is that it was very vague in stating just exactly when and where in Sedalia that it was delivered. The *Sedalia Democrat* version of the speech did not print the "brotherhood of man" portion of the speech, which begs the question as to whether the reporter just omitted this section from the newspaper account of the speech or is it possible that the speech reprinted in the *Appendix to the Congressional Record* was the speech that Truman delivered at the dedication of Sedalia's City Hospital No. 2? The evidence suggests the latter option because the description the reporter provided of the speech mirrors the layout of the speech that was reprinted in the *Record.*

The "brotherhood of man" speech was bold language for Truman to use in his Senate campaign; however, it would not be his last. In July of 1940 he was asked by Thompkins to address the National Colored Democratic Association meeting in Chicago, IL. It marked another important speech in his appeal for black political support. In this speech Truman defined what equality between the races meant to him:

> I wish to make it clear that I am not appealing for social equality of the Negro. The Negro himself, knows better than that, and the highest types of Negro leaders say quite frankly, that they prefer the society of their own people. Negroes want justice, not social relations. I merely wish to sound a note of warning. Numberless antagonisms and indignities heaped upon any race will eventually try human patience to the limit, and a crisis will develop. We will know the Negro is here to stay and in no way can be removed from our political and economic life, and we all should recognize his inalienable rights as specified in our Constitution. Can any man claim protection of our laws if he denies that protection to others?[25]

In August voters went to the polls and Truman narrowly defeated two other challengers to secure the Democratic nomination for the U.S. Senate. He coasted to victory in November defeating the Republican candidate by almost 25,000 votes in Kansas City and by 46,000 votes in St. Louis. Alonzo Hamby concluded that "he emerged definitively as a candidate of the cities, an urban liberal."[26] Part of being an "urban liberal" meant, at least to Truman, that he had to recognize the political significance of African American voters. However, when it came to the mixing of the races in public it was clear from his July 1940 address to the National Colored Democratic Association that he favored segregation.

Truman felt a certain amount of vindication in this election victory because he won the election on his own and the victory did allow him

During his Senate career, Truman served on the Interstate Commerce Committee and he helped Burton Wheeler, chair of the committee, draft the Transportation Act of 1940, which President Roosevelt signed into law in September.

the opportunity to shed the "Senator from Pendergast sign" that hung over his head during his first Senatorial term. In 1941 he supported the creation of the FEPC, which was proposed by President Roosevelt to A. Philip Randolph and Walter White, in order to forestall a March on Washington by African Americans who wanted the government to insure that blacks would not be discriminated against in wartime contracts. He also established a committee to investigate defense spending in February of 1941. The committee's work brought him name recognition and it also caught the eye of African American leaders. They wanted the committee to hold hearings on whether or not African Americans were being discriminated against in war contracts and in employment in war industry. Truman held hearings in Kansas City and St. Louis, but the committee, and Truman, did not vigorously pursue any charges because their main objective was looking at waste in the war industry and the committee was not focused so much on evaluating how human power was or was not effectively utilized in war industry.[27]

On October 13, 1942, Senator Truman introduced S. 2848 that eventually created the George Washington Carver National Monument, the first African American history monument that came to be managed by the National Park Service. He also supported an anti-poll tax bill and twice voted for cloture against filibustering the bill, but like the anti-lynching law, the Senate did not have the numbers to successfully pass the bills.[28]

Truman claimed that his Senate committee to investigate defense contracting saved the United States $15 billion.

Truman's political star within the ranks of the Democratic Party rose because of his work on the Truman Committee and he was successfully placed on the presidential ticket with Roosevelt in 1944. Since Roosevelt's health was failing, Truman essentially campaigned on behalf of the ticket. The NAACP and Walter White scrutinized his Senate voting record. On August 8, 1944, a member of the NAACP staff prepared a review of his Senate voting record since 1935 for Walter White. The NAACP staffer concluded that "If I were to characterize his Senatorial Record with respect to the Negro, I would say that it was a fair—in-and-out—record."[29]

In the closing weeks of the campaign, some newspapers began running stories that Harry Truman had once been a member of the Klan. Walter

White grew concerned about the situation and whether or not Truman was a person the NAACP could support. The Klan charge bothered White but so too did a remark made by the Governor of Alabama who reportedly said that "Senator Truman told me he is the son of a[n] unreconstructed rebel mother." Truman sat on White's telegram for about a week and a half before he responded with one of his own on October 30th. As to the Klan charge, Truman told White:

> In these closing days of the campaign I have been falsely accused of Klan membership by irresponsible newspapers actively supporting the Republican ticket, although the record shows that the Klan fought me and I fought the Klan. The Klan is repugnant to every policy and every principle I have advocated and struggled for all my life.

As to the remark made by the Governor of Alabama, Truman's response was specific:

> I am happy to be judged not only by what I say to you in this telegram but also by my lifelong public record. Whether anyone calls an issue one of state or national rights, you can turn to the Congressional Record and see exactly how I voted and what I have supported. You will find that I have fought for fair treatment of every minority, every labor group, every interest that has been underprivileged, specifically, I believe that on issues affecting fair treatment for Negroes there is no legislation which has not had my support. I supported FEPC. I voted for cloture on the anti-lynching bill. I voted for cloture on the anti-poll tax bill. I voted for the Murray–Gilgore Bill, the Soldier's Vote, the NYA [National Youth Administration] and every bill to give [a] fair deal to minorities . . . I cannot control the opinions of other people as to whether they think my voting record favors states' rights or national rights.[30]

White seemed to accept Truman's response because in a letter sent to David Selznick he told Selznick that the NAACP had conducted an "exhaustive inquiry" as to whether or not he had been a Klan member and concluded that "we have been unable to unearth any proof of Truman having been a member of the Klan." He advised Selznick that "Under these circumstances, . . . there seems to be no other course for us to take except to make public the exchange of telegrams and leave the decision to individuals regarding the veracity of Mr. Truman's unequivocal denial the he ever joined the Klan." He also told Selznick that Truman's statement about his voting record on minority issues, as outlined above, "is correct."[31]

Roosevelt easily won a fourth term and was sworn in along with Truman. The country faced the daunting challenge of ending World War II with a president who was very ill. Harry Truman had only met with Franklin Roosevelt twice before his death on April 12, 1945, and he inherited the challenge of ending the war in Europe, which meant that it would be increasingly challenging for him to deal with civil rights issues. Because these issues were not immediately on his radar screen it meant that African American leaders would have to remind him that the establishment of a permanent FEPC, the passage of anti-lynching laws, and anti-poll tax laws, as well as the integration of the military, were still important concerns. They at least knew that Truman was receptive to their concerns because as a County Judge and as a U.S. Senator he demonstrated a profound interest, but also an interest that had moved him to action, something many African American leaders had not seen in their lifetime.

April 1945 was a pivotal time; while the war still waged in Europe, racial tension in the United States and in the armed forces reached a fever pitch. The Tuskegee Airmen of the 477th Medium Bombardment Group encountered significant discrimination and segregation at Freeman Field, which was located just outside Seymour, Indiana. In April of 1945 army officials transferred the 477th from Midland Army Air Field to Freeman Field and the white commanders at Freeman created a separate officers' club prior to their arrival, which violated "War Department Memorandum No. 97 and Army Regulation 210–10," according to historian Todd Moye. Thirty-six Tuskegee airmen made their way into the white officers' club and asked to be served. They were summarily arrested. The next night thirty-five more airmen entered the club and they too were arrested. After the second round of arrests 110 men of the 477th signed a petition asking the army's inspector general to investigate to see whether or not the air field's commander had violated army air force policy. Robert R. Selway, the airfield commander, then asked all of the members of the 477th and the white officers to sign a form stating that they would abide by his policy of maintaining separate facilities. There were 101 members from the 477th out of 422 that refused to sign. Selway then threatened the 101 who didn't sign with violating the 64th Article of War, which prohibits "the willful disobeying of a lawful direct order from a superior in wartime."[32] There were penalties that could be assessed for violating Article 64, including death. Selway transported the 101 men who refused to sign to Godman Field, located just outside Louisville, Kentucky, where they were incarcerated. The NAACP intervened and on April 23 army Chief of Staff,

General George C. Marshall, ordered the 101 released; however, three officers who led the initial attempts to integrate the white officers' club remained arrested pending court-martial proceedings. Two of the three were acquitted of charges, but one, Lt. Roger C. "Bill" Terry, was found guilty and fined. Of the whole ordeal Terry believed that his court martial:

> broke the camel's back because they had to recognize the fact that 104 officers were arrested, and that they all defied this order, and the order was said to be illegal. We feel, and I think I speak for most of the guys, that it was our advantage that we gave to the Negro people, that there would be no discrimination in the Army Air Force from that time on. Up until that time, they treated us like children. As long as we were flying airplanes and minding our own business and helping them, it was OK, but if we wanted to manifest our own destiny, that was verboten.[33]

The McCloy committee (discussed in Chapter 2) weighed in on how the army air corps decided to interpret Army Regulation 210–10 and War Department Pamphlet 20–6 in a report that it issued in May 1945. The committee recommended that the army air corps comply with Army Regulation 210–10. Historian Todd Moye concluded:

> The Freeman 104 forced the War Department to define racial segregation as a discriminatory act by definition, and they placed the institution squarely on the side of integration. The movement toward full integration of the armed forces might be gradual and halting from that point forward, but there would be no going back.[34]

The discrimination that many African Americans faced in the war industry and in the military as symbolized by Lt. Terry's experience, and the experiences of many others who served in the segregated armed services, also culminated into a significant movement by April 1945. Walter White wrote in 1945 that "Negro militancy and implacable determination to wipe out segregation grew more proportionately during the years 1940 to 1945 than during any other period of the Negro's history in America."[35] Further proof of this was that by 1945 the membership of the NAACP had grown to 500,000.[36] Harry Truman would encounter a re-energized African American populace that after the war had little patience for discrimination and continued civil rights abuses. Blacks had contributed to the war that defeated fascism and now they wanted to defeat racism in their own country except that now they would be fighting for civil and human rights within the context of the Cold War.

CHAPTER 4

Post-War Utilization of the Military and the Creation of the President's Committee on Civil Rights, 1945–1947

It is impossible to decide who suffers the greatest moral damage from our civil rights transgressions, because all of us are hurt. This is certainly true of those who are victimized. Their belief in the basic truth of the American promise is undermined. But they do have the realization, galling as it sometimes is, of being morally in the right.

To Secure These Rights[1]

It was no surprise that on April 19, 1945, Walter White sent Harry Truman a letter asking when he might be available to meet to discuss "Negro-white relations" given the significant challenges the country had worked through during the war.[2] He closed his letter by stating that he was leaving that afternoon to attend the San Francisco conference. The San Francisco conference was the first meeting of the United Nations, which had been outlined by the United States, the United Kingdom, and the Soviet Union at their wartime meeting at Yalta. The United States had asked forty-two organizations to come to San Francisco to serve as consultants to the U.S. delegation and the NAACP was

> In 1945 the Daughters of the American Revolution (DAR) invited Bess Truman to attend a tea in her honor at Constitution Hall; however, the DAR refused to allow blacks into Constitution Hall. When Bess accepted the invitation, New York Congressman Adam Clayton Powell sent her a telegram and urged her to decline the invitation. Bess refused and Powell responded by referring to her as "the last lady."

William Edward Burghardt Du Bois

William Edward Burghardt Du Bois was born in 1868 and grew up in Great Barrington, MA. He received a B.A. from Fisk University and entered Harvard in 1888 where he earned another B.A. In 1892 he earned an M.A. in History from Harvard and left to study abroad in Germany. In 1896 he completed his Ph.D. from Harvard—the first African American to do so—and wrote his dissertation on "The Suppression of the African Slave Trade to the United States, 1638–1870." Du Bois taught at Atlanta University in 1899 before leaving his position to become one of the initial co-founders of the NAACP in 1909 and remained with the organization as editor of the *Crisis*.[3]

The *Crisis* was the official newspaper of the NAACP; however, it was separate from the organization until the Great Depression when financial difficulties forced the NAACP to take on an increasingly important financial role in the paper. Because the NAACP made a greater financial commitment to the paper the organization exerted more oversight over Du Bois, which created tension between White and Du Bois, and in 1934 Du Bois submitted his resignation and traveled to Atlanta University where he taught. Roy Wilkins took his place. By 1944 White wanted Du Bois back because he was knowledgeable about the problems people of color faced around the world as he was well traveled; White also wanted to utilize the U.N. as a forum to discuss human rights and colonialism. White made Du Bois the director for special research and he returned to oversee the NAACP's effort to draw attention to the problem of human rights within the context of colonialism.[4]

However, in the late 1940s White and Du Bois disagreed over how to address the challenge of civil rights and colonialism and Du Bois was dismissed from the organization in 1948. He was charged by the U.S. government of being an "unregistered agent of a foreign country" in the communist hysteria of the 1950s; however, he was acquitted of those charges in 1951. The U.S. government became increasingly concerned about his affiliation with communist groups and refused to issue him a passport that would allow him to leave the United States. He was finally cleared for travel and he made his way to Moscow in the heat of the Cold War to accept the Lenin Peace Prize. Du Bois continued his Pan-Africanist work and accepted the invitation of the President of the new African nation of Ghana to reside in his country, an invitation which Du Bois accepted. In 1961 Du Bois sold his house in Brooklyn and made his way to Ghana convinced that "the only answer to racial oppression in the United States" was "socialism in some form." Throughout his lifetime he had fought segregation, discrimination, lynchings, and racial violence and he felt like the U.S. government in its current democratic form would never fully address these issues and on October 1, 1961, he applied for membership in the Communist Party of the United States and left for Ghana on October 5. Because of his membership in the Communist Party, he was not allowed to return to the United States and he died in Ghana in 1963 at the age of ninety-five, just a few months before the passage of the Civil Rights Act of 1964.[5]

one of those organizations that sent Walter White, W. E. B. Du Bois, and Mary McLeod Bethune to serve as representatives from the NAACP.

At these initial U.N. meetings, White, Du Bois, and Bethune met with representatives from African and Asian countries and also with delegates from China and the Soviet Union. As Patricia Sullivan has written, "the NAACP contingent participated in the crafting of a human rights agenda that prioritized race discrimination and an end to colonialism." However, this agenda met with stiff resistance from officials within the U.S. government. John Foster Dulles, a member of the U.S. delegation, was concerned that if the U.N. supported a strong human rights provision that it might draw attention to America's problem with race in the South.[6]

The chair of the American delegation to the United Nations was Edward R. Stettinius, Jr. and White did not hesitate to weigh in on the issue of human rights; he told Stettinius in a May 15, 1945, memo that "I think we, as Americans, should be willing to have some of our own practices examined, as well as advocate examination, of the practices, colonialism and otherwise, of other nations." In a subsequent memo of conversation that White had with President Truman on May 25, 1945, he noted that the

> Secretary [White] discussed with the President [Harry Truman] the matter of colonial trusteeships and expressed disagreement at [the] action of the American delegation in voting against [the] proposals of China and Russia [that would have provided] . . . eventual independence for colonials and dependent peoples. The Secretary expressed disapproval at the United States siding with the United Kingdom and France as colonial powers who want to maintain their possessions.

White also encouraged the President to strengthen the International Bill of Human Rights and Commission of Human Rights "so that it would be effective in protecting human and civil rights of all people everywhere."[7]

By the time the United Nations charter was approved in San Francisco on June 26, 1945, the final document committed the U.N. and member states under Article 55(c) to work for "universal respect for, and observance of, human rights and fundamental freedoms for all without distinction as to race, sex, language, or religion."[8] However, John Foster Dulles had inserted language in the final charter that prohibited the U.N. from intervening "in matters which are essentially within the domestic jurisdiction of the State concerned." As historian Carol Anderson argued, the domestic jurisdiction clause of the charter would be invoked by

American representatives at the U.N. when petitions from organizations in the United States charged the United States government with violating Article 55(c) with respect to the country's African American population.[9]

What is significant is that African American leaders like White, Du Bois, and Bethune quickly recognized that the U.N. might afford them the opportunity to have human rights grievances aired before an international body, but the U.N. would also provide an international forum where oppressed peoples of color around the globe might have their grievances aired too. While White and Du Bois continued to push the U.N. and the Truman administration on these issues, White had plenty of other challenges that needed to be addressed within the United States. Those challenges included whether or not the FEPC would continue securing the passage of a federal anti-lynching law as well as legislation that would abolish the poll tax. However, there was one issue that was somewhat on the back burner at that time—integration of the military. In fact the U.S. military continued to try and craft policies that addressed the inclusion of blacks in their ranks even before World War II had come to a close.

During the early months of 1945 the War Department began to seriously consider its use of black troops at the request of Assistant Secretary John McCloy, who headed the War Department's Advisory Committee on Negro Troop Policy, which was also known as the McCloy committee. McCloy concluded that during the war the armed services had not drafted a comprehensive policy that governed how blacks should be utilized in the American military and that the army must draft a comprehensive policy that would define how blacks would be utilized in a post-World War II military. Secretary of War Stimson supported McCloy's plan.

> After World War II, the American fighting force fell from 12 million to just 1.4 million and the wartime draft ended.

Two weeks after Germany surrendered (May 22, 1945) a questionnaire was mailed to the top commanders at home and abroad and it asked the commanders a number of questions about their command of black troops. Truman Gibson, an African American member of the McCloy committee, did not believe that a questionnaire was the best way to poll the commanders in the field. He noted:

> Mere injunctions of objectivity do not work in the racial field where more often than not decisions are made on a basis of emotion, prejudice or pre-existing opinion . . . Much of the difficulty in the Army has arisen from improper racial attitudes

> on both sides. Indeed, the army's basic policy of segregation is said to be based principally on the individual attitudes and desires of the soldiers.

Gibson wanted a more scientific inquiry into how the military had utilized and commanded its black troops and he also wanted the American public to be polled about how they thought black troops should be utilized.[10]

The committee received comments from the commanders in the field and they also solicited feedback from the black troops themselves. Many of the comments surrounded the effectiveness of the 92nd Infantry Division, the only black regiment that served in the European theater. Some white military commanders believed the performance of the black infantry troops was inferior while other white military commanders said that other elements of the 92nd, like its artillery, technical, and administrative units, performed very well. When asked why the black infantry troops' performance was substandard the white military commanders offered different reasons. One commander said that many infantrymen in his division "would not fight" and another said his troops had "a lack of dedication to purpose" in combat. Lower level officers offered a different view as to why the black troops did not perform well. Lt. Col. Marcus H. Ray pointed the finger at the white officers of these black troops, who withheld promotions for black troops, and who humiliated those black troops under their command who "exhibited self-reliance and self-respect—necessary attributes of leadership."[11] MacGregor summed up the responses in this manner:

> Commanders tended to blame undisciplined troops and lack of initiative and control by black officers and non-commissioned officers as the primary cause of the difficulty. Others, particularly black observers, cited the white officers and their lack of racial sensitivity . . . but the underlying problem usually overlooked by observers was segregation.[12]

Truman Gibson urged his superiors to look at whether or not the performance of black troops could be improved if the forces were allowed to serve in integrated units. Furthermore, Gibson believed that:

> future policy should be predicated on an assumption that civilian attitudes will not remain static. The basic policy of the Army should, therefore, not itself be static and restrictive, but should be so framed as to make further progress possible on a flexible basis.

Gibson essentially called for a gradual integration of the military.[13]

In the summer and fall of 1945 the army discussed drafting a post-war policy on the use of blacks in the military; at the same time, Congress also debated the merits of universal military training and how African Americans could successfully serve in the military. Those discussions about universal military training continued into 1947.[14]

In September of 1945 John McCloy urged Secretary of War Stimson to turn the issue of the utilization of black troops in the military over to a board of general officers for their consideration. On September 27, 1945, Robert P. Patterson replaced Henry Stimson as the Secretary of War; he took McCloy's recommendation and instructed General Marshall to establish a board that would draft the post-war policy on the role blacks would play in the armed services. On October 1, 1945, the board met for the first time under the direction of Lt. Gen. Alvan C. Gillem, Jr. The board was instructed to:

> prepare a policy for the use of the authorized Negro manpower potential during the post-war period including the complete development of the means required to derive the maximum efficiency from the full authorized manpower of the nation in the event of a national emergency"

The group came to be known as the Gillem Board.[15]

General Gillem was from Tennessee and had commanded the XIII Corps in World War II. Others on the board included Maj. Gen. Lewis A. Pick from Virginia, Brig. Gen. Winslow C. Morse from Michigan, and Brig. Gen. Alan D. Warnock from Texas. The board worked quickly and within a month after their first meeting they had already achieved consensus on several issues. They wanted to craft a policy that would assign blacks tasks based on their individual merit and ability. The board studied the navy's attempt at partial integration and concluded that their policy had created competition among the troops, which in turn improved their performance. In contrast, the marine corps training, which utilized strict segregation, seemed to also mean that the training for their black recruits took longer. Unfortunately, the board's progress report did not contain a commitment to integration.[16]

On November 17, 1945, the Gillem Board completed its finishing touches on their progress report and sent it to the army Chief of Staff. According to MacGregor, "The board declared that its recommendations were based on two complementary principles: black Americans had a constitutional right to fight, and the Army had an obligation to make the most effective use of every soldier." The board discussed how smaller platoons of African American troops that were imbedded with white troops during World War II were more successful than large combat units because in the larger units their junior and non-commissioned officers had difficulty in leading their troops in combat.[17]

The board outlined eighteen recommendations. One of the most important recommendations included language that eliminated segregation in the overhead units; these were essentially administrative units of the army and during the war their ranks were virtually closed to African Americans. The decision to include blacks in the overhead units would also help the army "foster leadership, maintain morale, and encourage a competitive spirit among the better qualified." The army expected to maintain a fighting force that was at least 10 percent black, which reflected the fact that African Americans made up 10 percent of the nation's population. The circular recommended that black officers be incorporated into the army but the board neither set a number nor required that the officers be restricted to black units.[18]

John J. McCloy and Truman Gibson both weighed in on the board's proposal. McCloy described the report as a "fine achievement" and a "great advance" over previous attempts at crafting a policy. However, they also had some concerns: McCloy and Gibson wanted the army to eliminate the 10 percent quota because it could be used by the army to keep out well qualified blacks who wanted to re-enlist. McCloy was direct: "I do not see any place for a quota in a policy that looks to utilize Negroes on the basis of ability." Gibson was very concerned that the proposal did not directly outline a clear path to an integrated military. Ambiguity in the proposed plan, he thought, would favor those in the military that struggled with the thought of an integrated army.[19]

The Gillem Board met again in January 1946 to examine the feedback to their proposal and they made a few modifications and additions to the report, but most were minor. General Dwight D. Eisenhower, Chief of Staff, sent the proposed policy to Secretary Patterson for his approval. The secretary approved the policy on February 28, 1946, and the *Utilization of Negro Manpower in the Postwar Army Policy* was published as War Department Circular 124 on April 27, 1946. This circular guided the army's policy on the "Utilization of Negro Manpower" until Truman issued the Executive Order that would eventually result in the desegregation of the military in July of 1948.[20]

The black press reaction to the policy was one of skepticism. The *Pittsburg Courier* did not believe that much would change because the policy did not specifically state that segregation must end. MacGregor noted the same problem; however, he concluded that the:

> Gillem Board was a progressive step in the history of Army race relations. It broke with the assumption implicit in earlier Army policy that the black soldier was inherently inferior by recommending that Negroes be assigned tasks as varied and skilled as those handled by white soldiers. It also made integration the Army's goal by declaring as official policy the ultimate employment of all manpower without regard to race.[21]

While the army crafted its policy on the utilization of blacks in a post-World War II world, so did the navy. In the last year of the war the navy modified its racial policies by breaking up its large, segregated units and integrated African Americans into specialist and officer training schools, into the WAVES, its auxiliary fleet, and into its recruiting centers. In the post-World War II period the navy integrated its general service; however, the policy did not bring about the integration of the steward's branch, which remained exclusively black and it also did not apply to the marine corps, which remained segregated.[22]

During the time the armed services debated and crafted their post-war policies on blacks in the military, the armed services also crafted its policies on homosexuals in the military. Some within the ranks of the military, like Lieutenant Colonel Lewis Loeser, who oversaw a study of 270 homosexual patients at a military hospital in England titled "Utilization of the Sexual Psychopath in the Military Service," concluded that homosexuals could be effectively utilized in the military. Loeser's research was supported by the work of Dr. Clements Fry, director of the Yale University student clinic, and Edna Rostow, a social worker, who concluded that "homosexuals were no better or worse than other soldiers and that many 'performed well in various military jobs' including combat." Unfortunately, as Berube noted, Loeser, Fry, and Rostow completed their research at the end of the war, when manpower for the armed services was not a critical issue, and consequently Berube concluded that these studies did not influence the military to "integrate homosexuals into the armed services" during the post-World War II period.[23]

Many homosexuals who left the army after the war received a blue discharge that prevented them from receiving benefits under the 1944 GI Bill of Rights. Harry Truman expressed interest in helping those that received a blue discharge and finally from late 1945 until early 1947, under the advice of psychiatric consultant William Menninger, who did not advocate the use of the blue discharges, urged the adjutant general to issue a directive that would grant honorable discharges to homosexuals "who had committed no inservice acts." However, by May 1947 this period of "tolerance," as Berube described it, came to an end.[24]

In September of 1947 Secretary of the Navy, John L. Sullivan, established a committee that examined what to do with naval personnel who were involved in homosexual offenses. In August of 1949 the Defense Department's Personnel Policy board completed a study, called Project M-46. The board drew heavily from the work completed by the naval committee and drafted a service wide policy on homosexuality. The Defense Department accepted the recommendations of the committee and drafted a policy that stated "homosexual personnel, irrespective of sex, should not be permitted to serve in any branch of the Armed Services in any capacity, and prompt separation of known homosexuals from the Armed Forces is mandatory."[25] Furthermore, Project M-46 called upon armed forces personnel to give lectures about homosexuality and it proposed to divide homosexual cases into three categories. Those categories included those who used force, those cases that were consensual, and those cases where individuals demonstrated homosexual tendencies.[26]

At the same time the armed services drafted its policy on homosexuals, the Congress also passed the Uniform of Military Justice law in 1950. This law was supposed to grant individual military personnel due process rights. Congress also created the Court of Military Appeals, which was an all-civilian court that was tasked with reviewing court-martial decisions. According to Berube, the:

> Uniform Code, together with the Defense Department's uniform guidelines, established the basic policies, discharge procedures, and appeals channels for the disposition of homosexual personnel that remained in effect, with periodic modifications, in all branches of the armed forces for the next four decades.[27]

While the military tightened its anti-homosexual policies in the late 1940s, the focus on homosexuals also was swept up in the hunt for communists. On February 28, 1950, Under Secretary of State, John Peurifoy, testified before a Senate Committee that was investigating the loyalty of federal employees. Peurifoy admitted that ninety-one State Department officials had been dismissed because they were homosexual and that they posed a security risk to the country. The argument was that homosexuals were seen as being more susceptible to blackmail from Communist infiltrators than heterosexuals. In response to Peurifoy's testimony, two Senators—Republican Kenneth Wherry of Nebraska and Democrat Lister Hill from Alabama—formed a subcommittee to investigate the "Infiltration of Subversives and Moral Perverts Into the Executive

Branch of the United States Government." In June 1950, the Senate also authorized the creation of another committee under the leadership of Senator Clyde Hoey of North Carolina to investigate the "Employment of Homosexuals and Other Sex Perverts in Government." In December of 1950 the Hoey committee released a report that essentially argued that homosexuals posed a security risk.[28]

Berube argued that the strongest action taken against homosexuals occurred when President Dwight Eisenhower signed Executive Order 10450, which for the first time stated that "sexual perversion" was now grounds "for not hiring and for firing federal workers." Berube concluded: "With Eisenhower's executive order the government's antihomosexual policies and procedures, which had originated in the wartime military, expanded to include every agency and department of the federal government and every private company or corporation with a government contract."[29]

While the military crafted policies that would keep gays and lesbians out of the military in the immediate post-World War II period, the country had to readjust from a wartime to a peacetime environment. African American veterans returned home hoping to exchange their service in the war for a more democratic United States that respected their rights as citizens. Unfortunately, many returned to find that Jim Crow was entrenched even more and others encountered violence and a renewed effort by some whites to make sure that blacks still knew their place in a post-World War II world. This challenge would shake the nation and African Americans to their core.

The year 1946 opened with Truman facing a significant fight over the extension of the FEPC. Truman asked for the creation of a permanent FEPC in his State of the Union address that he delivered on January 21, 1946.[30] In February, the Senate took a cloture vote on the bill but it did not receive the necessary two-thirds vote so the FEPC bill did not move forward. In response, A. Philip Randolph traveled across the United States in protest and one protest at Madison Square Garden in New York City drew over 17,000 people and a telegram of support from Harry Truman.[31]

Also in February, the United Nations Commission on Human Rights (CHR) was created. The commission drafted an international bill of rights and established a Sub-Commission on Prevention of Discrimination and Protection of Minorities. According to historian Glenda Gilmore, "The commission found its authority in the non-discrimination clause in the U.N. Charter." The United States approved this clause when the U.N. was created in June of 1945. However, John Foster Dulles was concerned that the clause might enable outside groups to petition the U.N. to examine how the United States dealt with the civil rights of its African

American citizens. The creation of the CHR in February of 1946 did not have an immediate impact on Harry Truman although the Commission would later have to decide whether or not it would entertain petitions from groups within the United States that wanted America's civil rights record reviewed—the push for a review had much to do with the racial violence that exploded in February of 1946.

On February 13, 1946, Isaac Woodard, a newly returned African American veteran from the war, boarded a Greyhound bus in Camp Gordon, Georgia, and made his way home to Winnsboro, South Carolina. The bus pulled into Batesburg, South Carolina, for a break and Woodard got off and found the blacks only restroom. When he returned to the bus, the bus driver had alerted the police, having thought Woodard had taken too long of a break. Chief of Police Lynwood Shull arrived on the scene and confronted Woodard, but he was not pleased with the way in which Woodard responded to his questions so then proceeded to beat him with his night stick, severely damaging both of his eyes in the brutal attack.[32]

A couple of weeks later, on February 24, in Columbia, Tennessee, a dispute which started between a white radio repairman and a black mother and her son, who was a veteran of World War II, resulted in a white mob descending on the African American section of Columbia. The African Americans responded by shooting into the mob and wounded four police officers. The state highway patrol was called in and for the next two days they ransacked the black businesses and inflicted a reign of terror on black residents. They also arrested forty-two black residents of Columbia.

The NAACP immediately intervened in the situation and provided legal counsel for all of those who were arrested. The National Committee for Justice in Columbia (NCJC), Tennessee, was created and headed by Eleanor Roosevelt and Channing Tobias, of the NAACP. Trials were held and twenty-five of the forty-two who were arrested faced serious charges. An all-white jury was selected to hear the case. In the closing arguments of the case Z. Alexander Looby, defense attorney, put the case in an international perspective when he said:

> We have spent millions, yea billions of dollars to preserve democracy on earth; and why was democracy threatened? If I remember correctly, it was because of the existence of a so-called master race . . . we sacrificed thousands of our young men in the flower of youth . . . We did all of that that democracy shall not perish but take root and grow and cover the earth . . . but how can we go to the United Nations and demand and insist on democracy in other countries when we don't practice it ourselves? This is the question before us.

The jury returned a verdict that acquitted twenty-three of the twenty-five.[33] It was a significant victory for the NAACP.

On June 6, 1946, the NNC, which had remained dormant during the war and was now under the direction of Max Yergan, decided to petition the U.N. to call attention to the oppression that African Americans faced in the United States. The NNC was closely allied with the Civil Rights Congress (CRC), which was organized in May of 1946.[34] Both the NNC and the CRC challenged Harry Truman's administration to act on civil rights; some of their proposals were to the left of the NAACP. The FBI was quick to point out that the NNC was a Communist organization in order to try and discredit the NNC and their petition. While it was true that communists were involved with the organization, "red baiting," which is essentially accusing someone or some group of being Communist, was an easy way to silence individuals and groups who had legitimate complaints during the Cold War. Furthermore, some of the groups that were advocating for civil rights had to walk a fine line about how they criticized the government's policies for fear of being accused of sympathizing with Communism. The U.N. instructed the NNC to provide evidence that the allegations in their petition were true and so the NNC forwarded articles about lynching to the U.N. secretariat. They also organized "People's Tribunals" in several major cities to obtain testimony from African Americans that supported their petition; however, these tribunals only brought limited success.[35]

The challenge that the petition faced was that the American representatives to the U.N. CHR wanted to make sure that the domestic jurisdiction clause of the U.N. Charter would be invoked to prevent the CHR from addressing the NNC petition. The problem was that Third World countries and the Soviet Union did not agree with that interpretation. According to Carol Anderson, the General Assembly rejected the domestic jurisdiction argument and argued that every country that signed the U.N. Charter had renounced their sovereignty. This was an issue that continued to play out through the end of the year and into 1947.[36]

While the U.N. CHR was deciding the fate of the NNC petition, Harry Truman's Attorney General made a significant speech on civil rights. Speaking before the Chicago Bar Association on June 21, 1946, Tom C. Clark, a Texas native, revealed that in the first half of government fiscal year 1946 his department received 2,690 complaints from individuals who said their civil rights were violated. In response, Clark stated that the Department of Justice only had a "limited scope and jurisdiction" as a "protector of civil rights." He discussed that the Department only had two sections (Section 51 and Section 52) under which they could prosecute violations of a person's civil liberties. He described Section 51 and Section 52 of Title 18 of the criminal code:

> Section 51 of Title 18 provides: If two or more persons conspire to injure, oppress, threaten, or intimidate any citizen in the free exercise or enjoyment of any right or privilege secured to him by the Constitution or laws of the United States, or because of his having so exercised the same, or if two or more persons go in disguise on the highway, or on the premises of another, with intent to prevent or hinder his free exercise or enjoyment of any right or privilege so secured, they shall be fined not more than $5,000 and imprisoned not more than ten years, and shall, moreover, be thereafter ineligible to any office, or place of honor, profit, or trust created by the Constitution or laws of the United States.
>
> . . . Under such holdings as the *Slaughterhouse* cases, the rights to life, liberty, and property, encompassed in the 14th amendment, are not considered federal-secured rights since they flow for the most part from the States.
>
> They are incidents of State, not national, citizenship and have been held not to be within the scope of Section 51.
>
> A further weak point in this section is that the Constitution deals primarily with relationships between the private person and government, rather than with relationships of private persons, one to another.
>
> There are few constitutional rights protected against infringement by other individuals.
>
> In the absence of special circumstances, Section 51 does not protect the individual or the minority against mob or ruffian activity.
>
> While such attacks may amount to a deprivation of freedom of speech or other rights guaranteed by the Bill of Rights, these rights are rights protected only against official action, not private action.
>
> Among the rights which have been held to warrant protection against the acts of individuals as well as officials are the rights to run for federal office, to be free from involuntary servitude, to have access to the federal courts, to be a witness in the federal courts, to inform federal officers concerning federal offenses, to journey to the national capital on federal business, and possibly most important of all, the right to vote and to have that vote counted as cast.

The Civil Rights Section has always been in the vanguard of the struggle to insure that every qualified voter can freely and without fear, exercise his constitutional right and his first duty as a citizen—his right to vote.

Such landmarks in constitutional law as *Classic v. United States*, and *Smith v. Allwright*, [discussed in Chapter 1] making the right to vote real and meaningful for the negro in particular, but for all Americans in the larger sense, are among the more outstanding successes of the Civil Rights Section.

. . . I, as attorney General, will use every force at my command to see to it that in the primaries and forthcoming elections, no American citizen will be deprived of his vote because of his race or color.

. . . Section 52 of Title 18 includes the larger number of the constitutional guarantees—the 14th and 15th Amendments as well as the Bill of Rights. It reads as follows:

Depriving citizens of civil rights under color of State laws.

Whoever, under color of any law, statute, ordinance, regulation, or custom, willfully subjects, or causes to be subjected, any inhabitant of any State, Territory, or District to the deprivation of any rights, privileges, or immunities secured or protected by the Constitution and laws of the United States, or to different punishments, pains, or penalties, on account of such inhabitant being an alien, or by reason of his color, or race, than are prescribed for the punishment of citizens, shall be fined not more than $1,000, or imprisoned not more than one year, or both.

Under this section we prosecute anyone who, clothed with State or Federal power, willfully misuses that power to deprive any person of such liberties as freedom from personal restraint, freedom of speech, press, and religion, freedom to assemble peaceably, to petition the government, to pursue a lawful calling, to acquire and use knowledge, to establish a home, or to move freely from state to state.

Rights of due process are also included—the right to a real hearing, the right to real counsel in a criminal prosecution, the right to a jury from which members of the defendant's race have not been purposely excluded.

This statute has been a powerful weapon against local sheriffs, police officers and other officials who would set themselves above the law and substitute trial by ordeal, or the "kangaroo court", for trial by law in dealing with the friendless, the ignorant, the unpopular, or the unorthodox.

Clark noted that the court, in *Screws v. United States*, which was decided in 1945 under his watch as Attorney General, narrowly defined what "willfully" meant. The case involved a black prisoner in Georgia who was falsely arrested and brutally beaten by a sheriff and his deputy. The sheriff and the deputy were convicted of violating the civil rights of the black prisoner; however, the Supreme Court reversed their conviction and in the process defined "willfully" to mean that a:

> state official must, at the time he deprives another of some established federal right, have more than a general bad purpose or evil intent to do wrong.
>
> He must have the purpose at that time of depriving his victim of a specific federal right—that is, a right which "had been made specific either by the express terms of the Constitution or laws of the United States or by decision interpreting them."
>
> The immediate effect of the court's narrow interpretation of the statute is perhaps best evidenced in the verdict of acquittal returned by the jury in the retrial of the case.

Clark outlined the limited legal tools the Civil Rights Division of the Justice Department had in responding to individual civil rights complaints. It seemed to be a frustrating position to be in, with limited legal tools with which to fight these significant assaults which were taking place against returning African American veterans. Because of the limited legal tools at his disposal, Clark encouraged his listeners to practice "tolerance and fair play, which are our heritage and the hallmarks of our civilization."[37]

What happened in Monroe, Georgia, on July 25, 1946, did not represent "tolerance and fair play" but rather the actions that had been the "hallmark" of America's Jim Crow experience. Roger Malcolm had just been released on bond for stabbing a white man for "messing" with his wife, Dorothy. He was picked up by Dorothy and her brother George, a recently returned veteran from World War II, and his wife, Mae, who was seven months pregnant. As the couple made their way home a mob intercepted their vehicle and forced it to stop. What happened next was disturbing, graphic, and revolting. Both couples were executed by a hail of gunshot blasts.[38]

The Monroe lynchings unified the African American organizations in a way that had never been seen before. On July 29 the NNC led a protest in front of the White House and the next day fifty women from the NAACP took their place. Also on that day Walter White sent Attorney General Clark a telegram stating that he believed that a federal crime had been committed in the lynching.[39] A new organization, the CRC was also formed around this time; however, it had strong ties to the NNC. On August 6, 1946, the NAACP, along with some forty other civil rights, labor, religious, and veterans groups, established the National Emergency Committee Against Mob Violence (NECAMV). On September 12 Truman sent a letter to the annual conference of the NUL. In part it read:

> It is an obligation of government to see that the civil rights of every citizen are fully and equally protected. If the civil rights of even one citizen are abused, government has failed to discharge one of its primary responsibilities. We, as a people, must not, and I say to you we shall not, remain indifferent in the face of acts of intimidation and violence in our American communities.[40]

The NECAMV arranged to meet with Harry Truman on September 19.

The group, led by Walter White, presented a petition to the President that once again expressed outrage at what had happened in Monroe. They asked that Truman reconvene Congress to pass an anti-lynching bill. White also detailed other atrocities that had been committed against African Americans and according to one accounting of the meeting:

> Truman sat with clenched hands through the recounting, his face mirroring shock at the story of Isaac Woodard's blinding. When White had concluded, the President got up from his chair and said, "My God! I had no idea that it was as terrible as that! We've got to do something!"[41]

The very next day Truman drafted a letter to Attorney General Tom Clark. The letter encouraged Clark to "push with everything you have" to investigate whether or not the local officials in Monroe County had violated the two sections of civil rights law that Clark had outlined in his June, 1946, speech. Unfortunately the grand jury that was convened to look at the lynchings in Monroe concluded that "The members of this body are unanimous in reporting that we have been unable to establish the identity of any person or persons participating in the murders or in any violation of the civil rights statutes of the United States." This led Laura Wexler to conclude: "The federal government . . . responded to the worst incident of racial violence since the end of World War II with the most massive lynching investigation in the country's history. And yet, there was still no justice."[42]

Paul Robeson, head of the American Crusade to End Lynching and noted African American singer and entertainer, arranged to meet with the

Paul Robeson

Paul Robeson was born in 1898 in Princeton, New Jersey. He was the youngest of five children who attended Rutgers University where he was selected as an All-American in football. He briefly played professional football; however, his athletic ability was not his only talent. He was also musically gifted and traveled to Europe in the 1920s where he established an international reputation. It was during his travels that he came to compare and contrast the racism and segregation that was entrenched in the United States with what he saw in Europe. In 1934 he visited the Soviet Union and in 1936 he returned for a concert tour. During the 1940s he returned to the United States but refused to perform in segregated venues.

In 1947 Robeson halted his singing career to support Henry Wallace. Robeson, by this time, was considered by many to be a Communist and in 1949 he attended the Congress of the World Partisans for Peace in Paris where he denounced the United States for its racist and anti-Soviet policies. In 1950 the United States government seized his passport and prevented him from leaving the country; however, he eventually got his passport back and traveled to England, returning to the United States where he died in 1976.[43]

President on September 23, 1946. Representatives from the NNC, the SCHW, and the National Council of Negro Women were also present. One of the delegates suggested the climate in the United States was not unlike the climate that existed in Nazi Germany during World War II. At the time, the world was watching the Nuremberg trials unfold in Germany, which had prosecuted Nazi leaders for war crimes. The comparison was not far off the mark; however, it infuriated President Truman. Paul Robeson encouraged the President to bring mob action to an end in the United States, which further created tension. Robeson represented the left wing of the civil rights movement and because of the confrontation with the President he never received another offer to visit the White House.[44]

On July 13, 1946, Truman created the President's Commission on Higher Education to make sure that higher education was ready to enroll the large numbers of veterans that returned home after the war to take advantage of their benefits that were extended to them under the Veterans' Rehabilitation Act and the G. I. Bill of Rights. Truman "charged its members with the task of examining the functions of higher education in our democracy and the means by which they can best be performed." The committee released the first volume of a six volume report on December 11, 1947, which established the goals the committee wanted to achieve.[45] The second volume, titled "Equalizing and Expanding Individual Opportunity" was released a few days later on December 22 and had significant implications for Truman's civil rights program.[46]

The Commission on Higher Education report was overshadowed by the release of the President's Committee on Civil Rights report, a few months earlier; however, the report stated:

> Discrimination in the admission of college students because of an individual's race, creed, color, sex, national origin, or ancestry is an antidemocratic practice which creates serious inequalities in the opportunity for higher education. The Commission is opposed to discrimination and believes it should be abandoned.

The commission also did not shy away from the discussion of segregation in higher education. The report continued:

> This Commission concludes that there will be no fundamental correction of the total condition until segregation legislation is repealed.
>
> Deep-seated, long-standing forces of opinion and sentiment are obviously involved. Segregation laws cannot be wished away or eradicated by executive order. But influences looking to their repeal are at work; time and more vigorous effort will change public sentiment. White and Negro citizens will have to continue to work together to secure the necessary legislation and then implement it adequately so that the educational opportunity for white and Negro students will become equal. Until such action is taken, the opportunities for Negroes to qualify as leaders in education, law, medicine, the church, and other areas will be limited seriously. Our national life is made poorer by the lack of such leadership.
>
> Since legalized segregation still exists, this Commission urges that the separate educational institutions for Negroes be made truly equal in facilities and quality to those for white students.[47]

Not every committee member agreed with this section of the report. In fact, there were four committee members who insisted on publishing a dissenting view on what was identified as the "Racial Discrimination" section of the report. Their letter of dissent stated that while they understood "that many conditions affect adversely the lives of our Negro citizens" they believed that any changes must be made "within the established patterns of social relationships, which require separate educational institutions for whites and Negroes." The dissenting opinion continued: "We believe that pronouncements such as those of the Commission on the question of segregation jeopardize these efforts, impede progress, and threaten tragedy to the people of the South, both white and Negro."[48]

On November 20, 1946, Harry Truman appointed an Advisory Commission on Universal Training. The committee's membership included Joseph E. Davies from Washington who had been a former lawyer and ambassador; Dr. Daniel Poling from Boston, editor, *The Christian Herald*; Samuel I. Rosenman from New York, jurist and former Special Counsel to Roosevelt; Anna Rosenberg from New York, public and industrial relations consultant; Truman K. Gibson from Chicago, lawyer and former Civilian Aide to the Secretary of War; Dr. Harold W. Dodds, President of Princeton University; The Reverend Edmund A. Walsh, Vice-President of Georgetown University; Dr. Karl T. Compton, President of Massachusetts Institute of Technology; and Charles E. Wilson, president of General Electric. Dodd chaired the committee. The committee met for the first time on December 20 and Truman told the committee members that he purposely omitted the word "military" from the title of the commission because in his words:

> I want it to be a universal training program, giving our young people a background in the disciplinary approach of getting along with one another, informing them of their physical makeup, and what it means to take care of this temple which God gave us. If we get that instilled into them, and then instill into them a responsibility which begins in the township, in the city ward, the first thing you know we will have sold our republic to the coming generations as Madison and Hamilton and Jefferson sold it in the first place.[49]

Truman Gibson, who had served as a civilian aide on the McCloy committee, was asked to provide his expertise on the role of African Americans in a universal training program. Gibson remembered that the advisory commission sometimes met with President Truman in the oval office and on one occasion Gibson vividly recalled a conversation he had with the President, Sam Rosenman, Truman aide, and fellow committee member, Anna Rosenberg. Truman talked about the beating that Isaac Woodard had endured in February of 1946 and remarked that "This shit has to stop." According to Gibson, Truman continued: "I've been mulling over this issue of segregation . . . I'm going to take the bull by the horns. I'm going to help your people." He then told them that he was going to issue an executive order that would eliminate segregation in the armed services.[50]

The committee held hearings on universal training, which also included hearings on the role African Americans should play in universal training. Gibson, of course, urged his fellow committee members to eliminate segregation. Drawing upon his work on the McCloy committee, he shared with fellow committee members how segregation had a negative impact on military efficiency and argued that it was a significant hindrance to the morale of black troops. According to Gibson, the Commission, which released its final report on May 29, 1947, titled *A Program for National Security*, rejected segregation; however, the executive summary left the commission's position on integration vague. The position against segregration was contained within the body of the report which read:

> Neither in the training itself, nor in the organization of any phase of this program, should there be discrimination for or against any person or group because of his race, class, national origin, or religion. Segregation or special privilege in any form should have no place in the program. To permit them would nullify the important living lesson in citizenship which such training can give. Nothing could be more tragic for the future attitude of our people, and for the unity of our nation, than a program in which our federal government forced our young manhood to live for a period of time in an atmosphere which emphasized or bred class or racial differences.[51]

On April 15, 1947, Jackie Robinson stepped onto Ebbets Field in Brooklyn, New York to break the racial barrier that had divided white major leaguers from their black counterparts in the Negro Leagues. It was the same month that eight black men and eight white men embarked on the first freedom rides on behalf of the Congress of Racial Equality (CORE) in order to test whether or not states were complying with the *Morgan v. Virginia* decision which outlawed segregation in interstate transportation.[52]

> Jackie Robinson served as a second lieutenant in the U.S. army from 1942 to 1944. During boot camp, Robinson was arrested because he refused to go to the back of the bus because he was black. He was arrested and court-martialed for his actions; however, he was later acquitted of all charges, but he remained an outspoken critic of segregation and discrimination for the rest of his life.

The Advisory Commission on Universal Training was not the only important commission that Truman established in 1946 that addressed segregation in the armed

Anna Rosenberg

Figure 4.1 The President's Advisory Commission on Universal Training presents *A Program for National Security* to Harry Truman. Anna Rosenberg is pictured third from the right and Truman Gibson is second from the right. Truman Library.

The Advisory Commission on Universal Training membership included one woman, Anna Rosenberg. Rosenberg, who was a Jewish immigrant from Hungary, came to the United States in 1915 and settled in New York City. She became active in Tammany Hall, a political machine, and later the New Deal where she befriended Franklin Roosevelt. From August to September of 1944 she served as Roosevelt's "Special Representative to the European Theater of Operations" and was tasked with developing education and vocational programs that would benefit returning servicemen after the war. It was while she was in this capacity as special representative that she met General Eisenhower. Secretary of War Robert P. Patterson awarded her the Medal of Freedom in 1945.[53]

Congress refused to act on the commission's report and the commission remained in existence until the outbreak of the Korean War in 1950. At that point, George Marshall, who became the Secretary of Defense in September of 1950, was tasked with finding new ways to increase the number of Americans in the military. He established an office of the Assistant Secretary for Manpower and tried to revive the push for universal training and he asked Anna Rosenberg if she would fill that task. She received an interim appointment and was sworn in on November 15, 1950, and later in November the Senate Armed Services Committee confirmed her as Assistant Secretary. She became the first female Assistant Secretary of Defense and during the Korean War she helped implement Truman's order to desegregate the military.[54]

services. In September of 1946 at the meeting where Truman met with Walter White and the NECAMV he had already made up his mind that he wanted to establish a commission that would look at civil rights in the United States. In follow up conversations with White, Truman said that he would probably have to create the commission by executive order. The person on Truman's administrative staff that would be responsible for the committee was David K. Niles. Niles handled minority affairs for the President and he was assisted by Philleo Nash. Niles and Nash were the two individuals that black leaders contacted if they wanted something from the Truman administration.[55]

On October 11, 1946, Attorney General Clark submitted for Truman's approval a draft of an executive order that would create a commission to examine America's record on civil rights. After the midterm elections of November of 1946, which returned a Republican Congress for Harry Truman, he issued Executive Order 9808 on December 5, 1946, which created the PCCR. When he issued the executive order he also issued a statement:

> Freedom from Fear is more fully realized in our country than in any other on the face of the earth. Yet all parts of our population are not equally free from fear. And from time to time, and in some places, this freedom has been gravely threatened. It was so after the last war, when organized groups fanned hatred and intolerance, until, at times, mob action struck fear into the hearts of men and women because of their racial origin or religious beliefs.
>
> Today, freedom from fear, and the democratic institutions which sustain it, are again under attack. In some places, from time to time, the local enforcement of law and order has broken down, and individuals—sometimes ex-servicemen, even women—have been killed, maimed, or intimidated.
>
> The preservation of civil liberties is a duty of every Government—state, federal and local. Wherever the law enforcement measures and the authority of federal, state, and local governments are inadequate to discharge this primary function of government, these measures and this authority should be strengthened and improved.
>
> The Constitutional guarantees of individual liberties and of equal protection under the laws clearly place on the federal government the duty to act when state or local authorities abridge or fail to protect these Constitutional rights.
>
> Yet in its discharge of the obligations placed on it by the Constitution, the federal government is hampered by inadequate

> civil rights statutes. The protection of our democratic institutions and the enjoyment by the people of their rights under the Constitution require that these weak and inadequate statutes should be expanded and improved. We must provide the Department of Justice with the tools to do the job.
>
> I have, therefore, issued today an Executive Order creating the President's Committee on Civil Rights and I am asking this Committee to prepare for me a written report. The substance of this report will be recommendations with respect to the adoption or establishment by legislation or otherwise of more adequate and effective means and procedures for the protection of the civil rights of the people of the United States.[56]

The direction that he gave the committee was clear: they were to "inquire into and to determine whether and in what respect current law-enforcement measures and the authority and means possessed by federal, state, and local governments may be strengthened and improved to safeguard the civil rights of the people." Finally, they were to produce a report that would make recommendations as to how the federal government could more adequately protect the civil rights of all Americans. The Executive Order also outlined who would serve on the committee.

Truman appointed Charles E. Wilson, a white northerner who was also President of General Electric, to chair the committee. Wilson also served on the President's Advisory Commission on Universal Training. Franklin Roosevelt's son, Franklin D. Roosevelt Jr., served as vice-chair. Additional committee members included Sadie T. Alexander, James B. Carey, John S. Dickey, Morris L. Ernst, Rabbi Roland B. Gittelsohn, Dr. Frank P. Graham, The Most Reverend Francis J. Haas, Charles Luckman, Francis P. Matthews, The Right Reverend Henry Knox Sherrill, Boris Shishkin, M. E. Tilly, and Channing H. Tobias.

The committee was diverse racially, religiously, geographically, and included representatives from business and labor. Philleo Nash referred to the committee as the:

> 'Noah's Ark Committee,' because we were so meticulous to get balance that we wound up with two of everything; two women, two southerners, two business, two labor, and many people were there in more than one role, but it was a very carefully balanced commission, of around fifteen.[57]

Sadie Alexander and Channing Tobias were the two African American committee members and Sadie was a woman while Tobias was from the

South. The committee was also ecumenically balanced with Rabbi Roland Gittelsohn representing the Jewish faith, Episcopal bishop Henry Knox Sherrill representing Protestants, and Bishop Francis J. Haas, dean of Catholic University's School of Social Service, representing Catholics. Charles Wilson, president of General Electric; Charles Luckman, who was president of Lever; and Francis P. Matthews from Omaha, who served as an officer in the U.S. Chamber of Commerce, represented business interests, while they were balanced out by the presence of James Carey who was once president of a union that had tangled with Wilson's General Electric over collective bargaining and Boris Shishkin, a Russian Jewish immigrant who had worked for the AFL and served on the FEPC from 1942 to 1946. Rounding out the committee included John Dickey who was president of Dartmouth and Frank Porter Graham who was president of the University of North Carolina and who also had served as the first president of the SCHW. The final member, Morris Ernst, was born in Alabama and raised in New York City and he served as the co-counsel for the American Civil Liberties Union.[58]

The committee convened for the first time on January 15, 1947. Truman reflected back on his days when he was running for the Jackson County Court and he told those assembled that at the time "there was an organization in that county that met on hills and burned crosses and worked behind sheets." He continued: "I don't want to see any race discrimination. I don't want to see any religious bigotry break out in this country as it did then."[59]

The committee had to work fast because they were only given sixty days to prepare a report and they decided to break the work up by establishing three subcommittees. The first committee examined existing federal laws regarding civil rights and suggested new legislation to correct any deficiencies. The second subcommittee examined the public relations effect of America's civil rights record and the third assessed how America's civil rights record violated the individual civil rights of its citizens.[60]

According to McCoy and Ruetten, the committee received significant support from the Truman administration to complete their work and when more violent racial episodes erupted, the committee pledged to keep the incidents visible before Truman administration officials. Both David Niles and Philleo Nash assisted the committee as did the Department of Justice. The lynching of Willie Earle in South Carolina in February allowed the committee to intercede and the committee's role, according to Niles, took the President "off the hot seat."[61]

Under the direction of Chairman Wilson, the committee sent out letters to 194 groups and 112 individuals asking for their input about America's civil rights record. They also held hearings and invited members of the Justice Department, including Attorney General Clark and Turner Smith, chief of the Civil Rights Section, to testify before the committee. Attorney General Clark encouraged the committee to strengthen "the present Sections 51 and 52 of the civil rights statutes so that those who engage in mob activity or lynching activity . . . might be found guilty of a federal offense."[62]

The committee continued to meet throughout the spring and summer of 1947. On June 29, 1947, Harry Truman became the first President to address the NAACP on the steps of the Lincoln Memorial. It was a remarkable speech, with a setting that was as equally remarkable and it was carried live on the radio. Truman was accompanied by Walter White, Eleanor Roosevelt, and Senator Wayne Morse. The day before the speech Truman dashed off a letter to his sister and mother back home in Grandview, Missouri. He told his sister:

> I've got to make a speech to the Society for the Advancement of Colored People tomorrow and I wish I didn't have to make it. Mrs. R.[oosevelt] and Walter White, Wayne Morse, Senator from Oregon . . . are the speakers. Walter White is white in color, has gray hair and blue eyes, but he is a Negro. Mrs. Roosevelt has spent her public life stirring up trouble between whites and black[s]—and I'm in the middle. Mamma won't like what I say because I wind up by quoting old Abe. But I believe what I say and I'm hopeful we implement it.[63]

Oregon Senator Wayne Morse spoke first and told those gathered that "bigotry and democracy cannot be reconciled." Eleanor Roosevelt took the podium next and talked about the "blot of lynching" and said that "We [the United States] are now under the eyes of the whole world, which sees us as a nation built upon the contributions of many peoples." Walter White spoke next and described how William English Walling, a white Southerner, witnessed a race riot in Springfield, Illinois, and later became one of the founding members of the NAACP because he recognized that if a lynching could take place in Springfield, a place outside of the South, then lynchings could happen anywhere. White also described the successful efforts of the NAACP since its founding in securing human rights protections, including voting rights protections in primary elections.[64]

Truman took center stage and told the NAACP, the nation, and the world that:

> It is my deep conviction that we have reached a turning point in the long history of our country's efforts to guarantee freedom and

equality to all our citizens. Recent events in the United States and abroad have made us realize that it is more important today than ever before to insure that all Americans enjoy these rights.

When I say all Americans I mean all Americans.

There is no justifiable reason for discrimination because of ancestry, or religion, or race, or color.

Every man should have the right to a decent home, the right to an education, the right to adequate medical care, the right to a worthwhile job, the right to an equal share in making the public decisions through the ballot, and the fight to a fair trial in a fair court.

Many of our people still suffer the indignity of insult, the narrowing fear of intimidation, and, I regret to say, the threat of physical injury and mob violence. Prejudice and intolerance in which these evils are rooted still exist. The conscience of our Nation, and the legal machinery which enforces it, have not yet secured to each citizen full freedom from fear.

We cannot wait another decade or another generation to remedy these evils. We must work, as never before, to cure them now. The aftermath of war and the desire to keep faith with our Nation's historic principles make the need a pressing one.

Our case for democracy should be as strong as we can make it. It should rest on practical evidence that we have been able to put our own house in order. For these compelling reasons, we can no longer afford the luxury of a leisurely attack upon prejudice and discrimination. There is much that State and local governments can do in providing positive safeguards for civil rights. But we cannot, any longer, await the growth of a will to action in the slowest State or the most backward community.

Our national government must show the way.

This is a difficult and complex undertaking. Federal laws and administrative machineries must be improved and expanded. We must provide the Government with better tools to do the job. As a first step, I appointed an Advisory Committee on Civil Rights last December. Its members, fifteen distinguished private citizens, have been surveying our civil rights difficulties and needs for several months. I am confident that the product of their work will be a sensible and vigorous program for action by all of us.

We must strive to advance civil rights wherever it lies within our power. For example, I have asked the Congress to pass legislation extending basic civil rights to the people of Guam and American Samoa so that these people can share our ideals of

> freedom and self-government. This step, with others which will follow, is evidence to the rest of the world of our confidence in the ability of all men to build free institutions.
>
> The way ahead is not easy. We shall need all the wisdom, imagination and courage we can muster. We must and shall guarantee the civil rights of all our citizens. Never before has the need been so urgent for skillful and vigorous action to bring us closer to our ideal.
>
> We can reach the goal. When past difficulties faced our Nation we met the challenge with inspiring charters of human rights—the Declaration of Independence, the Constitution, the Bill of Rights, and the Emancipation Proclamation. Today our representatives, and those of other liberty-loving countries on the United Nations Commission on Human Rights, are preparing an International Bill of Rights. We can be confident that it will be a great landmark in man's long search for freedom since its members consist of such distinguished citizens of the world as Mrs. Franklin Roosevelt.[65]

After the speech Walter White told the President that he did an excellent job and the President reiterated that "I said what I did because I mean every word of it—and I am going to prove that I do mean it."[66]

The committee struggled to meet the sixty day deadline during the summer and fall of 1947; however, they did achieve consensus on a number of issues. The only issues that remained somewhat divisive included whether or not federal grants-in-aid to schools should be denied unless the schools adopted a non-segregation stipulation, strengthening FBI assistance in civil rights cases, and the role of federal loyalty programs. In September the PCCR released a draft report that was circulated among its members and the Justice Department and on October 29 the committee gathered at the White House to present the report to the President.

The release of the committee's report overshadowed two important events that had taken place a couple of weeks prior to October 29. On October 10, 1947, A. Philip Randolph and Grant Reynolds organized the Committee Against Jim Crow in Military Training and Service. The committee would play a role in Truman's decision to issue the executive order that resulted in the integration of the military. The creation of the committee was followed by the October 23 NAACP submission of a petition to the U.N. titled *An Appeal to the World: A Statement on the Denial of Human Rights to Minorities in the Case of Citizens of Negro Descent in the United States of America and an Appeal to the United Nations for Redress*. The NAACP, under the direction of W. E. B. Du Bois, had been working on this document since 1946. The introduction to the ninety-four page document linked the struggle that African Americans faced in the United States with a global struggle that other minority populations faced in other countries.

> We appeal to the world to witness that this attitude of America is far more dangerous to mankind than the Atom bomb; and far, far more clamorous for attention than disarmament or treaty. To disarm the hidebound minds of men is the only path to peace; and as long as Great Britain and the United States profess democracy with one hand and deny it to millions with the other, they convince none of their sincerity, least of all themselves. Not only that, but they encourage the aggression of smaller nations: so long as the Union of South Africa defends Humanity and lets two million whites enslave ten million colored people, its voice spells hypocrisy . . .
>
> Therefore, Peoples of the World, we American Negroes appeal to you; our treatment in America is not merely an internal question of the United States. It is a basic problem of humanity; of democracy; of discrimination because of race and color; and as such it demands your attention and action. No nation is so great that the world can afford to let it continue to be deliberately unjust, cruel and unfair toward its own citizens.
>
> This is our plea to the world; and to show it validity we are presenting you with the proof. The National Association for the Advancement of Colored People, with more than a half million members, has asked four scholars under my editorship to present chapters showing in detail the status of American Negros in the past and today, in law, administration and social condition; and the relation of this situation to the Charter of the United Nations.[67]

As historian David Levering Lewis has written, "Du Bois's petition was an early casualty of the new Cold War civil rights politics." The planning for the *Appeal* had gone on prior to Truman's creation of the PCCR and both Walter White and Roy Wilkins had supported Du Bois's work on the *Appeal* because they did not know what would become of it; however the PCCR delivered a document that White regarded as the "most courageous and specific document of its kind in American history" which led David Levering Lewis to conclude that "*To Secure These Rights* [PCCR's final report] made *An Appeal to the World* seem almost crankily obsolete" and that *An Appeal to the World* "by the fall of 1947" had lost "its appeal to Walter White and Roy Wilkins."[68]

The PCCR committee presented *To Secure These Rights* to the President and he thanked the committee for their service and told the nation that he hoped the document would be "an American charter of human freedom in our time." He continued:

> The need for such a charter was never greater than at this moment. Men of good will everywhere are striving, under great difficulties, to create a worldwide moral order, firmly established in the life of nations. For us here in America, a new charter of human freedom will be a guide for action; and in the eyes of the world, it will be a declaration of our renewed faith in the American goal—the integrity of the individual human being, sustained by the moral consensus of the whole Nation, protected by a Government based on equal freedom under just laws.[69]

The committee tried to define what they meant by civil rights and civil liberties and in fact used those words interchangeably when they described racial discrimination. Steven Lawson stated that when the term "civil rights" is used today that serves as a reference to civil rights that are outlined in the thirteenth, fourteenth, and fifteenth amendments of the Constitution whereas the term civil liberties is usually seen as something preserved in the Bill of Rights. During Truman's day the "categories were more fluid."[70] The PCCR centered their report on four basic rights, which included the right to safety and security of the person; the right to citizenship and its privileges; the right to freedom of conscience and expression; and the right to equality of opportunity.[71]

To Secure These Rights was divided into four sections. The first paragraph of the report stated that the committee was "not asked to evaluate the extent to which civil rights have been achieved in our county" but rather, "we have almost exclusively focused our attention on the bad side of our record—on what might be called the civil rights frontier." The first section titled "The American Heritage: The Promise of Freedom and Equality" discussed the four rights that were outlined in the previous paragraph and concluded that, while the country has had human slavery and religious persecution, the "civil rights of the American people—all of them—can be strengthened quickly and effectively by the normal processes of democratic, constitutional government."[72]

The second chapter, "The Record: Short of the Goal," described how the United States had fallen short in fulfilling its obligation to protect the rights of its minority citizens in all four of those categories outlined above. In discussing how the United States had not protected the "right to safety and security of the person", lynching, police brutality, administration of justice, involuntary servitude, and the internment of Japanese Americans during the War were discussed in significant detail. In the "right to citizenship and its privileges" portion of the chapter, the report outlined the problems of the white primary and the poll tax and declared that the "denial of suffrage on account of race is the most serious present interference with the right to vote."[73] The report also examined the role of minorities in the military under the subheading of the "Right to Bear Arms" and concluded that the "armed forces, in actual practice, still maintain many barriers to equal treatment for all their members."[74] The "Right to Freedom of Conscience and Expression" was included because some committee members believed that the Executive Order Truman issued that required federal employees to pledge their loyalty to the United States might inhibit free expression. In many ways this was an issue of civil liberties rather than an issue of civil rights; however, the committee wanted to include it in their report. The fourth right—the "Right to Equality of Opportunity"— discussed the problems of job discrimination and also the right to education, the right to housing, the right to health service, and the right to public services and accommodations. The chapter concluded by devoting a section to "Segregation Reconsidered" and called the doctrine of separate but equal a myth. The report read:

> In a democracy, each individual must have freedom to choose his friends and to control the pattern of his personal and family life. But we see nothing inconsistent between this freedom and a recognition of the truth that democracy also means that in going to school, working, participating in the political process, serving in the armed forces, enjoying government services in such fields as health and recreation, making use of transportation and other public accommodation facilities, and living in specific communities and neighborhoods, distinctions of race, color, and creed have no place.[75]

The third chapter, "Government's Responsibility: Securing the Rights," outlined five reasons why the "the federal government must play a leading role in our efforts as a nation to improve our civil rights record." The first reason given as to why the federal government must play a greater role was because local officials and private persons were not protecting the rights of their citizens. The belief that the federal government could provide leadership for local communities was the second reason given as to why the federal government must play an increased role and was made clear when the report noted that "leadership is available in the national government and it should be used." The committee argued as its third reason for an increased role for the federal government to play in civil rights matters was because "our civil rights record has growing international implications." The report went on to state: "The subject of human rights, itself, has been made a major concern of the United Nations." The committee was clearly aware that America's civil rights issues were seen in an international context when the report observed:

> A lynching in a rural American community is not a challenge to that community's conscience alone. The repercussions of such a crime are heard not only in the locality, or indeed only in our own nation. They echo from one end of the globe to the other, and the world looks to the American national government for both an explanation of how such a shocking event can occur in a civilized country and remedial action to prevent its recurrence.
>
> Similarly, interference with the right of a qualified citizen to vote locally cannot today remain a local problem. An American diplomat cannot forcefully argue for free elections in foreign lands without meeting the challenge that in many sections of America qualified voters do not have free access to the polls. Can it be doubted that this is a right which the national government must make secure?

The committee cited as the fourth reason for more federal involvement was that they believed there was a "steadily growing tendency of the American people to look to the national government for protection of their civil rights." Finally, the committee believed the federal government must assume greater leadership in the civil rights arena because it is the "largest single employer of labor in the country." This included the nation's armed forces and the committee was unequivocal when it wrote:

> government has the power, the opportunity and the duty to see that discrimination and prejudice are completely eliminated from the armed services, and that the American soldier or sailor enjoys as full a measure of civil liberty as is commensurate with military service.[76]

The final chapter of the report was titled "A Program of Action: The Committee's Recommendations." The committee members believed that the country was at a turning point in rethinking its commitment to civil rights. The report mentioned how the country reviewed what civil rights meant for the first time when the fledging nation drafted the Declaration of Independence and the Articles of Confederation between 1776 and

1791. The committee argued the country revisited the issue of civil righ[illegible] during the American Civil War for a second time and it was the committee's "profound conviction" that *To Secure These Rights* represented "a third re-examination of the situation." The report noted that "we have a moral reason, an economic reason, and an international reason for believing that the time for action is now."[77]

The moral reason for acting now had everything to do with the fact that the committee members believed there was a "pervasive gap between our aims and what we actually do" which created "a kind of moral dry rot which eats away at the emotional and rational bases of democratic beliefs." The report continued: "There are times when the differences between what we preach about civil rights and what we practice is shockingly illustrated by individual outrages." Those outrages included lynchings, the denial of voting rights privileges to both blacks and whites, and wartime segregation in the military. The economic reason for acting included the argument that discrimination "depresses the wages and income of minority groups," which reduces their purchasing power. Economic discrimination also manifests itself in keeping minorities out of skilled laboring positions, which keeps the workforce from being adequately prepared in the event of a national emergency. Discrimination embodied in the "separate but equal" doctrine required duplication of separate public schools for blacks and whites and also required public transportation to duplicate facilities, which created inefficiencies. The international reason to act was tied up in the committee's belief that:

> Our foreign policy is designed to make the United States an enormous, positive influence for peace and progress throughout the world. We have tried to let nothing, not even extreme political differences between ourselves and foreign nations, stand in the way of this goal. But our domestic civil rights shortcomings are a serious obstacle.
>
> . . . The international reason for acting to secure our civil rights now is not to win the approval of our totalitarian critics. We would not expect it if our record were spotless; to them our civil rights record is only a convenient weapon with which to attack us. Certainly we would like to deprive them of that weapon. But we are more concerned with the good opinion of the peoples of the world . . .[78]

The fourth chapter outlined thirty-four specific recommendations that the President needed to consider in order to make the federal government a leader in securing civil rights for all Americans. Some of the most important recommendations included reorganizing the civil rights section of the Department of Justice and strengthening Sections 51 and 52 of the United States Code that Attorney General Clark discussed in his June 1946 speech on civil rights. Other significant recommendations included the passage of a federal anti-lynching law, legislation that would end the use of poll taxes, enactment of a permanent Fair Employment Practices bill, and laws that would eliminate restrictive covenants. The report also included as one of its provisions the "enactment by Congress of legislation, followed by appropriate administrative action, to end immediately all discrimination and segregation based on race, color, creed, or national origin, in the organization and activities of all branches of the Armed Services."[79]

To Secure These Rights was a monumental indictment of America's civil rights record. Coupled with the President's Commission on Higher Education "Equalizing and Expanding Individual Opportunity" report that called for an end to segregation in higher education and the President's Advisory Commission on Universal Training that called for an integrated military, the President had three important commission reports that recommended fundamental changes going into 1948. Harry Truman had to engage with these reports and they offered civil rights leaders, like Walter White, a significant hope that real change could be realized; however, to other leaders, like W. E. B. Du Bois, the seeds of discontent were sowed and in the fall of 1947 and throughout the election year of 1948 all of the leaders had to make important decisions about how the United States would proceed with implementing the recommendations outlined in *To Secure These Rights*.

CHAPTER 5

Integration of the Military, 1948–1953

But Mr. Truman—Judge Fahy has told me this—said, "Go ahead and work it out, and I'll stand behind you." Now, he absolutely kept his word on this, he never tried to make any political capital out of it at all. And it was a great help.

E. W. Kenworthy, Executive Secretary of the Fahy Committee, Oral History[1]

And it took two presidential commissions to really make the Army realize that the President meant what he said. But the Fahy Commission really conveyed to them and really helped change them, for the Army realized finally that the President meant what he said . . . Because the Army really basically felt that integration interfered with military efficiency. They believed it. There is no need for integration. It would be too hard. And, really, in a popular sense you could not fault them too much because they were efficient officers. They conducted a great army, but it could have been a greater army.

Truman Gibson, Oral History[2]

The reaction to *To Secure These Rights* was significant. Walter White, writing in the *New York Herald Tribune*, called the report one of "the most uncompromising and specific pronouncement by a governmental agency on the explosive issue of racial and religious bigotry which has ever been issued."[3] In many ways the report said most of what W. E. B. Du Bois's *Appeal* had set out to do and Walter White and the NAACP strongly encouraged the Truman administration to focus on fulfilling the recommendations of the report. In contrast, the Southern reaction to the report was at times muted, but also very vigorous. Truman received letters like the one from a Virginia man that instructed the President that "If you do away with segregation, allow negro children in white schools, churches, etc. you might as well drop a few bombs on us and not prolong the agony."[4] Tension ran high and it would eventually spill over the top in the presidential election of 1948.

Truman wasted no time in making the PCCR's report an important component of his political agenda. In his January State of the Union address he announced that he would deliver a special message on civil rights. On February 2, 1948, Harry Truman delivered that message before Congress and outlined ten areas where legislation would be required to address particular deficiencies. The ten objectives included the first objective of establishing a permanent Commission on Civil Rights, a Joint Congressional Committee on Civil Rights, and a civil rights Division in the Department of Justice. Strengthening existing civil rights statutes, providing federal protection against lynching, and protecting the right to vote were the second, third and fourth objectives. The fifth and sixth objectives included establishing a FEPC to prevent unfair discrimination in employment and legislation that would prohibit discrimination in interstate transportation facilities. Providing home-rule and suffrage in Presidential elections for the residents of the District of Columbia and providing statehood for Hawaii and Alaska and greater self-government for America's territorial possessions comprised objectives seven and eight. Rounding out Truman's request included objective nine, which equalized opportunities for residents of the United States to become naturalized citizens and the final objective—settling the evacuation claims of Japanese-Americans. The integration of the military was not included as one of the ten objectives because as Truman noted in his speech, "the Executive branch is taking every possible action to improve the enforcement of the civil rights statutes and to eliminate discrimination in federal employment, in providing federal services and facilities, and in the armed forces."[5]

Three days after Truman's speech, A. Philip Randolph met with Democratic Party officials. At the time of the meeting, the Senate Armed Services Committee was conducting hearings on Harry Truman's proposed Universal Military Training bill and Randolph hoped the bill would have a strong commitment to an integrated military. On March 22 a group of African American leaders, including Randolph, called upon the President to discuss this issue and he told the President it would be difficult for blacks in the United States to "fight for democracy abroad unless they get democracy at home." Five days later the NAACP hosted a meeting in

New York of twenty African American organizations that pledged to support Truman's civil rights agenda.[6]

This did not satisfy A. Philip Randolph. On March 30 the Committee Against Jim Crow in Military Service and Training, which was represented by the organization's national chairman, Grant Reynolds and A. Philip Randolph, delivered testimony before the Senate Armed Services Committee. Randolph was still disappointed that the proposed draft universal training bill did not have a commitment to an integrated military. The testimony that A. Philip Randolph delivered before the committee garnered national attention. Randolph said that if the draft bill did not prohibit segregation in the military then he would encourage blacks not to register for the draft as would be required under the law. The Republican Senator from Oregon, Wayne Morse, who had accompanied Harry Truman to the Lincoln Memorial for his speech before the NAACP, told Randolph that what he said would be "treason" to which Randolph responded: "I would be willing to face that . . . on the theory . . . that we are serving a higher law than the law which applies to the act of treason."[7]

African American reaction to Randolph's pronouncement was mixed. The NAACP was concerned about Randolph's insistence on using civil disobedience as a way of dealing with the challenge of a segregated army; however, Walter White did not denounce Randolph. Army Chief of Staff, General Eisenhower, also testified before the Armed Services Committee on the issue and told the committee that "I do believe that if we attempt merely by passing a lot of laws to force someone to like someone else, we are just going to get into trouble."[8] In the wake of Eisenhower's testimony, Southern Senators seized on his remark and used it to justify the continuance of segregation in the military by arguing that blacks were inferior soldiers. As Richard Dalfiume wrote:

> Senator Burnet R. Maybank of South Carolina claimed that "the wars of this country have been won by white soldiers and I defy any member . . . to challenge this statement." Senator Allen Ellender of Louisiana proclaimed that the Negro was inherently inferior, and this was the reason he had proven to be a poor soldier in combat. Senator Russell of Georgia repeated these ideas, and said there was no doubt in his mind that the President was determined to end segregation in the armed forces.[9]

While the Southern Senators worked hard to keep a segregated military and language in the Universal Military Training bill devoid of any commitment to integration, another fight was being waged in the

United Nations. This involved *An Appeal to the World*, the petition that Du Bois had crafted and submitted to the U.N. Human Rights Commission for consideration.

The U.N. Human Rights Commission was chaired by Eleanor Roosevelt, who was considered to be a friend of the NAACP—in fact she had served on the organization's board of directors since 1945. She was chair of the Human Rights Commission when it drafted what came to be known as "The Universal Declaration of Human Rights," an international document that was committed to human rights. According to historian Carol Anderson, White wanted to use *An Appeal to the World* "to move the United States toward a more comprehensive, enforceable Declaration and Covenant."[10] Eleanor Roosevelt refused to push Du Bois's *An Appeal to the World* before the U.N. and Walter White acquiesced, which led to an open fight between White and Du Bois that ended in his dismissal from the NAACP in October of 1948. Du Bois came to be involved in the Council on African Affairs, an organization that was to the left of the NAACP and the Universal Declaration of Human Rights that Eleanor Roosevelt worked hard to craft was approved by the U.N. General Assembly on December 10, 1948.

According to Carol Anderson, there was more at stake to the fight between White and Du Bois other than Du Bois's removal from the NAACP. Anderson argued that White had traded the opportunity to push for human rights before the U.N. for the push for civil rights in the United States that was outlined in *To Secure These Rights*. Anderson argued that the Universal Declaration of Human Rights "was the first attempt to define and codify standards of human rights that were the inherent rights of all people, regardless of race, color, sex, nationality, or citizenship." She concluded that the Universal Declaration "could have helped transform the civil rights movement into a human rights movement. Instead, the feud between Du Bois and White had left the NAACP's petition [*Appeal to the World*] in the dustbin of history."[11]

The debate over human rights before the U.N. and the role of the NAACP in that debate was not the only significant issue that dominated the early part of 1948. The Supreme Court handed down decisions in two important civil rights cases in May of 1948. During Truman's tenure as President he appointed four people to the bench. On September 19, 1945, he appointed Republican Senator Harold Burton to the bench, followed by Fred Vinson on June 6, 1946, who became Chief Justice. These two justices participated in two unanimous court cases that were decided on May 3, 1948: *Shelly v. Kraemer* and *Hurd v. Hodge*. Both cases involved the use of restrictive covenants that were used to keep minorities from settling in predominately white neighborhoods. The PCCR had discussed the problems of the restrictive covenants and in a friend-of-the-court brief filed by Solicitor Perlman, the brief submitted in the *Shelley v. Kraemer* decision, quoted a line from the speech that Truman had delivered before the NAACP in June to support invalidating the continued use of restrictive covenants.

In the *Shelley v. Kraemer* decision the court ruled that "in granting judicial enforcement of the restrictive agreements in these cases, the States have denied petitioners the equal protection of the laws and that, therefore, the action of the state courts cannot stand." The *Hurd* case involved the use of restrictive covenants in Washington, D.C. and, like the *Shelley* case, dealt a blow to the use of restrictive covenants and according to Michael Gardner, "created important judicial momentum for the civil rights reform called for by President Truman" and "confirmed the new proactive civil rights direction of the Vinson Court."[12]

While the Supreme Court seemed to embrace Harry Truman's civil rights agenda, the issue of gender, which was not mentioned as a category of analysis in *To Secure These Rights*, came up for discussion in June of 1948 when Congress passed the Women's Armed Services Integration Act. Harry Truman signed the measure into law on June 12. In the House, Republican Congresswoman Margaret Chase Smith, who served on the House Armed Services Committee, oversaw the passage of the bill. The law allowed women to "serve as commissioned officers and enlisted women in the permanent regular and reserve of the Army, Navy, Marine Corps and Air Force."[13]

The Senate quickly passed the legislation for the Women's Armed Services Integration Act in July of 1947 with the support of the army Chief of Staff Dwight Eisenhower; however, the passage of the bill stalled in the House. The House Armed Services Committee decided to strip the permanent regular status for women out of the bill, which happened privately at the request of the navy. Other military officials also privately expressed concern that if women were granted permanent regular status it might "lead to a draft for women in another war, West Point's becoming coed, and women on board navy ships."[14] Congresswoman Smith lobbied Secretary of Defense James Forrestal to step in because officially the armed services supported granting permanent regular status to women, but unofficially some members of the military were dragging their feet and encouraging the chair of the House Armed Services Committee to delay moving forward with the bill. The secretary intervened and the legislation finally cleared the House almost a year after it was approved in the Senate and Chase was successful in restoring the permanent regular status back into the bill prior to its passage.[15]

The final bill included several important provisions. The first provision was that women could only make up 2 percent of the military's total strength. The bill created a director of the women's corps position that received a temporary commission of colonel. Additional provisions in the bill prohibited women from serving on ships or aircraft that were engaged in combat and that husbands and children of officers were not to be considered dependents. The bill did not address what would happen if a woman became pregnant while in service; however, members of the Conference committee decided they would leave that decision up to the new director of women's corps, but believed that the policy during the war would be followed, which required the woman to be discharged from service. The other issue was whether or not women could command men. Members of the committee agreed that the Secretary of War could provide guidelines for this issue.[16] One biographer noted the importance of Smith's role in the passage of the bill when she wrote:

> Because policy is collectively made, it is often impossible to assess the impact of one member of Congress on the progress of a particular piece of legislation. This instance is the exception . . . Smith demonstrated a mastery of important lessons in the art of politics.[17] The armed services established a peacetime quota of enlisting 18,000 women.

The army and the navy had the bulk of the quota while the air force agreed to enlist 4,000 women and the marines about 800.[18]

June of 1948 also witnessed a move by A. Philip Randolph to force Truman's hand on the integration of the military. On June 26 Randolph announced the formation of the League for Non-Violent Civil Disobedience Against Military Segregation. The purpose of the group was to get Truman to issue an executive order that would end segregation in the military. The group gave the President a deadline of August 16 to act because that was the date a new draft law was to take effect. Randolph informed the President that unless the Executive Order is issued, "Negro youth will have no alternative but to resist a law, the inevitable consequences of which would be to expose them to un-American brutality so familiar during the last war."[19]

In June of 1948 Truman was thinking about his re-election campaign. Truman had demonstrated his commitment to civil rights when he created the President's Committee on Civil Rights in 1946 and endorsed the committee's report, *To Secure These Rights* with his February 2, 1948, speech on civil rights; however, these actions came with a high political price: they angered one of the key constituencies of the Democratic Party—

white Southern Democrats. This was to be expected. In fact, one of Truman's advisors, Clark Clifford, had predicted this in a memo he sent to the President in November of 1947, which has since come to be known as the Clifford Memorandum.

Clifford looked at the various constituencies of the Democratic Party, which included, as he described it an "unhappy alliance of Southern conservatives, Western progressives and Big City Labor" and concluded that the success of the party in 1948 would hinge on whether or not the "Democratic leadership can . . . lead enough members of these three misfit groups to the polls" in November. Clifford also noted that key to a Democratic win in 1948 would be whether or not the party could successfully attract African American voters. The Republicans had put on a full court press to attract the black vote in 1944 when they put a number of planks in their political platform that would appeal to African American voters and other Republicans in Congress openly supported a permanent FEPC and an anti-poll tax measure. Clifford cautioned Truman that:

> Unless there are new and real efforts—the Negro vote is already lost. Unless there are new and real efforts (as distinguished from mere political gestures which are today thoroughly understood and strongly resented by sophisticated Negro leaders), the Negro bloc, which, certainly in Illinois and probably in New York and Ohio, *does* hold the balance of power, will go Republican.[20]

At the time the memo was written (November 1947) Clifford encouraged Truman:

> to have the President go as far as he feels he possibly could go in recommending measures to protect the rights of minority groups. This course of action would obviously cause difficulty with our Southern friends but that is the lesser of two evils.[21]

The Clifford Memo has been cited by some historians to argue that Truman's main motivation to act on civil rights was to attract African American voters to the Democratic Party. Unfortunately for Truman, Southern discontent with the President's civil rights agenda was not the only division in the Democratic Party in 1948.

There was a progressive and liberal faction in the party that was skeptical of Truman's commitment to civil rights. The leader of the progressive faction was Henry Wallace. Wallace had served as Franklin Roosevelt's Vice President from 1940 to 1944, when he was replaced with Harry Truman on the presidential ticket. The liberal faction was led by

Hubert Humphrey from Minneapolis, whose support could be found in the Americans for Democratic Action, who opposed Henry Wallace and painted him as a Communist because he disagreed with the foreign policy strategy of containment that the Truman administration had adopted at the beginning of the Cold War.[22]

The Democrats assembled at Philadelphia for their convention and on July 14, 1948, the Democratic Party Platform Committee met to draft a civil rights plank. Harry Truman, who still wanted to court the Southern white Democrats, supported a civil rights plank that the liberal faction of the party rejected. In opposition to Truman's moderate plank and the liberal plank, the Southern white Democrats, sometimes referred to as the conservatives, offered the Moody plank which argued for "the reserved powers of the states . . . to control and regulate local affairs and act in the exercise of police powers." This came to be known as the states' rights plank.[23]

The convention voted on the liberal civil rights plank, which came to be known as the Biemiller amendment, named after Congressman Andrew Biemiller from Wisconsin, and it passed. The Biemiller amendment also attracted support from Harry Truman's moderate faction. Truman was a little concerned that the more liberal amendment would offend the Southern Democrats and he referred to it as the "Crackpot Biemiller" amendment and noted in his diary that if it passed the convention "there would be a splintering off of the South or at least a portion of it."[24]

The convention platform that the Democrats adopted in part read:

> We highly commend President Harry S. Truman for his courageous stand on the issue of civil rights.
>
> We call upon the Congress to support our President in guaranteeing these basic and fundamental American Principles: (1) the right of full and equal political participation; (2) the right to equal opportunity of employment; (3) the right of security of person; (4) and the right of equal treatment in the service and defense of our nation.
>
> We recommend to Congress the submission of a constitutional amendment on equal rights for women.[25]

The "constitutional amendment on equal rights for women" was also included in the 1944 platform; however, little effort had been made between 1944 and 1948 to enact the ERA, which was proposed first by Alice Paul and the National Woman's Party in 1923. The ERA amendment simply read: "Equality of rights under the law shall not be denied or abridged by the United States or by any State on account of sex."[26] Furthermore, the issue of women serving in the military was never connected with the discussion of the ERA amendment for women and Harry Truman did very little to support the ERA from 1948 until 1953 despite the efforts from Alice Paul and the National Woman's Party to push the issue with the President.[27]

Truman supported the Biemiller amendment after its passage; however, for many in the Southern delegations, the civil rights plank was the last straw. They walked out of the convention and two days after Truman received the nomination to serve as the Democratic nominee for president, held their own convention and nominated Strom Thurmond, Governor of South Carolina, to run for President under the Dixiecrat Party or the States' Rights Party. Clark Clifford had not predicted this situation in the Clifford memorandum.[28]

A few days after the Dixiecrats met, the Progressive Party selected Henry Wallace to serve as their presidential candidate. Wallace had already signaled his intention of running in late December of 1947 and in August of 1948 he undertook a campaign swing through the South. His campaign, according to historian Patricia Sullivan, was loosely affiliated with the SCHW. Wallace launched an attack on segregation by embarking on a campaign that took him across the South where he was met with significant resistance when he established a policy that he would only deliver campaign speeches before non-segregated audiences.[29]

With the Democratic Party divided three ways, the political situation looked bright for the Republicans who nominated New York governor, Thomas Dewey, to run as their candidate. Like the Democrats, the Republicans adopted a strong civil rights plank in their platform that in part read:

> One of the basic principles of this Republic is the equality of all individuals in their right to life, liberty, and the pursuit of happiness. This principle is enunciated in the Declaration of Independence and embodied in the Constitution of the United States; it was vindicated on the field of battle and became the cornerstone of this Republic. This right of equal opportunity to work and to advance in life should never be limited in any individual because of race, religion, color, or country of origin. We favor the enactment and just enforcement of such federal legislation as may be necessary to maintain this right at all times in every part of this Republic.

> We favor the abolition of the poll tax as a requisite to voting. We are opposed to the idea of racial segregation in the armed services of the United States.[30]

The Republican platform was unequivocal in its call for an integrated military and it also called for the passage of the equal rights amendment. As governor of New York, Dewey had appointed blacks to state positions and endorsed a state version of the FEPC. Dewey and the Republican Party had taken a step forward in appealing to black voters by stressing Dewey's record on civil rights and pointing out their commitment to civil rights that was outlined in their 1948 platform. In May of 1948 the New York *Amsterdam News*, an African American newspaper, endorsed Dewey.[31]

In addition to Truman and Dewey, African American voters could have also picked Henry Wallace. Paul Robeson and W. E. B. Du Bois endorsed Wallace early in 1948; however, that endorsement was not shared by Walter White and the NAACP. The NAACP had vowed to remain neutral, but it never wavered in its support of Harry Truman and the African American newspaper, the *Chicago Defender*, declared its support too.[32]

In July the political pressure surrounding Harry Truman was intense. On July 22, 1948, Truman received a letter from Leon Henderson, who was national Chairman of the Americans for Democratic Action, which was associated with the liberal faction of the Democratic Party that urged him to issue an order to desegregate the military "so that the armed forces of the world's greatest democracy may become in truth the world's most democratic armed forces."[33] In fact, there were discussions about issuing an executive order prior to A. Philip Randolph's creation of the League for Non-Violent Civil Disobedience Against Military Segregation in June. After the Democratic convention Philleo Nash, Clark Clifford, and Oscar Ewing, all presidential advisors, drafted one executive order that banned discrimination in federal employment and another that ended segregation in the armed forces.[34]

On July 26, Harry Truman issued Executive Orders 9980 and 9981. Executive Order (EO) 9980 required the federal government to employ "a policy of fair employment throughout the federal establishment, without discrimination because of race, color, religion, or national origin" that would be overseen by a Fair Employment board in the Civil Service Commission. Executive Order 9981 called for "equality of treatment and opportunity for all persons in the armed services without regard to race, color, religion, or national origin" and created the Committee on Equality of Treatment and Opportunity in the Armed Services that would oversee the military's implementation of the Executive Order.[35]

Nash, Clifford, and Ewing quickly drafted EO 9981 and presented it to Secretary of Defense James Forrestal for comment. Forrestal requested that the services be allowed to draft their own programs of compliance with the EO and the Secretary specifically requested that the President's order not set a firm deadline for compliance and Truman agreed to both requests. On the morning of July 26 the draft was sent over to Forrestal's office for one last review, which the White House requested be completed by that afternoon. Forrestal suggested that the proposed EO acknowledge that since World War II the service branches had made some progress towards integration; however, the President rejected this request. The draft made its way to Secretary of the Air Force Stuart Symington, Secretary of the Navy John L. Sullivan, and Secretary of the Army Kenneth Royall, who all approved the language in the EO. The draft was also sent to Walter White and to A. Philip Randolph.[36]

The wording of the Executive Order was vague because it neither mentioned segregation or integration. Truman was asked to clarify the Executive Order in a press conference that was held on July 29 and he was unequivocal when he was asked by the press: "does your advocacy of equality of treatment and opportunity in the Armed Forces envision eventually the end of segregation?" He simply responded in the affirmative with, "Yes."[37] He was also asked about army Chief of Staff, General Omar N. Bradley's comments where he said that the army would have to retain segregation because it was practiced nationally. Truman responded by telling the press gallery that he had been assured by the Secretary of Defense that is not what General Bradley meant. Apparently, at the time of his remarks, Bradley was not aware that Truman had issued the EO.[38]

There was also other reaction to EO 9981. A. Philip Randolph announced on August 18 that he was disbanding his civil-disobedience campaign because of the executive order. Henry Wallace called it an "empty gesture." The *Chicago Defender*, which supported Harry Truman, called it "unprecedented since the time of Lincoln."[39]

President Truman continued his presidential campaign into the fall, but avoided campaigning in the South and campaigned in the border states, the Midwest, and the far west. He appealed to labor, farmers, and African Americans. Harry Truman lumbered into Harlem for a campaign event in the closing days of the campaign. It was the first time a President had delivered a speech in Harlem and he was presented with the Franklin D. Roosevelt Memorial Brotherhood Medal. The day he chose to speak was not a coincidence—October 29, which marked one year to the date when the PCCR released *To Secure These Rights*. The president re-emphasized the importance of that document and also reminded the crowd that when Congress had not implemented his plan for civil rights outlined in

Fahy Committee

EO 9981 called for the creation of a committee that would oversee the implementation of the EO; however, the committee was still not in place by September 1, 1948. Secretary of the Army Royall did not agree with some of the names that were recommended; but by September 16 a committee chair and five out of the six committee members had been named. Charles Fahy was selected to chair the committee. David Niles, advisor on minority affairs, suggested Fahy's name who he described as a "reconstructed southerner liberal on race." He was a lawyer and a former solicitor general from Georgia. Lester Granger, an African American who had served as an advisor on black affairs to Secretary Forrestal as well as the NUL, joined the committee as did John Sengstacke, the other African American on the committee, who was the publisher of the black newspaper, the *Chicago Defender*. Dwight Palmer, president of General Cable Corporation; Charles Luckman, president of Lever Brothers and a native of Kansas City; and Alphonsus J. Donahue, a business owner from Connecticut, joined the two African American appointees. William Stevenson, who served as president of Oberlin College, rounded out the committee.[40] Alphonsus Donahue grew ill and later died while the committee was still deliberating and Charles Luckman seemed to have great difficulty in adjusting his work schedule with the work of the committee and really did not play a significant role on the committee. E. W. Kenworthy, former secretary of the American Embassy in London, was selected as the committee's executive secretary.[41]

his February 1948 message to Congress he went ahead and issued EO 9980 and 9981 in July of 1948. He closed his speech with these lines: "Our determination to attain the goal of equal rights and equal opportunity must be resolute and unwavering. For my part, I intend to keep moving toward this goal with every ounce of strength and determination that I have."[42]

When the votes were cast on November 2, 1948, a clear winner was not declared until the wee hours of the next morning. Truman had squeaked by with a razor thin victory, winning only 49.5 percent of the popular vote compared to Thomas Dewey's 45.1 percent of the popular vote. Strom Thurmond captured 2.4 percent of the popular vote and won the states of Mississippi, Alabama, Louisiana, and South Carolina. By some estimates, Truman received 69 percent of the black vote and in places like Harlem, Truman polled more votes in this close election than Roosevelt had in 1944. The end of the white primary due to the Supreme Court ruling in *Smith v Allright*, 1944, had increased the number of eligible African

American voters from 250,000 in 1940 to 750,000 by 1948.[43] This led McCoy and Reutten to conclude that the election of 1948 "demonstrated that in a close contest the weight of America's most numerous racial minority could determine the electoral votes of large states and hence the election." It was certainly clear that the African American migrations of World War I through the post-World War II period had political implications for the Democratic Party.[44] However, other historians challenge the significance of the black vote and argue that the election swung on the fact that Truman made a successful appeal to the farm states of the Midwest. While he won some of those Midwestern and upper Midwestern states, he lost others; if he would have lost them all he would have lost the election.[45]

> On January 20, 1949, Harry and Bess hosted the first integrated presidential inaugural events. The inaugural parade featured Dixiecrat Strom Thurmond and, when his car passed the reviewing stand, Harry Truman turned his back to him.

The President's Committee on Equality of Treatment and Opportunity in the Armed Services, which came to be known as the Fahy Committee—after its chair, Charles Fahy—met for the first time on January 12, 1949. The committee met with President Truman, Secretary of Defense Forrestal and the secretaries of the army, navy, and air force. The President was particularly blunt and told the committee that he wanted "concrete results . . . not publicity" and that if needed he would not hesitate to "knock somebody's ears down" to accomplish the work of the committee.

The armed services had been operating under the Utilization of Negro Manpower in the post-war army policy that was approved by the secretary on February 28, 1946, and was published as War Department Circular 124 on April 27, 1946 (discussed in Chapter 4). From April of 1946 to July 26, 1948, when Harry Truman issued EO 9981, some of the armed services, notably the air force and the navy, had taken small steps that provided for greater equality in their ranks; however, the army had done very little to insure greater equality and equal treatment since circular 124 came out.[46]

On January 13 the committee held its first hearings and heard from representatives from each branch of the service. The army General Staff described that it was the intention of the army to "achieve maximum effective utilization of all its available manpower." The army contended that they were already complying with the EO 9981 and argued that segregation in the army for black soldiers "has been the thing that has given the Negro far greater opportunity than any business or profession in the United States can point to." When naval representatives testified before the committee they revealed that two thirds of the black sailors were still serving in the segregated Steward's Branch and there were only five black officers out of 45,000 that were on active duty. The marine corps, which was supposed to follow the navy's integration policy, could not explain to the committee why only one black officer could be found among the 8,200 black marines. When the air force representatives were called to testify they talked about their integration policy, which was being considered by the secretary of defense; however, committee members became concerned about a quota that the air force established which limited the number of blacks in any one unit to just 10 percent.[47]

The committee was not convinced that each branch was complying with the EO; however, the committee was also not certain whether their task was to make sure segregation in the military would end and also whether or not they should also seek to end discrimination.[48] At the outset, what was clear was that the armed services had to craft their own policies about how they would comply with EO 9981 and they would be submitted to the Fahy Committee for review. Fahy was committed to reviewing and recommending changes to the armed services policies on integration in a non-coercive way, which was stressed at the initial meetings of the committee members with the service secretaries and their subordinate staffs.[49]

The Fahy Committee had to find a way to demonstrate that the army's commitment to segregation impeded the efficiency of the organization. E. W. Kenworthy, executive secretary of the committee, sent Fahy a letter on March 10 which read:

> I wonder if the one chance of getting something done isn't to meet the military on their own ground—the question of military efficiency. They have defended their Negro manpower policies on the grounds of efficiency. Have they used Negro Manpower efficiently? . . . Can it be that the whole policy of segregation, especially in large units like the 92nd and 93rd Division, ADVERSELY AFFECTS MORALE AND EFFICIENCY?

To demonstrate that the army's policy of segregation was not efficient required Kenworthy to find proof to substantiate his claim. He turned to Roy K. Davenport, who managed the army's manpower affairs and who was also African American, for help. Kenworthy arranged a meeting between Fahy and Davenport, who agreed to testify before the Fahy Committee.[50]

On March 28 the Secretary of the Air Force, Stuart Symington, Secretary of the Navy John L. Sullivan, and Secretary of the Army,

Kenneth Royall, appeared before the committee to testify. It was also the same day that Secretary of Defense James Forrestal resigned from his duties as defense secretary due in part to his health and Louis Johnson succeeded him as secretary. Secretaries Symington and Sullivan expressed their opposition to segregation to the committee and they both noted that segregation had prohibited efficient use of their manpower. When Secretary Royall testified he remained committed to a segregated army and he utilized many of the same arguments that have already been discussed as to why black troops could not be fully integrated. He believed that African American troops were not suited to combat; however, they were qualified for manual labor. He invoked the old argument that the army should not be used as "an experiment for social evolution" and that an integrated army would, in contrast to the views expressed by Secretaries Symington and Sullivan, prohibit the army from fulfilling its objective of effectively providing for the national defense.[51]

Roy Davenport and Maj. James D. Fowler, a black West Point graduate who also worked as an army personnel officer, took the stand and led the committee on a step by step analysis of how the army's segregation policy was inefficient. MacGregor concluded:

> Davenport and others were able to prove to the committee's satisfaction that the Army's segregation policy could be defended neither in terms of manpower efficiency nor common fairness. With Davenport and Fowler's testimony, Charles Fahy later explained, he began to "see light for a solution." He began to see how he would probably be able to gain the committee's double objective: the announcement of an integration policy for the army and the establishment of a practical program that would immediately begin moving the army from segregation to integration.[52]

In the Defense Department the agency that was responsible for drafting the policies on how the branches would comply with the executive order was known as the Personnel Policy Board. On April 5, 1949, the Personnel Policy Board, chaired by Thomas R. Reid, approved a directive that was signed by Secretary Johnson the next day that reaffirmed the military's commitment to comply with EO 9981.[53]

On May 11, 1949, the secretary of defense approved the air force integration plan, but rejected plans submitted by the army and navy. The air force integration plan prohibited the use of quotas and made a commitment that individuals within its ranks would be promoted on the basis of individual merit, although some all-black units might be retained.

The air force agreed to abolish its all-black fighter wing at Lockbourne Field, Ohio, and to "reassign to white units most, but not all, of its Negro personnel."[54] The navy resubmitted its plan on May 23 and it was approved on June 7, 1949, which left the army without an approved integration plan.[55] Also in June of 1949 Gordon Gray replaced Royall as secretary of the army and Secretary Gray was tasked with drafting an integration plan.

The Fahy Committee met with the President on June 7, 1949, and presented "A Progress Report for the President." On July 27, 1949, the committee sent "An Interim Report to the President" that outlined several measures the committee believed the army needed to address in order to comply with EO 9981. Over the course of the next couple of months the army had addressed all of the issues except one: abolishing the racial quotas. The army had a commitment to maintaining a force that was 10 percent African American. While this sounds noble, the quota was also used to deny well qualified blacks the opportunity to serve. The reason why the army fought so hard to keep the quota could be found in the testimony that Secretary Royall had delivered before the Fahy Committee in March. In his testimony he said that:

> One of the prime reasons for this army quota is the higher enlistment standards of the other services, which standards tend to reduce the number of Negroes in the army, making the problem of utilization—as well as of segregation—the more serious for the army.[56]

What Secretary Royall was concerned about, and also his successor Secretary Gray, was that the navy and the air force had higher standards that recruits had to meet than the army and Secretary Royall was essentially arguing that the quota was needed in order to prevent the service from attracting too many recruits that were not on par with the recruits attracted to the navy and air force. After discussions between Secretary of Defense Louis Johnson and Secretary of the Army, Gordon Gray, the army announced on September 30, 1949, that the Secretary of Defense had approved its integration policy, with the racial quotas still intact. The approval was true; however, the army had not run its final program before the Fahy Committee prior to the announcement, which angered the committee.[57]

The discussions over the quota and other issues of compliance with EO 9981 continued into the fall when the army was considering revising Circular 124. Roy Davenport was able to convince Secretary Gray to rethink some of the army's other policies and the secretary made tremendous gains at a meeting the secretary attended with the committee on December 27. On January 16, 1950, the army issued Special Regulation 600–629–1, *Utilization of Negro Manpower in the Army*, with the support of the committee; however, the challenge remained over the army's insistence on the use of quotas.[58]

By February of 1950 one committee member, Dwight Palmer, had had enough of the battle between the committee and the army over their insistence on the use of quotas. In a letter to Chairman Fahy he wrote:

> Regardless of the fact that the air corps and the navy may have a more glamorous appeal and therefore be able to get all the white boys they want and the smartest negroes, it seems to me that the army's inability to attract such men, if that is the case, may in large part be due to the army's history, that is, how it has mistreated the portion of citizens about whom it complains. In other words, they have made their own bed and it is up to them not only to change the sheets but also to change the mattress of that bed. Those in the service who continue to object to equal opportunity for all citizens, in the main are carrying on the prejudice, misinformation and the traditions of their forebears. It is easy enough, with the handicaps that the army has seen to it that the Negro should have, for the Negro not to show up to advantage. Again, I say this is largely the army's own fault.[59]

The battle between the committee and the army was exacerbated by a report the army released in February of 1950. In the fall of 1949 another board began examining the army's racial policy. The board was headed by Lt. Gen. S. J. Chamberlain and the report they issued in February was known as the Chamberlain report. The Chamberlain report was essentially a rewording of the old Gillem Board report and it recommended that the army retain segregation and the 10 percent quota. The report made it harder for Secretary Gray to work out a compromise over the 10 percent quota with the Fahy Committee.[60]

Finally, Secretary Gray brokered a deal with the President. Secretary Gray told Truman that he would drop the racial quota if:

> as a result of a fair trial of this new system, there ensues a disproportionate balance of racial strengths in the army, it is my understanding that I have your authority to return to a system which will, in effect control enlistments by race.

Harry Truman agreed with the secretary's proposal and the Fahy Committee reluctantly agreed because they were concerned about whether or not the army would agree to their own proposal. That is why the committee, which was working on its final report for the President, agreed to suggest that the President retain a committee to continue to review the services compliance with the EO. This recommendation was at odds with Secretary Johnson who wanted the President to abolish the committee. Niles, who had worked directly with the committee, encouraged the committee to take that request out of the final report, which they did. Niles did not wish to see a watchdog committee created and neither did Clark Clifford.[61]

On May 22, 1950, the Fahy Committee presented the committee's report, *Freedom to Serve: Equality of Treatment and Opportunity in the Armed Services: A Report by the President's Committee* to the President. In accepting the committee's report Truman observed:

> I attach the highest importance to this Committee's assignment. In the Committee's own words, equality of treatment and opportunity in the armed services is right, it is just, and it will strengthen the Nation. That is true throughout our entire national life.
>
> As more and more of our people have shared the opportunity to enjoy the good things of life, and have developed confidence in the willingness of their fellow Americans to extend equal treatment to them, our country has grown great and strong.
>
> Today, the free people of the world are looking to us for the moral leadership that will unite them in a common purpose. The free nations of the world are counting on our strength to sustain them as they mobilize their energies to resist Communist imperialism.
>
> We have accepted these responsibilities gladly and freely. We shall meet them with the sure knowledge that we can move forward in the solution of our own problems in accordance with the noblest of our national ideals—the belief that all men are created equal.

The president closed his brief remarks by urging Congress to approve a fair employment practices bill, which never happened.[62]

Just because the army had agreed to abolish the quota system did not mean that segregation immediately ended in its ranks. Unlike the army, the air force, by the end of 1950 had:

> reduced the number of black units to nine with 95 percent of its black airmen serving in integrated units. The number of black officers rose to 411, an increase of 10 percent over the previous year, and black airmen to 25,523, an increase of 15 percent.[63]

Historians Discuss the Significance of the EO

Getting the military committed to integration was a significant step forward. Military historian Morris MacGregor, Jr., summarized the importance of the Fahy Committee:

> After protracted argument it won from the army an agreement to abolish the racial quota and to open all specialties in all army units and all army schools and courses to qualified Negroes. Finally, it won the army's promise to cease restricting black servicemen to black units and overhead installations alone and to assign them instead on the basis of individual ability and the army's need.
>
> As for the other services, the committee secured from the navy a pledge to give petty officer status to chief stewards and stewards of the first, second, and third class, and its influence was discernible in the navy's decisions to allow stewards to transfer to the general service. The committee also made, and the navy accepted, several practical suggestions that might lead to an increase in the number of black officers and enlisted men. The committee approved of the air force integration program . . . In regard to the marine corps, however, the committee was forced to acknowledge that the corps had not yet "fully carried out Navy policy."[64]

Richard Dalfiume concluded:

> The executive order . . . provided the impetus for the air force to move rapidly to a policy of integration. The committee's examination of the navy's failure to completely implement a progressive policy led that service to take steps to bring practice in line with policy. The committee's conviction and proof that segregation led to discrimination encouraged it to resist doggedly army pressure for something less than integration. Important in all of this was the initiative of the President. Truman's issuance of the executive order and his insistence that its purpose was to end segregation weakened resistance in the armed services.[65]

In the navy, the concentration of blacks in the navy's general service saw slight gains while the number of blacks in the Steward's Branch showed a slight decline. As noted in Mershon and Schlossman, "In 1949, 34.9 percent of all black sailors held non-steward positions, while 65.1 percent went in the Steward's Branch; by 1953, the comparable figures were 48.3 percent in non-steward positions and 51.7 percent in the Steward's Branch."[66]

The integration in the army was not made evident until the Korean War. Harry Truman was at home in Independence on June 25, 1950, when he received a phone call from Secretary of State Dean Acheson. Acheson informed the President that North Korea had invaded South Korea. The President made his way to the downtown airport where his plane took off for Washington, D.C. While the Korean War would bring some of the darkest moments to Truman's presidency, the war would have an impact on how quickly the army would integrate and it would also re-energize civil rights organizations to push for rights in wartime.

Walter White, writing in the *Chicago Defender*, argued that Korea "brought the United States face to face with the global race question." In the summer of 1951, Ralph Bunche asked the NAACP's annual meeting attendees a very pointed question in his address: "[is there any] greater devotion to flag and country than American Negroes fighting in Korea to protect rights and privileges for the Koreans which the Negroes who fight and die have never enjoyed at home?" A. Philip Randolph completely supported the war in Korea because it afforded African Americans the opportunity to push yet again for racial justice in wartime.[67] However, the black left refused to sign on to the war and W. E. B. Du Bois, who became chair of the new Peace Information Center, which was an organization that supported nuclear disarmament in the United States, wrote in the organization's newsletter, *Peacegram*, an article against the war and he was asked by the Justice Department to register the organization.[68]

Shortly after the war began, the black Twenty-Fourth Infantry Regiment, part of the Twenty-Fifth Infantry Division of the Eighth Army, was sent into combat. White officers of the unit alleged that the blacks in the Twenty-Fourth fled when they came under fire. The commander of the Twenty-Fifth division, Major General William Kean, concluded that the Twenty-Fourth was "untrustworthy and incapable of carrying out missions." Members of the unit disputed the Major General's conclusion about their combat effectiveness and sent their complaints to the black press and to the NAACP. In January of 1951 Thurgood Marshall went to Korea to investigate these charges. Marshall, after examining the records of the Twenty-Fifth Infantry Division, discovered that the Twenty-Fourth Infantry Regiment had the most court-martial cases in the division and that furthermore, blacks received harsher punishments than whites for the same offenses. Marshall argued that the high court-martial rate led to low morale and concluded that "racial segregation, which facilitated the isolation and subordination of blacks, was the root cause of the injustices that he had documented."[69]

The war also witnessed the deployment of women. When the Korean War started, 22,000 women were on active duty with 7,000 women

Cornelius H. Charlton

Figure 5.1 The family of Sgt. Cornelius H. Charlton, accepts posthumously the Congressional Medal of Honor for actions that he had taken in the Korean War. Cornelius's father, Van, is pictured second from the left and Army Secretary Frank C. Pace, Jr. is in the center. Truman Library.

Cornelius H. Charlton was the son of Van Charlton, a coal miner from Welch, West Virginia, who moved his family and wife to the Bronx in 1945. Cornelius was born in East Gulf, West Virginia, in 1929 and attended Theodore Roosevelt High School; he joined the army in 1946 and went to Korea in October of 1950.[70] When the Korean War broke out he was sent into action with Company C of the 1st Battalion. Cornelius was Sergeant in the 3rd Platoon in Company C and his platoon saw action in Korea on June 2, 1951. On that day, Sergeant Charlton advanced on the enemy's main position against heavy fire to reach the enemy; however, in the advance his lieutenant was wounded and Charlton immediately assumed command and led another attack, despite being wounded himself. According to Private Ronald Holmes, Charlton rallied his troops for another advance, and the private remembered: "I saw the Sergeant go over the top and charge a bunker on the other side. He got the gun but was killed by a grenade."[71]

In February of 1952 the army announced that Sgt. Cornelius H. Charlton would receive the Congressional Medal of Honor for the actions he had taken on June 2, 1951, in Korea. Secretary of Army, Frank C. Pace, Jr., presented Van Charlton with his son's Congressional Medal of Honor in a ceremony held on March 12 in Washington. Sgt. Charlton was the second African American member of the armed services to be awarded the Medal of Honor for actions taken in Korea.[72] In a February 1952 article in the *New York Times*, Cornelius's father stated: "My boy's action in combat and his death make a liar out of Paul Robeson, who said the Negroes would never fight for their country against the communists."[73]

In June of 1951 women only made up a little over 1 percent of all the fighting forces that were involved with the Korean War.

serving in the WAC, WAVES, WAF, and women marines. In November of 1951 Harry Truman sent out an urgent radio plea for more women to enlist and this coincided with Assistant Secretary of Defense, Anna M. Rosenberg's, June 1951 request to raise the 2 percent quota to allow more women to enter the ranks of the military. Harry Truman told the women:

> There are now 40,000 women on active duty in the Army, Navy, Air Force, and Marines. In the next 7 months, we hope at least 72,000 more will volunteer for service.
>
> Our Armed Forces need these women. They need them badly. They need them to undertake every type of work except duty in actual combat formations.
>
> Women are now serving in every branch of the Armed Forces. They serve in communications centers and supply organizations, and medical installations, and many, many other vital activities. They are continuing to do fine jobs as nurses and medical specialists. They have won for themselves a full place as regular members of our Armed Forces.
>
> This is a tribute to the young women of our country. But it is more than a tribute—it is a great opportunity, too. For the armed services have much to offer the young women who join our active forces. These women have an opportunity to make a vital contribution to our national security. They have an opportunity to learn new skills that will help them advance in their chosen fields of work.
>
> There is nothing more constructive that young women in the United States can do for themselves and for their country than answer the call to service with our Armed Forces.
>
> This is a way—a real, direct, and positive way—that they can help secure the peace and safeguard freedom in the world.[74]

The women responded to Truman's call because by war's end, 46,000 women were on active duty and that included 8,000 WACS, 8,000 WAVES, 13,000 WAFS, and 2,400 Women marines. Also by war's end, between 500 and 600 women U.S. army nurses had served in Korea. The 2 percent quota was reinstated on July 31, 1954.[75]

In January of 1951 Walter White sent a telegram to all of the armed services secretaries that encouraged them to take "immediate steps to eliminate segregation and discrimination from all phases of military life." On February 28 White and A. Philip Randolph called on the White House where they discussed with the President six things they wanted to see accomplished. The list included the creation of an "executive FEPC, elimination of segregation in the nation's capital, and abolition 'once and for all' of racial segregation in the army." The meeting demonstrates that African Americans were still very much engaged with these issues and continued to push for an end to segregation in the military even after the Fahy Committee and their report, *Freedom to Serve*, essentially declared that the armed services had secured "equal opportunity and treatment" for all its citizens serving in the military.[76]

In February of 1951 the military created a special board of three generals to examine how black manpower could be used most efficiently in Korea. There were some units that had integrated and evidence was presented to the committee that these efforts were successful; however, the board concluded that the racial quota should be reinstituted. The army staff was not content with the ruling of the panel and the Personnel and Administration Division agreed to seek the opinion of twenty-two officers and two civilian officials who had experience with integration. According to Dalfiume, "the general conclusion of the majority was that integration furnished the most effective way to utilize Negro soldiers." In fact seventeen members favored integration while only two favored maintaining segregation.[77]

These discussions over whether or not integration or segregation should continue happened at the same time there were critical shortages of soldiers on the battlefield and those critical shortages were tied directly to the continued policy of segregation. In fact, some units were "overstrength," which meant that they had too many people, while other units had shortages. Assistant Secretary of the Army Earl Johnson told the Secretary of the Army Frank Pace, who had succeeded Royall in the position, that the "obvious solution was to take the excess Negro strength and distribute it throughout the other units of the army." The army's top brass was conflicted over what to do. According to Dalfiume, the Army General Staff and General Mark Clark, Commander of the Army Field Forces, argued that integration had not proven successful and the best way to reduce overstrength in the black units was to reinstitute the quotas. However, Johnson and Pace refused to reinstitute the quotas.[78]

On March 18, 1951, the Pentagon announced that all basic training in the United States would be integrated; however, once some troops finished their basic training, they were assigned to segregated units. Also, in March the army called in a team of social scientists to study integration and segregation in the army. The code name for the project and the research team was "Project Clear." The research was overseen by the Operations Research Office of the Johns Hopkins University and they conducted surveys in Korea, Japan, and at ten army posts in the United States. Until the results of the research were in, the army embraced a position that was leaning towards integration, but it was a slight lean.[79]

In April of 1951 Harry Truman removed General Douglas MacArthur from his command as Far Eastern Commander because of insubordination and he was replaced with General Matthew B. Ridgway. Ridgway asked the Pentagon to allow him to integrate the troops under his command. The Pentagon studied his request for two months and Secretary of the Army Frank Pace secured the approval of the President. The Pentagon agreed to allow Ridgway to move forward with his plan and the reason why, as Dalfiume noted, was because the researchers working on Project Clear released a preliminary report that noted that integration was critical to the efficient use of forces and where it had been utilized it was successful. On July 26, 1951, which marked the three year anniversary of Truman's EO 9981, the army announced that integration of its forces in Japan, Korea, and Okinawa would be completed in six months and that the all-black Twenty-Fourth Infantry would disband.[80] In December of 1951 the army, without much publicity, ordered the integration of all its units.[81]

According to Dalfiume, "Project Clear ended most of the remaining opposition to integration among the Army General Staff." By October of 1953 the army announced that 95 percent of its forces were integrated. Dalfiume argued that the Fahy Committee's work for integration coupled with the Project Clear's reaffirmation that integration produced a more efficient army had "finally convinced" army leaders to support an integrated military.[82] On October 30, 1954, the army reported that all of its units were integrated except for a few detachments. In sharp contrast, the navy had fallen behind. The Stewards Branch was still segregated and 98 percent of its make up included either blacks or Filipinos. Lester Granger was brought back in as a consultant, but in June of 1954 he resigned in protest after the navy refused to go along with his recommendation of breaking up the branch. Granger was successful in getting the navy to stop recruiting African Americans specifically for messmen positions.[83] Over the course of the war, 600,000 African Americans had served in all branches of the military and, at the conclusion of the war, 25,000 black soldiers remained in Korea.[84]

The integration of the military was a significant victory for the Truman administration; however, it was not the only victory that Truman scored for his civil rights agenda in his second term. On June 5, 1950, the Supreme Court handed down three significant decisions. This Court featured the

In September of 1950 the Puerto Rican Sixty-Fifth Infantry regiment was assigned to the Third Division, which served in Korea. By the end of the war, 60,000 Puerto Ricans had served in Korea and members of the Sixty-Fifth received four Distinguished Service Crosses and more than 150 Silver Stars for gallantry. Like their fellow African American counterparts, the Sixty-Fifth Infantry was finally integrated by March 1953 in response to EO 9981.

third and fourth Supreme Court appointees that Truman made during his presidency: his former Attorney General, Tom Clark, and former U.S. Senator, Sherman Minton. Clark came on the bench after August 24, 1949, when he completed his tenure as Attorney General and Minton joined the court on September 15, 1949. The first case, *Henderson v. United States*, involved segregation in interstate travel. The Interstate Commerce Commission approved the railroad practice of allowing trains to have ten tables to serve whites while only having one table reserved for blacks. The ICC had also approved a requirement that a curtain be used as a partition between white and black passengers. Truman's Solicitor, General Perlman, filed an amicus brief (friend-of-the-court) along with Thurgood Marshall of the NAACP in support of the government's position, which was that the ICC could not have these provisions because they violated the "separate but equal" doctrine outlined in the *Plessy v. Ferguson* decision of 1896. As Gardner pointed out, the Supreme Court's decision in this case represented an "incremental assault on *Plessy*'s separate-but-equal doctrine."[85]

The second case was *Sweatt v. Painter*. This case dealt with segregation in higher education. In this case, Heman Sweatt, an African American man, was admitted into a state funded law school for blacks instead of being admitted to the all-white University of Texas Law school. Thurgood Marshall and Attorney General J. Howard McGrath believed that the alternative blacks-only law school was not equal to the whites-only University of Texas Law School. Harry Truman's appointed Chief Justice, Fred Vinson, wrote the majority opinion for the 8–0 decision which read:

> The law school, the proving ground for legal learning and practice, cannot be effective in isolation from the individuals and institutions with which the law interacts. Few students and no one who has practiced law would choose to study in an academic vacuum, removed from the interplay of ideas and the exchange of views with which the law is concerned. The law school to which Texas is willing to admit petitioner [Sweatt] excludes from its student body members of the racial groups which number

> 85 percent of the population of the State and include most of the lawyers, witnesses, jurors, judges and other officials with whom petitioner will inevitably be dealing with when he becomes a member of the Texas Bar. With such a substantial and significant segment of society excluded, we cannot conclude that the education offered petitioner is substantially equal to that which he would receive if admitted to the University of Texas Law School . . . We hold that the Equal Protection Clause of the Fourteenth Amendment requires that petitioner be admitted to the University of Texas Law School.[86]

In the final important civil rights case, *McLaurin v. Oklahoma State Regents*, G. W. McLaurin, a black graduate student who was pursuing his doctorate in education from the University of Oklahoma, was told that he could attend classes at the University of Oklahoma but that he had to sit in a section that was reserved for black students. McLaurin challenged this requirement. The University of Oklahoma also created separate seating arrangements in their library and cafeteria and McLaurin had to sit in those sections as well. Again, Chief Justice Vinson wrote the majority opinion and which read:

> These restrictions [seating arrangements] were obviously imposed in order to comply, as nearly as could be, with the statutory requirements of Oklahoma. But they signify that the State, in administering the facilities it affords for professional and graduate study, sets McLaurin apart from the other students. The result is that appellant is handicapped in his pursuit of effective graduate instruction. Such restrictions impair and inhibit his ability to study, to engage in discussions and exchange views with other students, and, in general, to learn his profession . . . State imposed restrictions which produce such inequalities cannot be sustained.
>
> It may be argued that appellant will be in no better position when these restrictions are removed, for he may still be set apart by his fellow students. This we think irrelevant. There is a vast difference—Constitutional difference—between restrictions imposed by the state which prohibit the intellectual commingling of students, and the refusal of individuals to comingle where the state presents no such bar. *Shelley v. Kraemer*, 334 U.S. I, 13–14 (1948). The removal of the state restrictions will not necessarily abate individual and group predilections, prejudices and choices. But at the very least, the state will not be depriving appellant of

the opportunity to secure acceptance by his fellow students on his own merits.[87]

Thurgood Marshall praised the court for its rulings when he wrote in the *Baltimore Afro-American* on June 5, 1950, that "the United States Supreme Court dealt a serious blow to white supremacy as it affects segregation in schools and in dining cars." He concluded: "the complete destruction of all enforced segregation is now in sight."[88] Michael Gardner argued that these three court cases combined with the Vinson court's previous rulings in *Shelley v. Kraemer* and *Hurd v. Hodge* "provided for sweeping structural civil rights reform that the Congress refused to embrace" and that they provided "the important judicial momentum for dismantling *Plessy*'s repugnant separate-but-equal doctrine."[89]

While the war to contain Communism waged in Korea, in November of 1950 the National CRC submitted a petition titled "We Charge Genocide" under the direction of William Patterson and with the support of the Communist Party, U.S.A., to the U.N. Convention on Genocide. The petition documented America's continued violation of the human rights of its African American citizens. After the petition was submitted to the U.N. committee American state department officials claimed, as historian Carol Anderson reported, that the petition could not move forward because "not enough blacks had been lynched to constitute genocide."[90]

Walter White and Channing Tobias, who served as alternate members of the U.S. delegation at the U.N. meeting in Paris where the petition was presented, challenged the CRC's petition. Initially, White called *We Charge Genocide* "a gross and subversive conspiracy" by "prominent American communists." He also challenged the well documented petition and called many of the specific incidents of racial violence "alleged instances."[91] However, after it was made clear that the information contained in the petition was correct, White took a different approach to refuting the *We Charge Genocide* petition by pointing out the "phenomenal gains in civil rights" that had occurred during the Truman administration. However, as Carol Anderson noted, his comments ignored some significant facts. Some black soldiers were convicted of cowardice during the war and racial violence was still prevalent in the United States.[92]

Roy Wilkins was dismayed at White's comments and so too was NAACP board member, Judge Hubert T. Delany. The State Department asked White to refute the *We Charge Genocide* petition; however the CRC petition was very similar to the NAACP petition, *An Appeal to Reason*, which was submitted to the UN in 1947. If White refuted the petition Judge Delany told him that "it means that instead of our being a militant organization fighting for first-class citizenship for the Negro, we are saying to the very people who are denying us [our] rights . . . that we are in effect satisfied."[93]

The NAACP board eventually approved White's rebuttal and both he and Tobias traveled to Paris to denounce *We Charge Genocide*. While the discussions were taking place in Paris over the CRC's petition, another grisly and graphic murder occurred in the United States in Florida. During 1949, 1950, and 1951 the state of Florida experienced the terror of the Ku Klux Klan as it fire bombed Jewish synagogues, Catholic churches, and black homes. The state director of the Florida NAACP, Harry T. Moore, publically challenged the authorities to rein in the Klan's reign of terror. On the night of December 25, 1951, the Klan placed a bomb under his bedroom and detonated it killing Moore and later his wife, who eventually succumbed to her injuries several days later. The violence created a flood of telegrams to the Truman White House but he seemed not to be moved by the violence.[94]

The renewed wave of violence sparked a short-lived renewed interest in the CRC's petition and also forced the NAACP to reassess some of its rhetoric that it used to refute the *We Charge Genocide* petition. William Patterson clearly captured the challenge that the civil rights movement of the 1940s was in, in a letter he sent to NAACP leadership in 1952 when he asked if we could "end once and for all the pitting of Negro against Negro?" Carol Anderson further refined what he meant when she wrote: "Rather Red Negro [under Communist influence] was pitted against American Negro so that no one articulated the comprehensive needs of African Americans." She also concluded that as the "Cold War intensified, the NAACP's once coherent quest for human rights was rapidly dissolving."[95]

There was little left for Harry Truman to do in the last couple of years of his presidency. In January of 1951 he asked Congress to pass his civil rights reforms, which he had asked for every year since his February 1948 address to the Congress. In February of 1951 he issued EO 10210 that declared there would be "no discrimination in work performed by contractors and subcontractors working for the Departments of Defense and Commerce" that were involved with providing the material needed to outfit the fighting forces in Korea. His commitment to insure that there would not be discrimination in the war contracts was supported further by EO 10308 that created a committee to insure the prevention and elimination of discrimination in the Korean War mobilization effort.[96]

On January 9, 1952, Harry Truman went before Congress and delivered his seventh and final State of the Union address. At this point, his approval rating hovered around 25 percent because of the American performance in Korea coupled with Truman's decision to replace Gen. MacArthur as leader of the U.N. forces in Korea. He did ask Congress to enact his much stalled civil rights program and he reminded Congress and the American people of the progress the "executive branch has been making . . . toward full equality of treatment and opportunity—in the Armed Forces, in the civil service, and in private firms working for the Government."[97]

At this point, Harry Truman was in the middle of deciding whether or not he wanted to seek re-election as President. On March 8, 1952, a group of African American leaders called on Truman and urged him to run for re-election. By the end of March, on the 29, Truman announced that he would not seek re-election; however, he continued to speak out on civil rights. On June 13, 1952, he spoke at Howard University and in the fall, on October 11, 1952, he returned to Harlem where he essentially took a trip down his own civil rights memory lane. He remembered:

> Now, many people have wondered how I came to have such a deep interest in civil rights. I want to tell you about that. Right after World War II, religious and racial intolerance began to show up just as it did in 1919. There were a good many incidents of violence and friction, but two of them in particular made a very deep impression on me. One was when a Negro veteran, still wearing this country's uniform, was arrested, and beaten and blinded. Not long after that, two Negro veterans with their wives lost their lives at the hands of a mob.
>
> It is the duty of the State and local government to prevent such tragedies. But, as President of the United States, I felt I ought to do everything in my power to find what caused such crimes and to root out the causes. It was for that reason that I created the President's Committee on Civil Rights. I asked its members to study the situation and recommend to the whole country what we should do.
>
> Their report is one of our great American documents. When it was handed to me, I said that it was a new charter of human freedom. Five years have passed, but I have never seen anything to make me change my mind. These 5 years have seen some hard fighting by those who believe in civil rights for all our people—women like that great lady, Mrs. Eleanor Roosevelt, men like your own good Senators, Herbert Lehman and Bob Wagner—and the fine Democrats you have sent from New York to the House of Representatives. These 5 years have seen a lot of

progress—progress in spite of obstacles that have been placed in our way.

I want to review that progress for you today.

Right after the Committee on Civil Rights made its report to me, I sent to the Congress a special message making 10 recommendations for new legislation. Only 2 of those 10 recommendations have been approved by the Congress. The opponents of civil rights in the Congress have blocked every effort to enact such important legislation as a fair employment practices law, an anti-poll tax law, and an anti-lynch law. Not only that, they have succeeded in changing the rules under which Congress operates, so as to make it impossible to stop a filibuster.

Who are the opponents of civil rights? All you have to do is to look at the record. Read the Congressional Record, and you'll find them. I sent a good FEPC bill to Congress; but the Republicans introduced the McConnell amendment—a toothless substitute for FEPC. And the Republicans in the House voted 2 to 1 for that amendment—beating the Democratic majority that wanted FEPC. The Republicans also introduced and got passed in the Senate the Wherry rule making it next to impossible to stop these filibusters. That is rule 22 that Governor Lehman was talking to you about.

It is no accident that these anti-civil rights measures bear the names of Republican legislators. Republicans introduced them, and Republicans approved them. The Republicans deserve this recognition, for they are always on tap to provide just enough votes to insure the defeat of civil rights measures.

When the Congress refused to act, I went ahead to do what I could within the executive branch itself. This fight of ours cannot stop just because we have been blocked in the United States Congress.

First, I acted to stop racial discrimination in the armed services. The Navy and the Air Force have now eliminated all racial distinctions. And for over 2 years, every soldier coming into an Army training unit in this country has been assigned on the basis of his individual merit—regardless of race or color. All the troops in Korea are now integrated, and integration is going forward elsewhere overseas.

I also had a fair Employment Board set up in the Civil Service Commission. Today, every federal agency has a fair employment practices program that is working. Any federal employee, or applicant for federal employment, who feels he has been discriminated against because of race can now ask for and receive justice.

At my request, the Solicitor General of the United States went before the Supreme Court to argue that Negro citizens have the right to enter State colleges and universities on exactly the same basis as any other citizens. And we won that fight. And more than a thousand Negro graduate and professional students have been accepted by 10 State universities that had barred their doors to Negroes before. This means that this country will have more men like Louis T. Wright and Ralph Bunche.

At my request, the Solicitor General again went before the Supreme Court and argued against the vicious, restrictive covenants that had prevented houses in many places from being sold to Negroes and to Jews. It was a great day in the history of civil rights when we won that case, also, before the Supreme Court.

As one result of that decision, more Negroes are homeowners today than ever before in American history.

Our locally-operated public housing projects are increasingly open to families of all races and creeds. The number of integrated projects has increased eightfold in 8 years. In the last few years, 9 States and 8 cities have forbidden discrimination or segregation in public housing.

In the last few years, 11 States and 20 cities have enacted fair employment practice laws. This is where the greatest gap exists in our federal laws on civil rights, and I have repeatedly urged the Congress to pass the kind of law we need. Such a statute must have enforcement powers if it is to mean anything. To talk about voluntary compliance with fair employment practice is just plain nonsense. Federal fair employment legislation with enforcement power is greatly needed and it ought to be on the books. And I am going to keep fighting for it, come hell or high water!

Progress has been made in assuring Negroes the opportunity to exercise their right to vote as citizens. The courts have made the infamous "white primary" a thing of the past. Thank God for that. And there are only five poll tax States left in this Union. Nevertheless, we still need laws to abolish the poll tax and otherwise protect the right to vote where intimidation or restrictions still exist.

In the last five years, two States have enacted anti-lynch laws. Five States and forty-five cities have passed laws against wearing masks in public—which will strip the hoods off the Ku Klux Klan. One of the finest things that has happened recently was the conviction and prosecution of those Ku Kluxers down in North Carolina and Southern States. This is splendid progress in the fight to guarantee our citizens protection against mob violence, but it is not enough. It is the clear duty of the federal government to stand behind local law enforcement agencies, and to step in if they fail to control mob action. That is exactly what we have been doing through the FBI and through the civil rights section of the Department of Justice.

Last year, a mob formed in Cicero, Illinois, and prevented a Negro veteran and his family from moving into an apartment house. Fortunately, Illinois was blessed with a great Governor, who is now your Democratic candidate for President.

Governor Stevenson, who believes in action in these matters, restored law and order with the National Guard. But a local grand jury did the incredible thing of indicting—not the ringleaders of the mob—but the Negro veteran's lawyer and the property owner. At this point the federal government stepped in to prevent a gross miscarriage of justice. It obtained an indictment of the city officials who had failed in their duty to assure equal justice under the law. And the officials who had abetted the mob were tried and convicted in a Federal Court.

It was also last year that the Nation was shocked by the bomb murder in Florida of Harry T. Moore and his wife. These tragic deaths came shortly after the bombings of synagogues and Catholic churches and of the housing project at Carver Village. For several months the FBI has been gathering evidence on the mobs responsible for these outrages. And this week the United States Government began to present that evidence to a federal grand jury at Miami.

These are examples of how your federal government—under a Democratic President—stands behind the constitutional guarantees of human rights. The federal government could do a better job if we had stronger civil rights laws—and we must never let down in fighting for those laws.[98]

In the November elections Adlai Stevenson, the Democratic candidate, captured 73 percent of the African American vote, which was the largest percentage of the black vote a Democratic candidate had ever captured up to that point in American history. Stevenson went on to lose to Republican challenger Dwight Eisenhower. In the waning days of the

Truman presidency on December 2, 1952, Harry Truman's attorney general J. Howard McGrath, who replaced Tom Clark, submitted an amicus curiae (friend-of-the-court brief) in support of five black students in what came to be known as the *Brown v. Board of Education of Topeka, KS* case.

CHAPTER 6

Historians Debate Truman's Civil Rights Record

[The] tendency to accept less and to clutch at civil rights straws as if they are the silk threads of democracy has created an anomaly in American society in the area of civil rights (and only in the area of civil rights), where the mere act of trying—and not necessarily succeeding—becomes more than enough. At some point, as a democracy, we must realize it is not.

Carol Anderson[1]

It is a curious fact that most Americans have failed to take note of President Truman's pioneering civil rights role. The general failure of the public to appreciate his moral leadership in this area may be due in large part to the fact that Truman was a modest man . . . Moreover, since the public often thinks of the civil rights movement in terms of the violent protests of the late 1950s and the 1960s, many scholars fail to realize that the frustrations evident in those protests had their roots in the liberating words and actions taken by President Truman from 1946 through the last days of his presidency . . . the ample record of the Truman presidency confirms that he was in fact this country's twentieth-century pioneering civil rights president.

Michael R. Gardner[2]

Harry Truman's record on civil rights, which included his decision to integrate the military, has been debated by historians. The early historians (the historians writing in the late 1960s and early 1970s) who found much to admire about Truman's civil rights legacy, focused their attention on his decision to integrate the military. The very first book that came out on Truman's civil rights legacy during this period was Richard Dalfiume's *Desegregation of the U.S. Armed Forces* in 1969 and it argued that the combined efforts of Harry Truman, the Fahy Committee, and civil rights groups, as well as the Korean War, led to the successful integration of the military. In 1973 Donald McCoy and Richard Ruetten, in their well-researched book, *Quest and Response*, examined Truman's civil rights record and regarded the President's decision to integrate the military as the "most stunning achievement of the Truman era in the field of civil rights."[3]

The accounts of Truman's civil rights record by Dalfiume and in McCoy and Ruetten were challenged by a group of other historians. Barton Bernstein published "The Ambiguous Legacy: The Truman Administration and Civil Rights" in 1970 in a group of essays published in *Politics and Policies of the Truman Administration* in which he argued that "Truman's rhetoric and his efforts fell far short of the promise of American democracy, and his actions were not even as bold as his words." However, Bernstein did credit Truman with being the first "president in the twentieth century to assail discrimination against Negroes, to condemn violence and intimidation directed at them, to proclaim their legal equality," but that Truman still did so because his "motives were frequently political."[4] William Berman supported Bernstein's conclusion in *The Politics of Civil Rights in the Truman Administration.* Berman saw Truman's decision to integrate the military in purely political terms and concluded that Truman "moved [on civil rights] only because he had no choice: Negro votes and the demands of the Cold War, not simple humanitarianism—though there may have been some of that."[5] Harvard Sitkoff's article, "Harry Truman and the Election of 1948: The Coming of Age of Civil Rights" was published in 1971 and argued that Truman was a "reluctant champion" on civil rights who was "often pressured by forces beyond his control."[6] These revisionist historians, according to Raymond Geselbracht:

> while often very appreciative of what Truman did to advance civil rights, were inclined to regard his achievement as meager, hesitantly undertaken, polluted by political motives, and when viewed from the perspective of the troubled late 1960s and early 1970s, terribly inadequate in view of what the race problem had become.[7]

At this point, the historiography surrounding Truman and civil rights and his decision to integrate the military shifted to military history. In 1981 Morris J. MacGregor Jr.'s *Integration of the Armed Forces, 1940–1965* was published by the United States Army's Center of Military History. In this book MacGregor provides the reader with a complex set of reasons why the services integrated. In addition to the reasons provided in Dalfiume and in McCoy and Ruetten as to why segregation happened when it did, MacGregor, up to this point in the historiography, provided the most detailed account as to the role various civil rights organizations played in pushing for integration. He called their advocacy of pushing for equal treatment and opportunity in the military "crucial" in influencing Roosevelt's decision to include African Americans in the navy's general service and in all branches of the army as well as Truman's decision to issue EO 9981. Likewise he cited the role of President Truman in issuing the executive order and the Fahy Committee's dogged determination to illustrate to the army that its continued policy of segregation impaired the overall efficiency of its fighting force as reasons why integration finally happened. MacGregor's analysis also took time out to mention those in the military, like Anna Rosenberg, who supported integration. Finally, MacGregor's analysis also discussed the fact that the Korean War, and its manpower shortages, forced the army to abandon its segregation policy, which it had already vowed to end as outlined in *Freedom to Serve*. MacGregor noted: "Gradual integration was disregarded, however, when the Army, fighting in Korea, was forced by a direct threat to the efficiency of its operations to begin wide-scale mixing of the races."[8]

Another significant work to appear just five years after MacGregor's work was Bernard C. Nalty's *Strength for the Fight: A History of Black Americans in the Military*. Although Nalty called Truman's EO 9981 a "marriage of politics and principle" he did not offer anything significantly new from either MacGregor or Dalfiume's coverage of integration. Nalty's contribution comes in his discussion of the overall role African Americans played in the U.S. military from the founding of the country up to 1984, the year when the book was published.

In 1998 Sherie Mershon and Steven Schlossman published *Foxholes and Color Lines: Desegregating the U.S. Armed Forces*. The book was released on the 50th anniversary year of Truman's decision to issue EO 9981. In many ways Mershon and Schlossman synthesized the previous research of Dalfiume, MacGregor Jr., and Nalty. The authors broke down the integration of the military into three phases. The first phase lasted from 1940 to the end of World War II where the army maintained its separate but equal segregation policy but did expand opportunities for African Americans, like creating the Tuskegee Airmen, who served in the army air corps. The second phase, which overlapped with the first, lasted from 1943 to 1953, when the army and the navy began to experiment with integrating small detachments of black troops into larger units and ended with the integration of the armed forces during the Korean War. The last phase, again, overlapping with the second, examined the impact of integration from the mid-1950s to the 1960s. The authors concluded as did Dalfiume, MacGregor, and Nalty that key to the integration of the military was the leadership of "President Truman, whose handling of the subject demonstrated his keen awareness of how important leadership was in effecting organizational change." The authors described the Fahy Committee as a committee that "provided a steady, central focus for the implementation process, helping military officials to understand what was required of them and mediating often bitter disputes."[9]

The 1990s also saw a wave of new Truman biographies that came out in rapid succession and all praised Truman's civil rights accomplishments. In 1992 David McCullough published his biography, *Truman*, and wrote:

> He had achieved less in civil rights than he had hoped, but he had created the epoch-making Commission on Civil Rights, ordered the desegregation of the armed services and the federal Civil Service, done more than any President since Lincoln to awaken American conscience to the issues of civil rights.[10]

He was followed by Robert Ferrell in 1994 who published *Harry S. Truman: A Life* and Ferrell called Truman an "unlikely supporter of civil rights" who "as senator in 1935–1944, . . . showed no major signs of racial consciousness" until September 1946 when Walter White and the NECAMV met with the President and informed him of the beating of Isaac Woodard. Ferrell then examined his civil rights record after that period and noted the role of the Vinson Court and concluded that "Truman did remarkably well with civil rights—through making brave and decent statements, raising issues when he had little personally to gain, and urging their adoption publicly and privately because it was the right thing to do."[11] The trilogy of the 1990s biographies on Truman concluded in 1995 when Alonzo Hamby published *Harry S. Truman: Man of the People* who described "civil rights" as one of the "two most important issues" that Harry Truman dealt with during his time in office with the "Soviet challenge" being the other and he pronounced that he was "magnificently right" on civil rights.[12]

The 1990s also saw historians evaluating Truman's civil rights agenda in geopolitical terms. In 1996 Brenda Gayle Plummer published *Rising Wind: Black Americans and U.S. Foreign Affairs, 1935–1960* and downplayed the significance of the PCCR report and Truman's EO 9981 when she noted that the PCCR report "did not address the U.S. Housing Authority's continued policy of housing segregation" and discussed Truman's decision to issue EO 9981 within the context of the pressure that A. Philip

Randolph exerted on the President to act on this issue through the League for Nonviolent Civil Disobedience Against Military Segregation.[13] Plummer's work was followed the next year by Penny M. Von Eschen's *Race Against Empire: Black Americans and Anticolonialism, 1937–1957* in which she argued that Truman's main reason for issuing EOs 9980 and 9981 was political and stemmed from the efforts on the left led by Paul Robeson, W. E. B. Du Bois, and Henry Wallace.[14]

The internationalist perspective on Truman's civil rights record continued to be examined after the turn of the twenty-first century by Mary Dudziak, Thomas Borstelmann, and Carol Anderson. Dudziak, writing in *Cold War Civil Rights*, in 2000 argued that "one of President Truman's most important civil rights accomplishments was initiating the desegregation of the armed services."[15] She then pushed her analysis further when she wrote: "Desegregation of the military is often thought of as Truman's principal civil rights accomplishment. Of great significance as well, however, was the Truman administration's participation in the landmark desegregation cases leading up to *Brown v. Board of Education*." Those cases included the decisions the Vinson court made in *Shelley*, *Hurd*, *Henderson*, *McLaurin*, and *Sweatt*. Dudziak went on to say that the "Truman administration's involvement in high-profile desegregation cases was a new practice" and that a Supreme Court "decision rendering segregation unconstitutional was potentially of the greatest symbolic value" in the Cold War.[16]

Borstelmann, writing one year after Dudziak, in 2001, also acknowledged the political framework within which Harry Truman created the PCCR and issued EO 9981 and added to Dudziak's argument that Truman's actions on civil rights within this international context were important because: "The Democrats, it must be remembered, had long been the party of the white South, of slavery and the lynching rope. It was Truman's rejection of racial discrimination that began to shatter that historic identification." He specifically singled out the international dynamics within which the issue of civil rights operated by citing Truman's February 2, 1948, civil rights message to Congress and he also noted that "Truman's executive orders for the integration of the armed forces and the civil service marked other milestones" and that the Korean War "hastened military desegregation."[17] Unlike Dudziak, Borstelmann's work did not put as much emphasis on the role Truman's Vinson's court played in leading up to the *Brown v. Board* decision of 1954.

Most recently, two scholars have added to the discussion surrounding Truman's civil rights legacy. Michael Gardner in *Harry Truman and Civil Rights: Moral Courage and Political Risks* looked at Truman's entire civil rights record, including his decision to integrate the military and while he considers Truman's decision to integrate the military an important part of Truman's civil rights program, he focuses more on the impact of the Supreme Court rulings in *Shelley*, *Hurd*, *Henderson*, *McLaurin*, and *Sweatt* that the Vinson court handed down during his administration and how, as he argued, those cases played important roles in eventually overturning the *Plessy v. Ferguson* decision of 1896 with the *Brown* decision of 1954. In this sense, Gardner essentially embraces Dudziak's argument in *Cold War Civil Rights* that the decisions that were handed down under the Vinson court paved the way for the *Brown v. Board* decision. Unlike Dudziak, Gardner's approach is also focused on demonstrating the moral courage Truman took in creating the President's Committee on Civil Rights, speaking before the NAACP in 1947, and in issuing EOs 9980 and 9981. In many ways Gardner's analysis was in the vein of those previous historians who wrote glowing reviews of Truman's civil rights initiatives in the early 1960s and 1970s; however, he worked hard to make sure that Truman received the credit for his conclusion that Harry Truman was "this country's twentieth-century pioneering civil rights president."[18]

Carol Anderson, writing in 2003, in *Eyes Off the Prize* and again in 2007 in an article titled: "Clutching At Civil Rights Straws" significantly took issue with Gardner's analysis and with Truman's civil rights legacy. She presented compelling evidence that Harry Truman and Eleanor Roosevelt worked to thwart the efforts of various groups, including the NAACP and the CRC, from presenting petitions to the United Nations that would have forced the U.S. to correct its human rights abuses. She wrote in *Eyes Off the Prize*: "[Eleanor] Roosevelt and Truman were clearly committed to some measure of civil rights, they were both unable and unprepared to fight for a world that embraced full equality for African Americans."[19]

In *Eyes Off the Prize* she pushed her analysis further and asked: is it fair to simply come to a verdict on Truman's civil rights record by comparing and contrasting his record on civil rights with the record of the presidents who came before and after him? She continued:

> Truman set out to implement his vision of equality for the black community. He issued executive orders to desegregate the federal bureaucracy and the military. He commissioned a study on the status of civil rights in the United States. He also had the Justice Department support a range of desegregation cases winding through the court system. And although this was an impressive start, especially compared with the sluggish civil rights efforts of Franklin Roosevelt and Dwight Eisenhower, Truman's efforts did not even come close to what needed to be done.

> Instead, it becomes evident that he often engaged in the politics of symbolic equality—executive orders issued with little or no funding to finance the endeavor; powerless commissions created to once again study "the Negro problem" and give the aura of action; and directives issued from on high with no enforcement mechanism and no serious repercussions for non-compliance.[20]

Anderson's evaluation of Truman's civil rights record continued in the "Clutching at Civil Rights Straws" essay. In contrast to Gardner, she found some serious problems with his commitment to equality. The PCCR report noted in one of its recommendations that the civil rights section of the Department of Justice needed to be strengthened and that the civil rights laws needed to be strengthened in order to prosecute abuses. Anderson argued that in 1950 the civil rights section of the Department of Justice still had only six attorneys, which was the same number the section had prior to the PCCR's recommendation. Furthermore, while sections 51 and 52 of the federal statutes dealing with civil rights were replaced in June of 1948 with sections 241 and 242, she argued that the reason they were replaced was not to strengthen existing civil rights statutes but to "make them more palatable and acceptable to the south."[21]

While Anderson clearly demonstrated the shortcomings of the Justice Department's civil rights division, she also took issue with the impact of the *Shelley v. Kramer* decision that was handed down by the Vinson court. She argued that even after the court handed down its verdict, that the restrictive covenants continued well into the 1960s and that under Harry Truman's watch he allowed the Federal Housing Administration, which was the responsible agency that would oversee compliance with the court ruling, to obfuscate compliance with the law. Anderson concluded: "when it came to the critical issue of housing and home ownership, the federal government threw off its sackcloth of timidity and impotence and became a strong, vigilant defender—of racial segregation, discrimination, and the creation of black, impoverished, resource-deprived slums."

Fundamentally Anderson did not understand why a President could be so "bold, innovative, and decisive" in charting a new course in world affairs by drafting the containment policy, creating NATO, and crafting the Marshall Plan and yet at home display a "consistent inability to secure the vote, end housing discrimination, and protect American citizens, including veterans, from lynching." Anderson was not alone in her criticism of Harry Truman's civil rights legacy. As she noted, in 1968, at a gathering of Truman scholars, Professor Flint Kellogg asked a similar question: Why did Truman find "it easier to move to integration in the armed forces than he did within the administration itself? What was the block here? Usually you'd think that would cause less uproar if he moved within administrative agencies than within the armed forces."[22]

While Anderson did not see the "moral courage" that Michael Gardner discussed in his analysis of Truman's civil rights record, Anderson did not consider the significance of the other Supreme Court rulings that were handed down by the Vinson court and that he and Dudziak argued paved the way to the *Brown v. Board* decision of 1954. Gardner also did not carry the analysis of Truman's moral courage on civil rights past his presidency and into his post presidential career. Truman left office in 1953 and died in 1972. He witnessed the civil rights revolution of the 1960s and he displayed a significant amount of ambivalence to it; part of that ambivalence was captured in one sound recording that was made prior to 1963, when another President, Lyndon B. Johnson, was drafting the Civil Rights Act of 1964 and the Voting Rights Act of 1965.

In the early 1960s a series of documentary films was made about the important decisions Truman made during his presidency. The television series was called *Decision: the Conflicts of Harry S. Truman*. After the series aired in 1964 Truman had all of the outtakes shipped back to the Truman Library and beginning in 2003 Truman Library archivists began reviewing some of these outtakes. One of these outtakes stood out and it reflects Harry Truman's ambivalent civil rights legacy:

> A foreigner, when he comes to this country, is usually always puzzled to find that there is to some extent bigotry in regard to the treatment of the Negro. Usually, the matter is explained to him on this basis, which I expect to do now and I hope it'll explain a great many things to people. He'll understand the situation. The South in the War Between the States . . . eleven of those states left the Union, and about three and a half million Negroes were freed and turned loose. And Abraham Lincoln was assassinated before he had a chance to implement the situation that he had in mind. And the freed Negroes felt that due to their emancipation and the amendments to the Constitution that were passed in 1868 [they] had the same rights as the white people.
>
> Well, the Southerners, having been raised in the slave time, just couldn't see it. And if the men from the North would have patience and stay out of the situation down South—they're always sticking their noses in someplace where they're not wanted and stirrin' up trouble. The Southerners are not bigots. They understand the situation. They know that eventually the situation will have to develop so there is equality among the races, and when that equality comes you'll find those Southern

> Negroes who came up here to New York—there's a million of 'em here—and who went to Chicago—there's a million and a half of 'em in Chicago—are now wishing they were back home, for the simple reason that they found that they don't get any better treatment from these so-called Northern friends of theirs, not half as good treatment as they get down South because a Southerner understands 'em, and if they'll approach this thing in a level-headed, easy manner, in the long run the whole thing will work out as it should.
>
> The Southerners believe in the equality of opportunity. They believe in equality of the political approach to the Government of the United States, and they understand that the constitution provides for just that, and that the civil rights law which had been passed to implement that—and I got that law through the Congress after about four years fight—and it has now been, to some extent but not entirely, implemented. There is another civil rights law now in contemplation, and eventually the whole situation will be worked out. But it takes patience and understanding, and the people in New York, Chicago, and Boston, particularly, can't understand the attitude of the Southerners in this matter. If they'd stayed home and tended their own business and the niggers who'd been invited to go up there and have find [sic] out that they're not half as well treated as they are down South. And after a while, there won't be any difficulty with it because I *know*—I come from a state, as I told you, a Southern state.

Juxtapose this outtake with an exchange of letters Truman had with Ernie Roberts who was President of the Faultess Starch Company in Kansas City, Missouri, during the 1948 election campaign. Ernie Roberts told the President:

> You can win the South without the "Equal Rights Bill" but you cannot win the South with it. Just why? Well you, Bess and Margaret, and shall I say, myself, are all Southerners and we have been raised with the Negroes and we know the term "Equal Rights." Harry, let us let the South take care of the Niggers, which they have done, and if the Niggers do not like the Southern treatment, let them come to Mrs. Roosevelt.
>
> Harry, you are a Southerner and a D—— good one so listen to me. I can see, you do not talk domestic problems over with Bess? You put equal rights in Independence and Bess will not live with you, will you Bess?

Harry Truman forcefully responded to his friend:

> I am going to send you a copy of the report of my Commission on Civil Rights and then if you still have that antebellum proslavery outlook, I'll be thoroughly disappointed in you.
>
> The main difficulty with the South is that they are living eighty years behind the times and the sooner they come out of it the better it will be for the country and themselves. I am not asking for social equality, because no such thing exists, but I am asking for equality of opportunity for all human beings and, as long as I stay here, I am going to continue that fight. When the mob gangs can take four people out and shoot them in the back, and everybody in the country is acquainted with who did the shooting and nothing is done about it, that country is in [a] pretty bad fix from a law enforcement standpoint.
>
> When a Mayor and a City Marshal can take a Negro Sergeant off a bus in South Carolina, beat him up and put out one of his eyes, and nothing is done about it by the state authorities, something is radically wrong with the system.
>
> . . . I can't approve of such goings on and I shall never approve it, as long as I am here, as I told you before. I am going to try to remedy it and if that ends up in my failure to be re-elected, that failure will be in a good cause.

What had changed between 1948 and 1963, when Harry Truman continued to freely use the word "nigger" to describe African Americans? He had witnessed the civil rights movement of the 1960s and he was very uncomfortable at what he saw, but he had not changed his views on civil rights—they stayed the same. What had changed was the civil rights movement. The movement had pushed beyond Truman's

On June 24, 1962, John F. Kennedy announced the creation of the President's Committee on Equality of Opportunity in the Armed Forces and the committee came to be known as the Gesell Committee, named after committee chair, Gerhard A. Gesell. Unlike the Fahy Committee, the committee was not created by an Executive Order, but rather operated under the authority of the secretary of defense; the committee uncovered that discrimination still existed within the armed services and also in areas just off base. The Committee recommended that the armed forces enforce economic sanctions against private businesses that discriminated against members of the military and Secretary of Defense Robert McNamara included this recommendation in a directive he issued on July 26, 1963, on the fifteenth anniversary of EO 9981.

view of civil rights, which in his mind only included "equal opportunity" and not social equality. In 1960 he was asked to comment on the sit-ins that were underway at lunch counters across the United States to protest segregation and he responded that they were Communist inspired. Dr. Martin Luther King responded back to the former president and described his remarks as "unfortunate" and that the sit-ins served to "dramatize the indignities and injustices that Negroes are facing."[23] There were limits to Truman's approach on civil rights. He was willing to use the power of the executive branch to address civil rights, but he grew increasingly uncomfortable when African Americans took the lead.

> By 1980 African Americans made up about one-third of the enlisted ranks in the military.

There were also other limits on "equal opportunity" as it applied to women and those with a different sexual orientation that served in the military. It is interesting that the Fahy Committee, when it discussed the quotas for the African American troops, never entertained the thought of removing the quota for women enlistees. This was temporarily done during the Korean War because of manpower shortages and it was put back in place after the war and remained in place until 1967, when the quota was finally abolished.[24]

One lasting legacy of the Truman administration was that the Defense Department Advisory Committee on Women in the Services (DACOWITS) that was formed in 1951, while not very influential during Truman's administration, became a strong advocate for women in the 1970s. In 1980 the Defense Officer Personnel Management Act was passed that abolished the women's army corps and incorporated women into the regular army, which meant women no longer served in segregated units away from men. The act also permitted women to command men.[25]

In the 1990s the discussion of women in the military shifted to whether they should serve in combat and whether or not they were physically capable of completing some tasks required in some of the branches. In 1991, under a Defense Authorization Act, women were allowed to fly in combat and in 1993, under another Defense Appropriation Act, women were authorized to serve on combat ships; however, in 1992 and 1993 the House and Senate held hearings about women in combat. In those hearings individuals who were called to testify before the committee offered up some of the same arguments as to why women could not serve as were offered when the military were debating the merits of an integrated armed services in the 1940s and 1950s. Those who testified against allowing women a greater role in military service resurrected the arguments about how women might impact military efficiency and that the armed services should not be used as a laboratory for social change. One of the new arguments to emerge regarding women serving surrounded their physical stamina; however, as one observer noted: "This argument only applies to a small number of jobs, such as infantry or combat engineers."[26]

In 1993 the navy requested that Congress repeal the legislation that had been passed that prohibited women from serving on combatant ships. Naval officers wanted the legislation repealed because it prohibited the service's effectiveness and they did not wish to establish a quota based on gender to determine how many women the navy would accept. Ironically the focus on mission effectiveness, which had been utilized in the debate over segregation in the military, had found its voice again, except this time mission effectiveness was being used to allow women to serve in its ranks. In November of 1993 Congress passed the Defense Authorization Bill, which allowed women to serve on combatant ships; however, women were still excluded from serving on submarines and patrol craft.[27]

Current Department of Defense rules, sometimes referred to as the collocation rule, requires that "women be assigned to all positions where they are qualified but excludes them from assignments to 'units below the brigade level whose primary mission is to engage in direct combat on the ground.'" Furthermore, a separate army policy, drafted in 1992, "excludes women from jobs that are 'assigned a routine mission to engage in direct combat, or which collocate routinely with units assigned to a direct combat mission.'" So the use of women in combat remains subject to continued debate.[28]

By 2010, 15.1 percent of the officers in the military were women and 14.2 percent of the enlisted ranks were comprised of women. This figure is up significantly from the year 1973, when an all-volunteer army was reinstituted and when women comprised only 1.6 percent of the force. According to one observer: "Minority women make up a large part of the female force—35.3 percent of women officers and 52.8 percent of enlisted women."[29]

Gay men and lesbians continued to be denied the opportunity to serve openly in the military. Historian Allan Berube noted that in 1966 gay men and lesbian organizations organized one of the first nationwide protests that called attention to the military's continued policy of discrimination against gay soldiers and veterans. Little changed in the 1970s and in 1982, according to Berube, the Department of Defense:

> stated that homosexuality was never compatible with military service and catalogued all the antihomosexual arguments the military had accumulated since World War II: the presence of

> homosexuals constituted a serious threat to discipline, good order, morale, mutual trust, privacy, recruitment, security, and public relations.[30]

These were some of the same arguments that had been used to argue against allowing black men to serve in integrated units as well as allowing women to serve alongside men in the ranks of the military. Berube noted that since 1941 the military's policy of not allowing gays and lesbians to serve had, by the late 1980s, resulted in the discharge of about 100,000 individuals from the military. That averaged about 1,500 to 2,000 people per year.[31]

In October of 1989 the Defense Department's Personnel Security Research and Education Center completed a report that Congressional members released to the press. The report "concluded that homosexuals were no more of a security risk and no more susceptible to blackmail than heterosexuals, and that the military should consider accepting homosexuals." The report also suggested that the military begin integrating homosexuals into the ranks similar to the way in which African Americans were integrated into the service after Truman's EO 9981. Officials in the Defense Department did not embrace these findings.[32] High ranking African Americans in the military, like General Colin Powell, did not agree with the idea that allowing homosexuals to serve was akin to the integration of African Americans into the military because blacks were discriminated against because of their color, which was something that they could not control; whereas, a person who was homosexual could, at least in their opinion, control and conceal their sexuality.[33] In 1993 the RAND corporation completed a report about homosexuality and these reports eventually forced a rethinking of the policy of exclusion for homosexuals and in 1993 President Bill Clinton implemented the "Don't Ask Don't Tell" policy regarding gays and lesbians in military service. This policy was officially reversed in 2010 when President Barak Obama rescinded the policy, which allowed gays and lesbians to finally serve openly in the military.

> President Bill Clinton's "don't ask, don't tell, don't pursue" policy was released on July 19, 1993, and required that service members who demonstrated homosexual acts like holding hands or kissing be relieved of their military service.

Truman's decision to issue EO 9981 was a turning point in American history for the integration of black troops into the nation's military. It was part of Truman's civil rights program; however, the success of his civil rights program has been hotly debated by historians and his decision to integrate the military must be evaluated alongside his other civil rights initiatives and it also must be evaluated within the context of who was not covered by his Executive Order—women and gays and lesbians. Clearly, Truman's EO was a turning point for Colin Powell and many other black men who served; however, for other Americans their turning point would come much later as Americans and its military struggled well into the twenty-first century to expand the definition of equality of treatment and opportunity in the armed services to include women and individuals with a different sexual orientation.

Documents

DOCUMENT 1

To Secure These Rights: The Report of the President's Committee on Civil Rights, 1947

On December 5, 1946, Harry Truman issued EO 9808 that created the President's Committee on Civil Rights. The PCCR released To Secure These Rights *to the President and the public on October 29, 1947.*

> Note: Because of space concerns, we couldn't reproduce the whole document in the book. Here you will find an excerpt that includes the most important details. Readers interested in reading the full document will find a PDF copy of the entire text on the book's companion website. We urge you to read the entire document in order to understand what was communicated.

To Secure These Rights

THE REPORT OF THE PRESIDENT'S COMMITTEE ON CIVIL RIGHTS

"to secure these rights governments are instituted among men"
The Declaration of Independence

United States Government Printing Office
Washington: 1947

Table of Contents

Assignment from the President

MR. PRESIDENT:

This is the report which we have prepared in accordance with the instructions which you gave to us in your statement and Executive Order on December 5, 1946:

> Freedom From Fear is more fully realized in our country than in any other on the face of the earth. Yet all parts of our population are not equally free from fear. And from time to time, and in some places, this freedom has been gravely threatened. It was so after the last war, when organized groups fanned hatred and intolerance, until, at times, mob action struck fear into the hearts of men and women because of their racial origin or religious beliefs.
>
> Today, Freedom From Fear, and the democratic institutions which sustain it, are again under attack. In some places, from time to time, the local enforcement of law and order has broken down, and individuals—sometimes ex-servicemen, even women—have been killed, maimed, or intimidated.
>
> The preservation of civil liberties is a duty of every Government—state, federal and local. Wherever the law enforcement measures and the authority of federal, state, and local governments are inadequate to discharge this primary function of government, these measures and this authority should be strengthened and improved.
>
> The Constitutional guarantees of individual liberties and of equal protection under the laws clearly place on the federal government the duty to act when state or local authorities abridge or fail to protect these Constitutional rights.
>
> Yet in its discharge of the obligations placed on it by the Constitution, the federal government is hampered by inadequate civil rights statutes.

The protection of our democratic institutions and the enjoyment by the people of their rights under the Constitution require that these weak and inadequate statutes should be expanded and improved. We must provide the Department of Justice with the tools to do the job.

I have, therefore, issued today an Executive Order creating the President's Committee on Civil Rights and I am asking this Committee to prepare for me a written report. The substance of this report will be recommendations with respect to the adoption or establishment by legislation or otherwise of more adequate and effective means and procedures for the protection of the civil rights of the people of the United States.

EXECUTIVE ORDER 9808 ESTABLISHING THE PRESIDENT'S COMMITTEE ON CIVIL RIGHTS

WHEREAS the preservation of civil rights guaranteed by the Constitution is essential to domestic tranquility, national security, the general welfare, and the continued existence of our free institutions; and

WHEREAS the action of individuals who take the law into their own hands and inflict summary punishment and wreak personal vengeance is subversive of our democratic system of law enforcement and public criminal justice, and gravely threatens our form of government; and

WHEREAS it is essential that all possible steps be taken to safeguard our civil rights:

Now, THEREFORE, by virtue of the authority vested in me as President of the United States by the Constitution and the statutes of. (sic) the United States, it is hereby ordered as follows:

1. There is hereby created a committee to be known as the President's Committee on Civil Rights, which shall be composed of the following-named members, who shall serve without compensation:

   Mr. C. E. Wilson, chairman; Mrs. Sadie T. Alexander, Mr. James B. Carey, Mr. John S. Dickey, Mr. Morris L. Ernst, Rabbi Roland B. Gittelsohn, Dr. Frank P. Graham, The Most Reverend Francis J. Haas, Mr. Charles Luckman, Mr. Francis P. Matthews, Mr. Franklin D. Roosevelt, Jr., The Right Reverend Henry Knox Sherrill, Mr. Boris Shishkin, Mrs. M. E. Tilly, Mr. Channing H. Tobias.
2. The Committee is authorized on behalf of the President to inquire into and to determine whether and in what respect current law-enforcement measures and the authority and means possessed by federal, state, and local governments may be strengthened and improved to safeguard the civil rights of the people.

3. All executive departments and agencies of the federal government are authorized and directed to cooperate with the Committee in its work, and to furnish the Committee such information or the services of such persons as the Committee may require in the performance of its duties.
4. When requested by the Committee to do so, persons employed in any of the executive departments and agencies of the federal government shall testify before the Committee and shall make available for the use of the Committee such documents and other information as the Committee may require.
5. The Committee shall make a report of its studies to the President in writing, and shall in particular make recommendations with respect to the adoption or establishment, by legislation or otherwise, of more adequate and effective means and procedures for the protection of the civil rights of the people of the United States.
6. Upon rendition of its report to the President, the Committee shall cease to exist, unless otherwise determined by further Executive Order.

HARRY S. TRUMAN
The White House, *December 5, 1946.*

The Committee's first task was the interpretation of its assignment. We were not asked to evaluate the extent to which civil rights have been achieved in our country. We did not, therefore, devote ourselves to the construction of a balance sheet which would properly assess the great progress which the nation has made, as well as the shortcomings in the record. Instead, we have almost exclusively focused our attention on the bad side of our record-on what might be called the civil rights frontier.

This necessary emphasis upon our country's failures should not be permitted to obscure the real measure of its successes. No fair-minded student of American history, or of world history, will deny to the United States a position of leadership in enlarging the range of human liberties and rights, in recognizing and stating the ideals of freedom and equality, and in steadily and loyally working to make those ideals a reality. Whatever our failures in practice have been or may be, there has never been a time when the American people have doubted the validity of those ideals. We still regard them as vital to our democratic system.

If our task were to evaluate the level of achievement in our civil rights record, mention would have to be made of many significant developments in our history as a nation. We would want to refer to the steady progress toward the goal of universal suffrage which has marked the years between 1789 and the present. We would want to emphasize the disappearance of brutality from our society to a point where the occurrence of a single act of violence is a shocking event precisely because it is so out of keeping with our system of equal justice under law. And we would want to point to the building of our present economy which surely gives the individual greater social mobility, greater economic freedom of choice than any other nation has ever been able to offer.

But our purpose is not to praise our country's progress. We believe its impressive achievements must be used as a stimulus to further progress, rather than as an excuse for complacency.

At an early point in our work we decided to define our task broadly, to go beyond the specific flagrant outrages to which the President referred in his statement to the Committee. We have done this because these individual instances are only reflections of deeper maladies. We believe we must cure the disease as well as treat its symptoms. Moreover, we are convinced that the term "civil rights" itself has with great wisdom been used flexibly in American history.

For our present assignment we have found it appropriate to consolidate some individual freedoms under a single heading, to omit others altogether, and to stress still others which have in the past not been given prominence. Our decisions reflect what we consider to be the nation's most immediate needs. Civil rights, after all, are statements of aspirations, of demands which we make on ourselves and our society. We believe that the principles which underlie them are timeless. But we have selected for treatment those whose implementation is a pressing requirement. Throughout our report we have made use of specific data for illustrative purposes.

This report deals with serious civil rights violations in all sections of the country. Much of it has to do with limitations on civil rights in our southern states. To a great extent this reflects reality; many of the most sensational and serious violations of civil rights have taken place in the South. There are understandable historical reasons for this. Among the most obvious is the fact that the greater proportion of our largest, most visible minority group—the Negroes—live in the South.

In addition to this seeming stress on the problems of one region, many of our illustrations relate to the members of various minority groups, with particular emphasis upon Negroes. The reasons are obvious; these minorities have often had their civil rights abridged. Moreover, the unjust basis for these abridgements stands out sharply because of the distinctiveness of the groups. To place this apparent emphasis in its proper perspective one need only recall the history of bigotry and discrimination. At various times practically every region in the country has had its share of disgraceful interferences with the rights of some persons. At some time, members of practically every group have had their freedoms curtailed.

In our own time the mobility of our population, including minority groups, is carrying certain of our civil rights problems to all parts of the country. In the near future it is likely that the movement of Negroes from rural to urban areas, and from the South to the rest of the country, will continue. Other minority groups, too, will probably move from their traditional centers of concentration. Unless we take appropriate action on a national scale, their civil rights problems will follow them.

The protection of civil rights is a national problem which affects everyone. We need to guarantee the same rights to every person regardless of who he is, where he lives, or what his racial, religious or national origins are.

This report covers a broad field and many complex and controversial matters. It is not to be expected that every member of the Committee would personally put every statement just as it appears here. The report does represent a general consensus of the Committee except on those two specific matters where a substantial division of views is reported.

The Committee held a series of public hearings at which the spokesmen for interested groups made statements and were questioned. We heard some witnesses in private meetings. A number of staff studies gave us additional information. Hundreds of communications were received from interested private citizens and organizations who were anxious to help us with their information and advice.

From all of this and our own discussions and deliberations we have sought answers to the following:

(1) What is the historic civil rights goal of the American people?
(2) In what ways does our present record fall short of the goal?
(3) What is government's responsibility for the achievement of the goal?
(4) What further steps does the nation now need to take to reach the goal?

Our report which follows is divided into four sections which provide our answers to these questions.

Sadie T. Alexander
James B. Carey
John S. Dickey
Morris L. Ernst
Roland B. Gittelsohn
Frank P. Graham
Francis J. Haas
Charles Luckman
Francis P. Matthews
Franklin D. Roosevelt, Jr.
Henry Knox Sherrill
Boris Shishkin
Dorothy Tilly
Channing Tobias
Charles E. Wilson, *Chairman*

DOCUMENT 2

Special Message to the Congress on Civil Rights, February 2, 1948

On February 2, 1948, Harry Truman delivered a Special Message to Congress that outlined his plan to implement the recommendations in To Secure These Rights. *Source*: Public Papers of the Presidents: Harry Truman 1948.

February 2, 1948

To the Congress of the United States:

In the State of the Union Message on January 7, 1948, I spoke of five great goals toward which we should strive in our constant effort to strengthen our democracy and improve the welfare of our people. The first of these is to secure fully our essential human rights. I am now presenting to the Congress my recommendations for legislation to carry us forward toward that goal.

This Nation was founded by men and women who sought these shores that they might enjoy greater freedom and greater opportunity than they had known before. The founders of the United States proclaimed to the world the American belief that all men are created equal, and that governments are instituted to secure the inalienable rights with which all men are endowed. In the Declaration of Independence and the Constitution of the United States, they eloquently expressed the aspirations of all mankind for equality and freedom.

These ideals inspired the peoples of other lands, and their practical fulfillment made the United States the hope of the oppressed everywhere. Throughout our history men and women of all colors and creeds, of all races and religions, have come to this country to escape tyranny and discrimination. Millions strong, they have helped build this democratic Nation and have constantly reinforced our devotion to the great ideals of liberty and equality. With those who preceded them, they have helped to fashion and strengthen our American faith—a faith that can be simply stated:

We believe that all men are created equal and that they have the right to equal justice under law.

We believe that all men have the right to freedom of thought and of expression and the right to worship as they please.

We believe that all men are entitled to equal opportunities for jobs, for homes, for good health and for education.

We believe that all men should have a voice in their government and that government should protect, not usurp, the rights of the people.

These are the basic civil rights which are the source and the support of our democracy.

Today, the American people enjoy more freedom and opportunity than ever before. Never in our history has there been better reason to hope for the complete realization of the ideals of liberty and equality.

We shall not, however, finally achieve the ideals for which this Nation was rounded so long as any American suffers discrimination as a result of his race, or religion, or color, or the land of origin of his forefathers.

Unfortunately, there still are examples—flagrant examples—of discrimination which are utterly contrary to our ideals. Not all groups of our population are free from the fear of violence. Not all groups are free to live and work where they please or to improve their conditions of life by their own efforts. Not all groups enjoy the full privileges of citizenship and participation in the government under which they live.

We cannot be satisfied until all our people have equal opportunities for jobs, for homes, for education, for health, and for political expression, and until all our people have equal protection under the law.

One year ago I appointed a committee of fifteen distinguished Americans and asked them to appraise the condition of our civil rights and to recommend appropriate action by federal, state and local governments.

The committee's appraisal has resulted in a frank and revealing report. This report emphasizes that our basic human freedoms are better cared for and more vigilantly defended than ever before. But it also makes clear that there is a serious gap between our ideals and some of our practices. This gap must be closed.

This will take the strong efforts of each of us individually, and all of us acting together through voluntary organizations and our governments.

The protection of civil rights begins with the mutual respect for the rights of others which all of us should practice in our daily lives. Through organizations in every community—in all parts of the country—we must continue to develop practical, workable arrangements for achieving greater tolerance and brotherhood.

The protection of civil rights is the duty of every government which derives its powers from the consent of the people. This is equally true of local, state, and national governments. There is much that the states can and should do at this time to extend their protection of civil rights. Wherever the law enforcement measures of state and local governments are inadequate to discharge this primary function of government, these measures should be strengthened and improved.

The federal government has a clear duty to see that Constitutional guarantees of individual liberties and of equal protection under the laws are not denied or abridged anywhere in our Union. That duty is shared by all three branches of the Government, but it can be fulfilled only if the Congress enacts modern, comprehensive civil rights laws, adequate to the needs of the day, and demonstrating our continuing faith in the free way of life.

I recommend, therefore, that the Congress enact legislation at this session directed toward the following specific objectives:

1. Establishing a permanent Commission on Civil Rights, a Joint Congressional Committee on Civil Rights, and a Civil Rights Division in the Department of Justice.
2. Strengthening existing civil rights statutes.
3. Providing federal protection against lynching.
4. Protecting more adequately the right to vote.
5. Establishing a Fair Employment Practice Commission to prevent unfair discrimination in employment.
6. Prohibiting discrimination in interstate transportation facilities.
7. Providing home-rule and suffrage in Presidential elections for the residents of the District of Columbia.
8. Providing Statehood for Hawaii and Alaska and a greater measure of self-government for our island possessions.
9. Equalizing the opportunities for residents of the United States to become naturalized citizens.
10. Settling the evacuation claims of Japanese-Americans.

Strengthening the Government Organization

As a first stop, we must strengthen the organization of the federal government in order to enforce civil rights legislation more adequately and to watch over the state of our traditional liberties.

I recommend that the Congress establish a permanent Commission on Civil Rights reporting to the President. The Commission should continuously review our civil rights policies and practices, study specific problems, and make recommendations to the President at frequent intervals. It should work with other agencies of the federal government, with state and local governments, and with private organizations.

I also suggest that the Congress establish a Joint Congressional Committee on Civil Rights. This Committee should make a continuing study of legislative matters relating to civil rights and should consider means of improving respect for and enforcement of those rights.

These two bodies together should keep all of us continuously aware of the condition of civil rights in the United States and keep us alert to opportunities to improve their protection.

To provide for better enforcement of federal civil rights laws, there will be established a Division of Civil Rights in the Department of Justice. I recommend that the Congress provide for an additional Assistant Attorney General to supervise this Division.

Strengthening Existing Civil Rights Statutes

I recommend that the Congress amend and strengthen the existing provisions of federal law which safeguard the right to vote and the right to safety and security of person and property. These provisions are the basis for our present civil rights enforcement program.

Section 51 of Title 18 of the United States Code, which now gives protection to citizens in the enjoyment of rights secured by the Constitution or federal laws, needs to be strengthened in two respects. In its present form, this section protects persons only if they are citizens, and it affords protection only against conspiracies by two or more persons. This protection should be extended to all inhabitants of the United States, whether or not they are citizens, and should be afforded against infringement by persons acting individually as well as in conspiracy.

Section 52 of Title 18 of the United States Code, which now gives general protection to individuals against the deprivation of federally secured rights by public officers, has proved to be inadequate in some cases because of the generality of its language. An enumeration of the principal rights protected under this section is needed to make more definite and certain the protection which the section affords.

Federal Protection Against Lynching

A specific federal measure is needed to deal with the crime of lynching—against which I cannot speak too strongly. It is a principle of our democracy, written into our Constitution, that every person accused of an offense against the law shall have a fair, orderly trial in an impartial court. We have made great progress toward this end, but I regret to say that lynching has not yet finally disappeared from our land. So long as one person walks in fear of lynching, we shall not have achieved equal justice under law. I call upon the Congress to take decisive action against this crime.

Protecting the Right to Vote

Under the Constitution, the right of all properly qualified citizens to vote is beyond question. Yet the exercise of this right is still subject to interference. Some individuals are prevented from voting by isolated acts of intimidation. Some whole groups are prevented by outmoded policies prevailing in certain states or communities.

We need stronger statutory protection of the right to vote. I urge the Congress to enact legislation forbidding interference by public officers or private persons with the right of qualified citizens to participate in primary, special and general elections in which federal officers are to be chosen. This legislation should extend to elections for state as well as federal officers insofar as interference with the right to vote results from discriminatory action by public officers based on race, color, or other unreasonable classification.

Requirements for the payment of poll taxes also interfere with the right to vote. There are still seven states which, by their constitutions, place this barrier between their citizens and the ballot box. The American people would welcome voluntary action on the part of these states to remove this barrier. Nevertheless, I believe the Congress should enact measures insuring that the right to vote in elections for federal officers shall not be contingent upon the payment of taxes.

I wish to make it clear that the enactment of the measures I have recommended will in no sense result in federal conduct of elections. They are designed to give qualified citizens federal protection of their right to vote. The actual conduct of elections, as always, will remain the responsibility of State governments.

Fair Employment Practice Commission

We in the United States believe that all men are entitled to equality of opportunity. Racial, religious and other invidious forms of discrimination deprive the individual of an equal chance to develop and utilize his talents and to enjoy the rewards of his efforts.

Once more I repeat my request that the Congress enact fair employment practice legislation prohibiting discrimination in employment based on race, color, religion or national origin. The legislation should create a Fair Employment Practice Commission with authority to prevent discrimination by employers and labor unions, trade and professional associations, and government agencies and employment bureaus. The degree of effectiveness which the wartime Fair Employment Practice Committee attained shows that it is possible to equalize job opportunity by government action and thus to eliminate the influence of prejudice in employment.

Interstate Transportation

The channels of interstate commerce should be open to all Americans on a basis of complete equality. The Supreme Court has recently declared unconstitutional state laws requiring segregation on public carriers in interstate travel. Company regulations must not be allowed to replace unconstitutional state laws. I urge the Congress to prohibit discrimination and segregation, in the use of interstate transportation facilities, by both public officers and the employees of private companies.

The District of Columbia

I am in full accord with the principle of local self-government for residents of the District of Columbia. In addition, I believe that the Constitution should be amended to extend suffrage in Presidential elections to the residents of the District.

The District of Columbia should be a true symbol of American freedom and democracy for our own people, and for the people of the world. It is my earnest hope that the Congress will promptly give the citizens of the District of Columbia their own local, elective government. They themselves can then deal with the inequalities arising from segregation in the schools and other public facilities, and from racial barriers to places of public accommodation which now exist for one-third of the District's population.

The present inequalities in essential services are primarily a problem for the District itself, but they are also of great concern to the whole Nation. Failing local corrective action in the near future, the Congress should enact a model civil rights law for the Nation's Capital.

Our Territories and Possessions

The present political status of our Territories and possessions impairs the enjoyment of civil rights by their residents. I have in the past recommended legislation granting statehood to Alaska and Hawaii, and organic acts for Guam and American Samoa including a grant of citizenship to the people of these Pacific Islands. I repeat these recommendations.

Furthermore, the residents of the Virgin Islands should be granted an increasing measure of self-government, and the people of Puerto Rico should be allowed to choose their form of government and their ultimate status with respect to the United States.

Equality in Naturalization

All properly qualified legal residents of the United States should be allowed to become citizens without regard to race, color, religion or national origin. The Congress has recently removed the bars which formerly prevented persons from China, India and the Philippines from becoming naturalized citizens. I urge the Congress to remove the remaining racial or nationality barriers which stand in the way of citizenship for some residents of our country.

Evacuation Claims of the Japanese-Americans

During the last war more than one hundred thousand Japanese-Americans were evacuated from their homes in the Pacific states solely because of their racial origin. Many of these people suffered property and business losses as a result of this forced evacuation and through no fault of their own. The Congress has before it legislation establishing a procedure by which claims based upon these losses can be promptly considered and settled. I trust that favorable action on this legislation will soon be taken.

The legislation I have recommended for enactment by the Congress at the present session is a minimum program if the federal government is to fulfill its obligation of insuring the Constitutional guarantees of individual liberties and of equal protection under the law.

Under the authority of existing law, the Executive branch is taking every possible action to improve the enforcement of the civil rights statutes and to eliminate discrimination in federal employment, in providing federal services and facilities, and in the armed forces.

I have already referred to the establishment of the Civil Rights Division of the Department of Justice. The Federal Bureau of Investigation will work closely with this new Division in the investigation of federal civil rights cases. Specialized training is being given to the Bureau's agents so that they may render more effective service in this difficult field of law enforcement.

It is the settled policy of the United States Government that there shall be no discrimination in federal employment or in providing federal services and facilities. Steady progress has been made toward this objective in recent years. I shall shortly issue an Executive Order containing a comprehensive restatement of the federal non-discrimination policy, together with appropriate measures to insure compliance.

During the recent war and in the years since its close we have made much progress toward equality of opportunity in our armed services without regard to race, color, religion or national origin. I have instructed the Secretary of Defense to take steps to have the remaining instances of discrimination in the armed services eliminated as rapidly as possible. The personnel policies and practices of all the services in this regard will be made consistent.

I have instructed the Secretary of the Army to investigate the status of civil rights in the Panama Canal Zone with a view to eliminating such discrimination as may exist there. If legislation is necessary, I shall make appropriate recommendations to the Congress.

The position of the United States in the world today makes it especially urgent that we adopt these measures to secure for all our people their essential rights.

The peoples of the world are faced with the choice of freedom or enslavement, a choice between a form of government which harnesses the state in the service of the individual and a form of government which chains the individual to the needs of the state.

We in the United States are working in company with other nations who share our desire for enduring world peace and who believe with us that, above all else, men must be free. We are striving to build a world family of nations—a world where men may live under governments of their own choosing and under laws of their own making.

As a part of that endeavor, the Commission on Human Rights of the United Nations is now engaged in preparing an international bill of human rights by which the nations of the world may bind themselves by international covenant to give effect to basic human rights and fundamental freedoms. We have played a leading role in this undertaking designed to create a world order of law and justice fully protective of the rights and the dignity of the individual.

To be effective in those efforts, we must protect our civil rights so that by providing all our people with the maximum enjoyment of personal freedom and personal opportunity we shall be a stronger nation—stronger in our leadership, stronger in our moral position, stronger in the deeper satisfactions of a united citizenry.

We know that our democracy is not perfect. But we do know that it offers freer, happier life to our people than any totalitarian nation has ever offered.

If we wish to inspire the peoples of the world whose freedom is in jeopardy, if we wish to restore hope to those who have already lost their civil liberties, if we wish to fulfill the promise that is ours, we must correct the remaining imperfections in our practice of democracy.

We know the way. We need only the will.

HARRY S. TRUMAN

DOCUMENT 3

Letter from Mrs. Amelia A. Dixon to Harry Truman, March 12, 1948

Mrs. Amelia A. Dixon from Walton, Kentucky, sent Harry Truman a letter encouraging him to issue an Executive Order that would desegregate the military.
Source: Folder: June 1948 [1 of 2], OF 93–B, Truman Papers, Truman Library.

March 12, 1948

Dear Mr. President

I am not dictating to you. I am merely stating facts. If you want to be in the White House four more years be the man we think you are. You can win the re-election if you end racial segregation in the armed forces, discrimination in all federal departments and Jim Crowism in all the United States. You have the power to do that without new legislation. Be presumptuous. We Negro people will back you up. You can prevail, now is your probability. Send out your proclamation. You could start here in the White House, half of your body guards could be black. I served in World War II. I will die gladly before I will serve in world war III under the present conditions. This is the way we all feel.

Very truly yours,

Mrs. Amelia A. Dixon

DOCUMENT 4

A. Philip Randolph's Testimony on Civil Disobedience, March 31, 1948

On March 31, 1948, A. Philip Randolph testified before the Senate Armed Services Committee about the Universal Military Training (UMT) bill that was being considered by the Senate. The testimony he delivered became controversial because he advocated that African Americans not register for Universal Military Training if the bill did not contain a clause that prohibited segregation. He specifically said that he was drawing upon the teachings of Gandhi to support the use of civil disobedience in response to segregation.
Source: A. Philip Randolph Papers, Library of Congress.

Testimony of A. Philip Randolph, National Treasurer of the Committee Against Jim Crow in Military Service and Training and President of the Brotherhood of Sleeping Car Porters, AFL, Prepared for delivery before the Senate Armed Services Committee, Wednesday, March 31, 1948, 10 A.M., Washington D.C.

Civil Disobedience
Mr. Chairman:

Mr. Grant Reynolds, national chairman of the Committee Against Jim Crow in Military Service and Training, has prepared for you in his testimony today a summary of wartime injustices to Negro soldiers—injustices by the military authorities and injustices by bigoted segments of the police and civilian population. The fund of material on this issue is endless, and yet, three years after the end of the war, as another crisis approaches, large numbers of white Americans are blissfully unaware of the extent of physical and psychological aggression against and oppression of the Negro soldier.

Without taking time for a thorough probe into these relevant data—a probe which could enlighten the nation—Congress may now heed Mr. Truman's call for Universal Military Training and Selective Service, and in the weeks ahead enact a Jim Crow conscription law and appropriate billions for the greatest segregation system of all time. In a campaign year, when both major parties are playing cynical politics with the issue of civil rights, Negroes are about to lose the fight against Jim Crowism on a national level. Our hard-won local gains in education, fair employment, hospitalization, housing are in danger of being nullified—being swept aside, Mr. Chairman, after decades of work—by a federally enforced pattern of segregation. I am not beguiled by the army's use of the word "temporary." Whatever may pass in the way of conscription legislation will become permanent, since the world trend is toward militarism. The army knows this well. In such an eventuality, how could any permanent Fair Employment Practices Commission dare to criticize job discrimination in private industry if the federal government itself were simultaneously discriminating against Negro youth in military installations all over the world?

There can be no doubt of my facts. Quite bluntly, Chairman Walter G. Andrews of the House Armed Service Committee told a delegation from this organization that the War Department plans segregated white and Negro battalions if Congress passes a draft law. The *Newark Evening News* of March 26, 1948, confirmed this in a Washington dispatch based on official memoranda sent from Secretary Forrestal's office to the House Armed Services Committee. Nine days ago when we called this to the attention of the Commander-in-Chief in a White House conference, he indicated that he was aware of these plans for Jim Crow battalions. This despite his civil rights message to Congress . . .

With this background, gentlemen, I reported last week to President Truman that Negroes are in no mood to shoulder a gun for democracy abroad so long as they are denied democracy here at home. In particular, they resent the idea of fighting or being drafted into another Jim Crow Army. I passed this information on to Mr. Truman not as a threat, but rather as a frank, factual survey of Negro opinion.

Today I should like to make clear to the Senate Armed Services Committee and through you, to Congress and the American people that passage now of a Jim Crow draft may only result in a mass civil disobedience movement along the lines of the magnificent struggles of the people of India against British imperialism. I must emphasize that the current agitation for civil rights is no longer a mere expression of hope on the part of Negroes. On the one hand, it is a positive, resolute outreaching for full manhood. On the other hand, it is an equally determined will to stop acquiescing in anything less. Negroes demand full, unqualified first-class citizenship.

In resorting to the principles and direct-action techniques of Gandhi, whose death was publicly mourned by many members of Congress and President Truman, Negroes will be serving a higher law than any passed by a national legislature in an era when racism spells our doom. They will be serving a law higher than any decree of the Supreme Court which in the famous Winfred Lynn case evaded ruling on the flagrantly illegal segregation practiced under the wartime Selective Service Act. In refusing to accept compulsory military segregation, Negro youth will be serving their fellow man throughout the world.

I feel qualified to make this claim because of a recent survey of American psychologists, sociologists and anthropologists. The survey revealed an overwhelming belief among these experts that enforced segregation on racial or religious lines has serious and detrimental psychological effects both on the segregated groups and on those enforcing segregation. Experts from the South, I should like to point out gentleman, were as positive as those from other sections of the country as to the harmful effects of segregation. The views of these social scientists were based on scientific research and their own professional experience.

So long as the Armed Services propose to enforce such universally harmful segregation not only here at home but also overseas, Negro youth have a moral obligation not to lend themselves as world-wide carriers of an evil and hellish doctrine. Secretary of the Army Kenneth C. Royall clearly indicated in the New Jersey National Guard situation that the Armed Services do have every intention of prolonging their anthropologically hoary and untenable policies.

For 25 years now the myth has been carefully cultivated that Soviet Russia has ended all discrimination and intolerance, while here at home the American Communists have skillfully posed as champions of minority groups. To the rank-and-file Negro in World War II, Hitler's racism posed a sufficient threat for him to submit to Jim Crow Army abuses. But this factor of minority group persecution in Russia is not present, as a popular issue, in the power struggle between Stalin and the United States. I can only repeat that this time Negroes will not take Jim Crow draft lying down. The conscience of the world will be shaken as by nothing else when thousands and thousands of us second-class Americans choose imprisonment in preference to permanent military slavery.

While I cannot with absolute certainty claim results at this hour, I personally will advise Negroes to refuse to fight as slaves for a democracy they cannot possess and cannot enjoy. Let me add that I am speaking only for myself, not even for the Committee against Jim Crow in Military Service and Training, since I am not sure that all its members would follow my position. But Negro leaders in close touch with GI grievances would feel derelict in their duty if they did not support such a justified civil disobedience movement—especially those of us whose age would protect us from being drafted. Any other course would be a betrayal of those who place their trust in us. I personally pledge myself to openly counsel, aid and abet youth, both white and Negro, to quarantine any Jim Crow conscription system, whether it bear the label of UMT or Selective Service.

I shall tell youth of all races not to be tricked by any euphonious election-year registration for a draft. This evasion, which the newspapers increasingly discuss as a convenient way out for Congress, would merely presage a synthetic "crisis" immediately after November 2nd when all talk of equality and civil rights would be branded unpatriotic while the induction machinery would move into high gear. On previous occasions I have seen the "national emergency" psychology mow down legitimate Negro demands.

From coast to coast in my travels I shall call upon all Negro veterans to join this civil disobedience movement and to recruit their younger brothers in an organized refusal to register to be drafted. Many veterans, bitter over Army Jim Crow, have indicated that they will act spontaneously in this fashion, regardless of any organized movement. "Never again," they say with finality.

I shall appeal to the thousands of white youth in schools and colleges who are today vigorously shedding the prejudice of their parents and professors. I shall urge them to demonstrate their solidarity with Negro youth by ignoring the entire registration and induction machinery. And finally I shall appeal to Negro parents to lend their moral support to their sons—to stand behind them as they march with heads high to federal prisons as a telling demonstration to the world that Negroes have reached the limit of human endurance—that, in the words of the spiritual, we'll be buried in our graves before we will be slaves.

May I, in conclusion, Mr. Chairman, point out that political maneuvers have made this drastic program our last resort. Your party, the party of Lincoln, solemnly pledged in its 1944 platform a full-fledged Congressional investigation of injustices to Negro soldiers. Instead of that long overdue probe, the Senate Armed Services Committee on this very day is finally hearing testimony from two or three Negro veterans for a period of 20 minutes each. The House Armed Services Committee and Chairman Andrews went one step further and arrogantly refused to hear any at all! Since we cannot obtain an adequate Congressional forum for our grievances, we have no other recourse but to tell our story to the peoples of the world by organized direct action. I don't believe that even a wartime censorship wall could be high enough to conceal news of a civil disobedience program. If we cannot win your support for your own Party commitments, if we cannot ring a bell in you by appealing to human decency, we shall command your respect and the respect of the world by our united refusal to cooperate with tyrannical injustice.

Since the military, with their Southern biases, intend to take over America and institute total encampment of the populace along Jim Crow lines, Negroes will resist with the power of non-violence, with the weapons of moral principles, with the good-will weapons of the spirit, yes with the weapons that brought freedom to India. I feel morally obligated to disturb and keep disturbed the conscience of Jim Crow America. In resisting the insult of Jim Crowism to the soul of black America, we are helping to save the soul of America. And let me add that I am opposed to Russian totalitarian communism and all its works. I consider it a menace to freedom. I stand by democracy as expressing the Judean-Christian ethic. But democracy and Christianity must be boldly and courageously applied for all men regardless of race, color, creed, or country.

We shall wage a relentless warfare against Jim Crow without hate or revenge for the moral and spiritual progress and safety of our country, world peace and freedom.

Finally let me say that Negroes are just sick and tired of being pushed around and we just don't propose to take it, and we do not care what happens.

DOCUMENT 5

EO 9980, Regulations Governing Fair Employment Practices within the Federal Establishment, July 26, 1948

On July 26, 1948, Harry Truman issued two Executive Orders: EO 9980 and EO 9981. EO 9980 prohibited discrimination in federal employment and EO 9981 prohibited segregation in the armed services.
Source: Truman Library.

Executive Order 9980 Regulations Governing Fair Employment Practices within the Federal Establishment
July 26, 1948

WHEREAS the principles on which our Government is based require a policy of fair employment throughout the federal establishment, without discrimination because of race, color, religion, or national origin; and

WHEREAS it is desirable and in the public interest that all steps be taken necessary to insure that this long-established policy shall be more effectively carried out:

NOW, THEREFORE, by virtue of the authority vested in me as President of the United States, by the Constitution and the laws of the United States, it is hereby ordered as follows:

1. All personnel actions taken by federal appointing officers shall be based solely on merit and fitness; and such officers are authorized and directed to take appropriate steps to insure that in all such actions there shall be no discrimination because of race, color, religion, or national origin.
2. The head of each department in the executive branch of the Government shall be personally responsible for an effective program to insure that fair employment policies are fully observed in all personnel actions within his department.
3. The head of each department shall designate an official thereof as Fair Employment Officer. Such Officer shall be given full operating responsibility, under the immediate supervision of the department head, for carrying out the fair-employment policy herein stated. Notice of the appointment of such Officer shall be given to all officers and employees of the department. The Fair Employment Officer shall, among other things:

(a) Appraise the personnel actions of the department at regular intervals to determine their conformity to the fair-employment policy expressed in this order.

(b) Receive complaints or appeals concerning personnel actions taken in the department on grounds of alleged discrimination because of race, color, religion, or national origin.

(c) Appoint such central or regional deputies, committees, or hearing boards, from among the officers or employees of the department, as he may find necessary or desirable on a temporary or permanent basis to investigate, or to receive, complaints of discrimination.

(d) Take necessary corrective or disciplinary action, in consultation with, or on the basis of delegated authority from, the head of the department.

4. The findings or action of the Fair Employment Officer shall be subject to direct appeal to the head of the department. The decision of the head of the department on such appeal shall be subject to appeal to the Fair Employment Board of the Civil Service Commission, hereinafter provided for.

5. There shall be established in the Civil Service Commission a Fair Employment Board (hereinafter referred to as the Board) of not less than seven persons, the members of which shall be officers or employees of the Commission. The Board shall:

(a) Have authority to review decisions made by the head of any department which are appealed pursuant to the provisions of this order, or referred to the Board by the head of the department for advice, and to make recommendations to such head. In any instance in which the recommendation of the Board is not promptly and fully carried out the case shall be reported by the Board to the President, for such action as he finds necessary.

(b) Make rules and regulations, in consultation with the Civil Service Commission, deemed necessary to carry out the Board's duties and responsibilities under this order.

(c) Advise all departments on problems and policies relating to fair employment.

(d) Disseminate information pertinent to fair-employment programs.

(e) Coordinate the fair-employment policies and procedures of the several departments.

(f) Make reports and submit recommendations to the Civil Service Commission for transmittal to the President from time to time, as may be necessary to the maintenance of the fair-employment program.

6. All departments are directed to furnish to the Board all information needed for the review of personnel actions or for the compilation of reports.

7. The term "department" as used herein shall refer to all departments and agencies of the executive branch of the Government, including the Civil Service

Commission. The term "personnel action," as used herein, shall include failure to act. Persons failing of appointment who allege a grievance relating to discrimination shall be entitled to the remedies herein provided.

8. The means of relief provided by this order shall be supplemental to those provided by existing statutes, Executive orders, and regulations. The Civil Service Commission shall have authority, in consultation with the Board, to make such additional regulations, and to amend existing regulations, in such manner as may be found necessary or desirable to carry out the purposes of this order.

HARRY S. TRUMAN
THE WHITE HOUSE,
July 26, 1948

DOCUMENT 6

Letter from Joseph Beauhamais to Louis A. Johnson, Secretary of Defense, June 24, 1949

Joseph Beauhamais of Chicago, IL, sent this letter to Louis A. Johnson, Secretary of the Defense, regarding Truman's decision to integrate the military. Source: Folder July 1948—June 1949 [2 of 2], OF 93–B, Truman Library.

June 24, 1949

I pridefully state that I am a normal white man and I feel deeply within me as an instinct of racial pride. By cross-examining hundreds of white men and women whom I know personally, find that they also, without exception, are distinctly aware of this same instinct of racial pride. Therefore, you will not be surprised to learn that we were all sickened and disgusted to learn from the press reports that you are an advocate of non-segregation in the armed forces of the United States, which in plain blunt language means that because of your military authority and high-ranking power, you feel that you can change or enforce long-standing social edicts and customs by issuing directives to white men who are in the majority in the armed forces that they must eat, sleep and work with negroes, without their consent and against their wills. I think your decree is outrageous and I would never voluntarily enlist now in any branch of the armed forces under any circumstances.

In my opinion, and I am sure that this is the consensus of opinion of . . . the white men in America, the white man does not desire to live intimately with negroes, and we feel that he should not be forced to do so against his will. The very most the armed forces should do would be to mix those whites who do not object to it with the negroes, and maintain all-white organizations for those who prefer it. The white man who objects to it should not be forced into it. To quote an example—I may desire to associate intimately with Mr. Louis A. Johnson, Secretary of Defense, but if Mr. Johnson does not want my association, he should not be forced to live with it, just because I wanted it . . .

I maintain your decree issued to the armed forces to abolish all segregation . . . will be regretted and will cause many racial tensions and antagonisms resulting in shootings, stabbings clubbing and man murders that otherwise would not have occurred. These clashes are inevitable because it is a violation and a desecration of natural law to regiment the two races together and expect harmony to ensue. Experiments in Chicago for the past thirty years have proven beyond any doubt that when negroes are mixed with whites in schools, factories, offices or any mixed social basis that there are a hundred more times more racial incidents and hatreds than if the two races were kept strictly segregated . . .

I submit these remarks for your consideration, as a student, citizen and humanitarian. Henceforth, I shall work unceasingly to conserve the white man's dignity and rights in America.

DOCUMENT 7

Freedom to Serve: Equality of Treatment and Opportunity in the Armed Services, 1950

The Fahy Committee released Freedom to Serve *to President Truman and the public on May 22, 1950.*

Note: Because of space concerns, we couldn't reproduce the whole document in the book. Here you will find an excerpt that includes the most important details. Readers interested in reading the full document will find a PDF copy of the entire text on the book's companion website. We urge you to read the entire document in order to understand what was communicated.

Freedom To Serve

EQUALITY OF TREATMENT AND OPPORTUNITY IN THE ARMED SERVICES

A Report by
The President's Committee

UNITED STATES GOVERNMENT PRINTING OFFICE
WASHINGTON: 1950

Contents

Letter of Transmittal

MAY 22, 1950

MR PRESIDENT:
The President's Committee on Equality of Treatment and Opportunity in the Armed Services herewith reports to the President.

Executive Order 9981 of July 26, 1948, states: "It is hereby declared to be the policy of the President that there shall be equality of treatment and opportunity for all persons in the armed services without regard to race, color, religion, or national origin. This policy shall be put into effect as rapidly as possible, having due regard to the time required to effectuate any necessary changes without impairing efficiency or morale." This order further authorized the Committee "to examine into the rules, procedures and practices of the armed services in order to determine in what respect such rules, procedures and practices may be altered or improved with a view to carrying out the policy of this order."

The Committee appointed by the President has conducted such an inquiry and has made recommendations to the President, the Secretary of Defense, and the Secretaries of the three services. It was the judgment of the Committee that these recommendations, when put into actual practice, would bring an end to inequality of treatment and opportunity. All of the Committee's recommendations have been approved and accepted by the President, the Secretary of Defense and the service Secretaries. They are now in effect.

This submission, therefore, is a report of the work of the Committee and of the measures adopted by the services to carry out the President's policy. Chapter I contains the Committee's interpretation of its mission; an account of its method of work; and a summary of the progress which has been made.

Chapters II, III, IV, and V present a more detailed description of the racial policies and practices in the services at the beginning of the Committee's inquiry; the Committee's estimate of those policies and practices as measured against the President's policy; the recommendations of the Committee and the reasons for them.

It is the Committee's conviction that the present programs of the three services are designed to accomplish the objectives of the President. As the programs are carried out, there will be, within the reasonably near future, equality of treatment and opportunity for all persons in the armed forces with a consequent improvement in military efficiency.

In submitting its report, the Committee desires to express its appreciation to the White House staff, the Department of Defense and the Departments of the Army, Navy, and Air Force and to all organizations and individuals that have facilitated the work of the Committee.

Respectfully submitted,
Lester B. Granger
Dwight R. G. Palmer
John H. Sengstacke
William E. Stevenson
Charles Fahy, *Chairman*

Executive Order 9981

Establishing the President's Committee on Equality of Treatment and Opportunity in the Armed Services

Whereas it is essential that there be maintained in the armed services of the United States the highest standards of democracy, with equality of treatment and opportunity for all those who serve in our country's defense:

Now, therefore, by virtue of the authority vested in me as President of the United States, by the Constitution and the statutes of the United States, and as Commander in Chief of the armed services, it is hereby ordered as follows:

1. It is hereby declared to be the policy of the President that there shall be equality of treatment and opportunity for all persons in the armed services without regard to race, color, religion or national origin. This policy shall be put into effect as rapidly as possible, having due regard to the time required to effectuate any necessary changes without impairing efficiency or morale.

2. There shall be created in the National Military Establishment an advisory committee to be known as the President's Committee on Equality of Treatment and Opportunity in the Armed Services, which shall be composed of seven members to be designated by the President.

3. The Committee is authorized on behalf of the President to examine into the rules, procedures and practices of the armed services in order to determine in what respect such rules, procedures and practices may be altered or improved with a view to carrying out the policy of this order. The Committee shall confer and advise with the secretary of defense, the Secretary of the Army, the Secretary of the Navy, and the Secretary of the Air Force, and shall make such recommendations to the President and to said Secretaries as in the judgment of the Committee will effectuate the policy hereof.

4. All executive departments and agencies of the federal government are authorized and directed to cooperate with the Committee in its work, and to furnish the Committee such information or the services of such persons as the Committee may require in the performance of its duties.

5. When requested by the Committee to do so, persons in the armed services or in any of the executive departments and agencies of the federal government shall testify before the Committee and shall make available for the use of the Committee such documents and other information as the Committee may require.

6. The Committee shall continue to exist until such time as the President shall terminate its existence by Executive Order.

HARRY S. TRUMAN

The WHITE HOUSE, *July 26, 1948.*

The President appointed the following to be members of the Committee:

Charles Fahy, *Chairman*
Alphonsus J. Donahue
Lester B. Granger
Charles Luckman
Dwight R. G. Palmer
John H. Sengstacke
William E. Stevenson

Mr. Alphonsus J. Donahue died in July 1949. Mr. Charles Luckman has not actively participated in the work of the Committee.

Toward the Goal: A Summary of Progress

Executive Order 9981, issued on July 26, 1948, declared it to be "the policy of the President that there shall be equality of treatment and opportunity for all persons in the armed services without regard to race, color, religion or national, origin."

"This policy," the President directed, "shall be put into effect as rapidly as possible, having due regard to the time required to effectuate any necessary changes without impairing efficiency, or morale."

By the same order the President announced there would be created in the National Military Establishment a committee of seven members with authority "to examine into the rules, procedures and practices of the armed services" in order to determine what changes were necessary to carry out the President's policy.

In discharging its duties, the Committee was directed by the President to confer and advise with the Secretary of Defense and the Secretaries of the three services, and finally to make recommendations to the President and the aforementioned Secretaries.

The Committee Interprets Its Mission

At the outset of its deliberations the Committee was agreed that the problem with which it was charged was not merely one of simple justice. In addition to the factor of equality of treatment and opportunity was the factor of military efficiency, the making of a better armed service.

In the Committee's view the task could not be accomplished solely on the basis of information gathered in formal testimony, though such testimony must be a necessary step in the Committee's inquiry. The President had directed the Committee to examine into the procedures and practices of the three services. Such an examination, the Committee decided, required three lines of inquiry, each one of which would provide a check upon the other two.

First, it was necessary for the Committee to have a comprehensive understanding of the whole field of personnel policy and administration in the three services, including recruitment, basic training, technical training, assignment, promotion, and the so-called career guidance programs. Without such information the Committee did not feel competent to judge (a) whether the services were denying opportunity to any of their personnel solely on account of race and (b) whether their racial policies and practices promoted or reduced military efficiency.

Second, the Committee needed to make a study of the historical experience of the three services with racial groups, for it was on the basis of this experience that the services largely explained and rationalized their present policies and practices.

Third, the Committee wished to supplement its technical and historical studies with field trips so that it would have first-hand information.

One other problem concerned the Committee. This was how best to secure the endorsement by the armed services of those measures which, in the Committee's judgment, might be needed to effect the President's policy. The Committee believed that progress could be made most readily by a presentation of the facts, by suggestions for corrective measures, and by convincing the services of the reasonableness and effectiveness of its recommendations.

The services, though subject to civilian control, are old institutions with long-established customs and habits. The Committee believed that reforms would be more readily accepted and make headway faster if they represented decisions mutually agreed upon. Imposed decisions can be enforced by discipline but joint decisions engage the loyalty of those who have concerted them.

Therefore the Committee decided that it would confer with the services at each step of the way, confident that its recommendations would win support as the services became convinced they were sound in principle and would improve the efficiency of the military establishment. If this could be accomplished, the Committee contemplated that its recommendations would be implemented concurrently with their acceptance, and that a report to the President would then represent not a future objective but a program in being. This plan of work had the President's approval.

The Course of the Inquiry

At the beginning of its inquiry the Committee heard testimony from 67 witnesses, including the Secretaries and Assistant Secretaries of the Army, Navy, and Air Force, as well as the Army Chief of Staff; the Deputy Chief of Naval Operations for Personnel, the Air Force Director of Personnel Planning, the Army Director of Personnel and Administration; a former Assistant Secretary of War who headed the Special Troop Policies Committee in World War II; the chairman of the board of general officers that in 1945 formulated a new Army racial policy; civilian personnel experts from the three services; and individuals and representatives of civilian organizations concerned with minority group interests.

The testimony of these witnesses, totaling 1,025 pages, has been bound and indexed. Copies are being deposited with the Secretary of Defense, the Secretaries of the Army, Navy, and Air Force, the General Staffs of the Army and Air Force, the Bureau of Personnel of the Navy, the Library of Congress, and the Archives.

Through the cooperation of the Navy Bureau of Personnel, the office of the Director of Personnel Planning in the Air Force, the Army general staff divisions of Personnel and Administration and Organization and Training, the Personnel Research and Procedures Branch of the Army Adjutant General's Office and the Historical Records Section of the Army, the Committee has been able to secure a comprehensive understanding of the personnel policies and operations of the three services and a thorough knowledge of the policies governing minority groups.

These agencies made freely available to the Committee and its staff all the historical and technical information necessary to the Committee's study, and representatives of the services were always available to the Committee for guidance and consultation. The day-to-day conferences and collaboration of the Committee's staff and the technical experts of the services greatly facilitated the work of the Committee.

Finally, the Committee and its staff made field investigations covering eight Navy ships and stations, seven Air Force bases, and ten Army posts. In addition the Committee itself has held more than 40 meetings.

The scope of the executive order required that there be equality of treatment and opportunity for all persons in the armed services without regard to race, color, religion, or national origin. Members of various minority groups have asserted the existence of discrimination on these grounds, but no evidence was presented to the Committee and no specific facts were found indicating formally defined service policies denying equality of treatment and opportunity except with respect to Negroes. In their case practices resulting in inequality of treatment and opportunity had the sanction of official policy and were embodied in regulations.

The Committee felt, therefore, that its examination should leave room for gathering facts and developing conclusions affecting all minorities, but that it should proceed with the material on hand concerning the specific status of Negroes in the services. Once this racial factor should be satisfactorily disposed of, the Committee believed, a formula would be evolved applicable to all minorities. For this reason specific mention is limited throughout the report to recommendations and changes affecting Negroes.

There follows a summary account of the extent to which the President's executive order presently is being implemented, with an indication of the policy changes that have been put into effect by the services since the order was issued in July 1948.

The Navy

All jobs and ratings in the naval general service now are open to all enlisted men without regard to race or color. Negroes are currently serving in every job classification in general service.

All courses in Navy technical schools are open to qualified personnel without regard to race or color and without racial quotas. Negroes are attending the most advanced technical schools and are serving in their ratings both in the fleet and at shore installations.

Negroes in general service are completely integrated with whites in basic training, technical schools, on the job, in messes and sleeping quarters, ashore and afloat.

Chief, first-, second-, and third-class stewards now have the rate of chief, first-, second-, and third-class petty officers. (Policy change adopted June 7, 1949.)

Stewards who qualify for general ratings now can transfer to general service.

The Marine Corps, which as a part of the Navy is subject to Navy policy, has abolished its segregated Negro training units. (Policy change adopted June 7, 1949.) Marine Corps training is now integrated, although some Negro marines are still assigned to separate units after basic training. In this respect the effectuation of Navy policy in the Marine Corps is yet to be completed.

The Air Force

The Air Force announced its new racial policy on May 11, 1949. As a result of this policy, the all-Negro 332d Fighter Wing at Lockbourne Field, Ohio, has been broken up, and its personnel either sent to school for further training, transferred to white units in other commands, or separated under current regulations.

A majority of other Negro units has also been abolished. As of January 31, 1950, only 59 Negro units remained, and 1,302 units were racially integrated, as compared with 106 Negro units and only 167 mixed units on June 1, 1949, when the Air Force policy went into effect.

Approximately 74 percent of the 25,000 Negroes in the Air Force on January 31, 1950, were serving in integrated units; and 26 percent still were serving in Negro units. This integration process is continuing.

All Air Force jobs and schools are open to qualified personnel without racial restriction or quotas. Six percent of the total personnel attending technical training schools in January 1950 were Negro.

Negroes serving in mixed units and attending service schools are integrated with whites in living conditions.

The Army

All Army jobs now are open to Negroes. (Policy change adopted September 30, 1949.)

All Army school courses are open to Negroes without restriction or quota. (Policy change adopted September 30, 1949.)

For the first time Negroes no longer are limited in assignment to Negro and overhead (housekeeping) units, but are to be assigned according to their qualifications to any unit, including formerly white units. (Policy change adopted January 16, 1950.)

Negroes serving in mixed units will be integrated on the job, in barracks and messes. (Policy change adopted January 16, 1950.)

The 10 percent limitation on Negro strength in the Army has been abolished, and there no longer are Negro quotas for enlistment. (Policy change adopted March 27, 1950.)

The succeeding chapters contain a more detailed account of the Committee's recommendations to the services and the extent to which the President's policy is being implemented.

DOCUMENT 8

Letter from Harry Truman to A. Philip Randolph, August 22, 1950

Letter from Harry Truman to A. Philip Randolph describing the importance of black troops fighting in Korea.
Source: Truman Library.

August 22, 1950

Dear Mr. Randolph:

I have great pleasure in extending warm felicitations and hearty congratulations to the Brotherhood of Sleeping Car Porters, A.F. of L., on the occasion of the Silver Jubilee Convention.

Once again those who cherish freedom and individual dignity are involved in a great struggle for the minds, hearts and loyalties of millions of human beings all over the world. In this struggle, America's Negroes are destined to play an ever more historic role.

All America is proud of the valorous performances of our Negro fighters in Korea. Their courage, skill and high morale will give new impetus to the measures we have undertaken to insure that America's armed forces will be the most democratic in the world. Their achievements on the battlefield presage the more important role which American Negroes are destined to play in our new program to help the long-oppressed peoples of Asia and Africa help themselves toward freedom, dignity and self-government.

I am especially grateful for your organization's continued support and encouragement in the achievement of effective civil rights legislation, which I still regard as one of the major pieces of unfinished business before the Congress . . .

Very sincerely yours,
Harry S. Truman

DOCUMENT 9

Letter from Roy Wilkins, NAACP, to Harry Truman, January 12, 1953

Letter from Roy Wilkins, NAACP, to Harry Truman that congratulates Truman on his "many accomplishments," including his civil rights legacy.
Source: OF-596 (July 1950–53), Official File, Truman Papers, Truman Library.

January 12, 1953

President Harry S. Truman
The White House
Washington, D. C.

Dear Mr. President:

You must be receiving many letters and your hours in these last days of office must be filled with many duties, but I felt that I could not see you leave Washington without telling you how I feel about one phase of your administration.

I want to thank you and to convey to you my admiration for your efforts in the civil rights field, for your pronouncements and definitions of policy on racial and religious discrimination and segregation.

You have many accomplishments on record during your tenure of the White House (many more by far than is admitted publicly by the Republicans or the majority of the nation's press) but none more valuable to our nation and its ideals than your outspoken championing of equality of opportunity for all Americans without regard to race, color or national origin.

Mr. President, no Chief Executive in our history has spoken so plainly on this matter as yourself, or acted so forthrightly. We have had in the White House great men—great diplomats, great politicians, great scholars, great humanitarians, great administrators. Some of these have recognized inequality as undesirable, as being at variance with the democratic principles of our country; but none has had the courage, either personal or political, to speak out or act in the Truman manner.

You spoke, Sir, when you knew that many powerful influences in your own party (and in the party of the opposition) would not heed you. You reiterated your beliefs and restated your demands for legislation when political expediency dictated a compromise course. This is sheer personal courage, so foreign to the usual conduct in political office—high or low—as to be unique in the annals of our government. But it was worthy of the Presidency of the United States of America. No little man, no mere politician would have sensed the fitness of such conduct in the nation's leader.

Your great desire to achieve peace. Your sincere efforts toward this goal have saved us from a Third World War thus far and have laid a foundation on which others, if equally devoted, can bring peace to the world.

In urging that America erase inequality between its citizens, as citizens, you were outlining a component of the complex mosaic for peace in the world: the hope, dignity and freedom that democracies offer mankind in contrast to the offerings of totalitarianism. Your sure realization of the truism that preachment without practice would be powerless as a force for peace is a measure of the quiet greatness you brought to your high office.

As you leave the White House you carry with you the gratitude and affectionate regard of millions of your Negro fellow citizens who in less than a decade of your leadership, inspiration and determination, have seen the old order change right before their eyes.

Their sons are serving their country's armed forces in pride and honor, instead of humiliation and despair.

A whole new world of opportunity in education is opening to their children and young people.

The barriers to employment and promotion on the basis of merit have been breached and will be destroyed.

Some of the obstacles in the way of enjoyment of decent housing have been removed and others are under attack.

Restrictions upon the precious citizenship right of casting a ballot have been reduced and soon this right will be unfettered.

Some of the cruel humiliations and discriminations in travel and accommodation in public places have been eliminated and others are on the way out.

But in addition to these specifics, Mr. President, you have been responsible through the pronouncements from your high office, for a new climate of opinion in this broad area of civil rights. By stating a government policy, by relating that policy to the cherished ideals of our nation, you have recalled for the American people that strength of the spirit, that devotion to human welfare and human liberties, that made our country man's best hope for the things all men hold dear.

In their prayers for your health and long life, Negro Americans are joined, I am sure, by hosts of other citizens who have had their spirits renewed and their convictions strengthened by your espousal of the verities of our way of life.

You have said often that the people will act when they have understanding. The people who have had their faith fanned fresh by you will not fail to press toward the goals you have indicated. No change of personnel or party labels will stay them.

May God's blessing and guidance be with you in your new endeavors.

Respectfully yours,

Roy Wilkins
(Administrator, National Association for the Advancement of Colored People)

Notes

Introduction

1 Colin Powell, "Truman, Desegregation of the Armed Forces, and a Kid from the South Bronx," in Raymond Geselbracht, ed., *The Civil Rights Legacy of Harry S. Truman*, 120–122. What was reprinted here is a modification of the speech that Powell delivered at the RLDS Auditorium in Independence, Missouri, on July 24, 1998.

2 Ibid., 122.

1 Franklin Roosevelt, African Americans and the Coming of World War II

1 Harvard Sitkoff, *A New Deal for Blacks: The Emergence of Civil Rights as a National Issue, the Depression Decade*. New York: Oxford University Press, 1978, 35, 37–38.

2 Ibid., 41.

3 Ibid., 77–79.

4 Ibid., 60.

5 Ibid., 66–67.

6 For quote see ibid., 93–94.

7 Ibid., 94–97.

8 Patricia Sullivan, *Lift Every Voice: The NAACP and the Making of the Civil Rights Movement*. New York: The New Press, 2009, 146, 156.

9 Ibid., 159–160.

10 Ibid, 160.

11 Ibid, 160–161.

12 Paul Finkelman, ed., *Encyclopedia of African American History: 1896 to the Present, Vol. II*, New York: Oxford University Press, 2009, 459.

13 Sullivan, *Lift Every Voice*, 168–169.

14 Ibid., 195.

15 John B. Kirby, *Black Americans in the Roosevelt Era: Liberalism and Race*. Knoxville, TN: The University of Tennessee Press, 1980, 99–103.

16 Sitkoff, *A New Deal for Blacks*, 249.

17 Sullivan, *Lift Every Voice*, 219–221.
18 Sitkoff, *A New Deal for Blacks*, 260–261.
19 Patricia Sullivan, *Days of Hope: Race and Democracy in the New Deal Era*. Chapel Hill, NC: University of North Carolina Press, 1996, 63–65, 98–101.
20 There are other organizations that fought for civil rights as well. See Sitkoff, *A New Deal for Blacks* and Sullivan, *Days of Hope*.
21 Sitkoff, *A New Deal for Blacks*, 62, 65–66.
22 Ibid., 134.
23 Audrey Thomas McCluskey and Elaine M. Smith, eds., *Mary McLeod Bethune: Building a Better World: Essays and Selected Documents*, Bloomington, IN: Indiana University Press, 1999, xii, 4–9.
24 Sullivan, *Lift Every Voice*, 231–233.
25 The preceding three paragraphs were based on MacGregor, Jr., *Integration of the Armed Forces, 1940–1965*, Defense Studies Series. Washington DC: Center of Military History, U.S. Army, 1981, 4–7 and MacGregor, Jr., "Minorities in the Armed Services," in John E. Jessup, ed., *Encyclopedia of the American Military*, Vol. III., New York: Charles Scribner's Sons, 1994, 2050–2054.
26 Quoted in Sitkoff, *A New Deal for Blacks*, 301.

2 Politics and the Quest for an Integrated Military, 1937–1945

1 Quoted in Evelyn M. Monahan and Rosemary Neidel-Greenlee, *A Few Good Women: America's Military Women from World War I to the Wars in Iraq and Afghanistan*, New York: Alfred A. Knopf, 2010, 96.
2 Ulysses Lee, *The United States Army in World War II, Special Studies: The Employment of Negro Troops*, 37–50. Washington, DC: Office of the Chief of Military History United States Army, 1966. For the quotes see 49–50.
3 Sitkoff, *A New Deal for Blacks*, 303–304.
4 Phillip McGuire, ed., *Taps for a Jim Crow Army: Letters from Black Soldiers in World War II*. Lexington, KY: The University Press of Kentucky, 1983, xxvi.
5 Sitkoff, *A New Deal for Blacks*, 305–306.
6 As quoted in Lee, *Employment of Negro Troops*, 76.
7 As quoted in Sitkoff, *A New Deal for Blacks*, 307.
8 Quoted in Richard Dalfiume, *Desegregation of the U.S. Armed Forces: Fighting on Two Fronts, 1939–1953*. Columbia, MO: University of Missouri Press, 1969, 43.
9 Nancy J. Weiss, *Farewell to the Party of Lincoln: Black Politics in the Age of FDR*, 294.
10 Ernest Obadele-Starks, "A. Philip Randolph," in Paul Finkleman, ed., *Encyclopedia of African American History: 1896 to the Present*, Vol. IV, New York: Oxford University Press, 2009, 177–181.
11 Sitkoff, *A New Deal for Blacks*, 312.
12 Sullivan, *Lift Every Voice*, 253–255.
13 Ibid., 255.
14 Quoted in Sullivan, *Lift Every Voice*, 255.
15 For the white primary see Sullivan, *Lift Every Voice*, 145 and for the desegregation of the military see Sitkoff, *A New Deal for Blacks*, 302.

16 Marc A. Sennewald, "Thurgood Marshall," in Paul Finkelman, ed., *Encyclopedia of African American History: 1896 to the Present, Vol. III*, New York: Oxford University Press, 2009, 263–266.
17 Sullivan, *Lift Every Voice*, 244–246, 282–283.
18 Sitkoff, *A New Deal for Blacks*, 302. For the founding date for the Committee for the Participation of Negroes in the National Defense see Richard Dalfiume, *Desegregation of the U.S. Armed Forces*, 26.
19 Sitkoff, *A New Deal for Blacks*, 249.
20 Quoted in Lee, *Employment of Negro Troops*, 66.
21 Quoted in Morris J. MacGregor, Jr., *Integration of the Armed Forces, 1940–1965*. Defense Studies Series. Washington DC: Center of Military History, U.S. Army, 1981, 22–23.
22 Quoted in Sitkoff, *A New Deal for Blacks*, 324.
23 Neil A. Wynn, ed., *The A to Z of the Roosevelt–Truman Era*, Lanham, MD: Scarecrow Press, 2009, 31. MacGregor, Jr., *Integration of the Armed Forces*, says 800,000 served, 56.
24 Carolyn M. Feller and Constance J. Moore, eds., *Highlights in the History of the Army Nurse Corps*, Washington, DC: U.S. Army Center of Military History, 1996, 16–18.
25 Ibid., 13.
26 Quoted in Mattie B. Treadwell, *The Women's Army* Corps, Washington, DC: Office of the Chief of Military History, 1954, 13.
27 Ibid., 14.
28 Quoted in Treadwell, *Women's Army Corps*, 17.
29 Ibid., 16–17.
30 Ibid., 20–23.
31 Ibid., 193.
32 Ibid., 204–205.
33 For an extensive treatment of the campaign against the WAAC see Treadwell, *Women's Army Corps*, 191–218. For the quote from the WAAC official see ibid., 218.
34 For the conversion date see Treadwell, *The Women's Army Corps*, 220–221.
35 Jerold E. Brown, ed., *Historical Dictionary of the U.S. Army*, Westport, CT: Greenwood Press, 2001, 518–519. For more on the role of the WAC see Bettie J. Morden, *The Women's Army Corps, 1945–1978*. Washington, D.C.: Center of Military History, U.S. Army, 1990.
36 Morden, *The Women's Army Corps*, 25.
37 Charles D. Bright, ed., *Historical Dictionary of the U.S. Air Force*, New York: Greenwood Press, 1992, 628–630.
38 Morden, *The Women's Army Corps*, 5.
39 Ibid., 6.
40 Lee, *Employment of Negro Troops*, 421–424.
41 Allan Berube, *Coming Out Under Fire: The History of Gay Men and Women in World War II, 20th Anniversary Edition*. Chapel Hill, NC: University of North Carolina Press, 2010, for the numbers see 3; for the screening see 8–33.
42 Ibid., 33.
43 Ibid., 139–145.

44 For the three-fourths see Lee, *Employment of Negro Troops*, 138.
45 MacGregor, Jr., *Integration of the Armed Forces*, 20.
46 Lee, *Employment of Negro Troops*, 136.
47 Ibid., 139.
48 Quoted in Lee, *Employment of Negro Troops*, 140–141.
49 J. Todd Moye, *Freedom Flyers: The Tuskegee Airmen of World War II*. New York: Oxford University Press, 2010, 77–78.
50 Quoted in Moye, *Freedom Flyers*, 91. For the combat actions of these troops see ibid, 98–122, and Bernard C. Nalty, *Strength for the Fight: A History of Black Americans in the Armed Forces*. New York: Free Press, 1989, 143–183.
51 Lee, *Employment of Negro Troops*, 175.
52 Maggi M. Morehouse, *Fighting in the Jim Crow Army: Black Men and Women Remember World War II*. New York: Roman & Littlefield Publishers, 2000, 41–47.
53 Moye, *Freedom Flyers*, 72. For the date of Gibson's appointment see Lee, *Employment of Negro Troops*, 178.
54 Richard Goldstein, "Truman Gibson, 93, Dies; Fought Army Segregation," *New York Times*, January 2, 2006, B7.
55 Morehouse, *Fighting in the Jim Crow Army*, 41, 87.
56 Ibid., 87–112.
57 MacGregor, Jr., *Integration of the Armed Forces*, 45.
58 Ibid., 42.
59 Ibid., 42–43.
60 Command of Negro Troops, p. 1, General Printed Material [1 of 2], Box 7, RG 220, President's Committee on the Equality of Treatment and Opportunity in the Armed Services, Records, 1949–1950, Truman Library.
61 Ibid., 3–6.
62 Ibid., 6–8.
63 Ibid., 9–10.
64 Ibid., 19.
65 As quoted in MacGregor, Jr., *Integration of the Armed Forces*, 45.
66 Ibid., 43.
67 Ibid., 45–46.
68 *Leadership and the Negro Soldier: Army Service Forces Manual, M5*. Washington, D.C.: United States Government Printing Office, 1944, 9.
69 MacGregor, Jr., *Integration of the Armed Forces*, 76.
70 Ibid., 84.
71 Ibid., 86–88, 95–96.
72 Ibid., 92.
73 Ibid., 92–93.
74 Ibid., 98.
75 Ibid., 100–101.
76 Ibid., 103.
77 Ibid., 111–112.
78 Ibid., 112–116.
79 Ibid., 116–122.

3 Harry Truman and Civil Rights, 1884–1945

1 Roy Wilkins with Tom Mathews, *Standing Fast: The Autobiography of Roy Wilkins*, New York: Viking Press, 1982, 193.
2 Alonzo Hamby, *Man of the People: A Life of Harry S. Truman*. New York: Oxford University Press, 1998, 4–5.
3 Quoted in Robert H. Ferrell, ed., *Dear Bess: The Letters from Harry to Bess Truman, 1910–1959*. New York: Norton, 1983, 39.
4 Quoted in Jon E. Taylor, *Truman's Grandview Farm*, Charleston, SC: The History Press, 2011, 58.
5 For the number of African American voters see Donald R. McCoy and Richard T. Ruetten, *Quest and Response: Minority Rights and the Truman Administration*, Lawrence, KS: University Press of Kansas, 1973, 14.
6 David McCullough, *Truman*, New York: Simon & Schuster, 1992, 164–165.
7 Larry Grothaus, "Kansas City Blacks, Harry Truman and the Pendergast Machine," *Missouri Historical Review* 69, no. 1 (October 1974): 71–72.
8 David McCullough, *Truman*, 174.
9 See Sherry Lamb Schirmer, *A City Divided: The Racial Landscape of Kansas City, 1900–1960*, Columbia, MO: University of Missouri Press, 2002, 162–164 and Charles E. Coulter, "*Take Up the Black Man's Burden" Kansas City's African American Communities, 1865–1939*, Columbia, MO: University of Missouri Press, 2006, 209–213. For the quote see Coulter, 213.
10 Quoted in Coulter, "*Black Man's Burden*," 213.
11 Grothaus, "Kansas City Blacks," 76–81.
12 Ibid., 80.
13 Robert Sweeney, interview by Carol Briley, transcript of tape recorded interview, December 12, 1977, Truman Library.
14 Sitkoff, *A New Deal for Blacks*, 41.
15 Quoted in Grothaus, "Kansas City Blacks," 82.
16 Gary Kremer, "William J. Thompkins: African American Physician, Politician, and Publisher," *Missouri Historical Review* 101, no. 3 (April 2007): 168–182.
17 Wilkins and Mathews, *Standing Fast*, 96–110.
18 See Wilkins, *Standing Fast*, 192–193.
19 Sullivan, *Lift Every Voice*, 194–197.
20 McCoy and Ruetten, *Quest and Response*, 14–15.
21 Lawrence H. Larsen and Nancy J. Hulston, *Pendergast!* Columbia: University of Missouri Press, 1997, 146–147. For more on the Pendergast machine see Lyle Dorset, *Pendergast Machine*, New York: Oxford University Press, 1968, and Robert H. Ferrell, *Truman and Pendergast*, Columbia: University of Missouri Press, 1999.
22 "Dedicate Ground for Hospital," June 16, 1940, p. 1, *Sedalia Democrat*.
23 Ibid, p. 7.
24 *Congressional Record*. 76th Cong., 3rd sess, 1940, 86, pt. 16: 4546–4547.
25 Ibid., pt. 17: 5367–5369.
26 Hamby, *Man of the People*, 247.
27 For the Truman Committee see Hamby, *Man of the People*, 248–260. For the role of African Americans see Roy Wilkins to Ira Lewis, September 10, 1941, Folder: Bills-Truman, Harry S., 1941, Box II A 122, NAACP Papers, Library of Congress.

28 McCoy and Ruetten, *Quest and Response*, 37.
29 Grant to Walter White, August 8, 1944, Folder: Harry S. Truman, 1944, Box II A 632, NAACP Papers, Library of Congress.
30 Harry S. Truman to Walter White, October 29, 1944, Folder: Harry S. Truman, 1944, Box II A 632, NAACP Papers, Library of Congress.
31 Walter White to David O. Selznick, October 30, 1944, Folder: Harry S. Truman, 1944, Box II A 632, NAACP Papers, Library of Congress.
32 For an extensive account of the Freeman incident see Moye, *Freedom Flyers*, 132–144. For the quote see ibid., 135.
33 Quoted in Moye, *Freedom Flyers*, 142–143.
34 Moye, *Freedom Flyers*, 144.
35 Quoted in McCoy and Ruetten, *Quest and Response*, 17.
36 For the membership figure see Sullivan, *Lift Every Voice*, 288.

4 Post-War Utilization of the Military and the Creation of the President's Committee on Civil Rights, 1945–1947

1 *To Secure These Rights: The Report of the President's Committee on Civil Rights*, Washington, D.C.: U.S. Government Printing Office, 1947, 141.
2 Walter White to Harry S. Truman, April 19, 1945, Folder: Harry S. Truman, 1945, Box II A 632, NAACP Papers, Library of Congress.
3 Jon–Christian Suggs, "W. E. B. Du Bois," in Paul Finkelman, ed., *Encyclopedia of African American History: 1896 to the Present, Vol. II*, 96–99.
4 Carol Anderson, *Eyes off the Prize: The United Nations and the African American Struggle for Human Rights*, 1944–1955, Cambridge: Cambridge University Press, 2003, 32–35.
5 Suggs, "W. E. B. Du Bois," 99–102.
6 Sullivan, *Lift Every Voice*, 308–309.
7 Walter White memo to Edward Stettinius, May 15, 1945, Folder: Harry S. Truman, 1945, Box II A 632, NAACP Papers, Library of Congress.
8 Quoted in McCoy and Ruetten, *Quest and Response*, 20.
9 For the quote see Anderson, *Eyes off the Prize*, 48–49.
10 Quoted in MacGregor, Jr., *Integration of the Armed Forces*, 132.
11 Ibid., 133–135.
12 Ibid., 137.
13 Ibid., 142.
14 Ibid., 142.
15 Ibid., 153.
16 Ibid., 154–155.
17 Ibid., 155–156.
18 Ibid., 156–157.
19 Ibid., 157–158.
20 Ibid., 162.
21 Ibid., 165–166.
22 Ibid., 166–175.
23 Berube, *Coming Out Under Fire*, 170–173.
24 Ibid., 242.

25 Quoted in Berube, *Coming Out Under Fire*, 261.

26 Ibid., 261.

27 Ibid., 262. For more on the development of the Universal Code of Military Justice see Jonathan Lurie, *The U.S. Court of Appeals for the Armed Forces, 1775–1980*, Lawrence, KS: University of Kansas Press, 2001 and William Allison, *Military Justice in Vietnam: The Rule of Law in an American War*. Lawrence, KS: University of Kansas Press, 2006, especially Chapter 1.

28 Berube, *Coming Out Under Fire*, 265–268.

29 Ibid., 269. For more analysis of the impact of the Cold War on gay federal employees see David K. Johnson, *The Lavender Scare: The Cold War Persecution of Gays and Lesbians in the Federal Government*. Chicago, IL: University of Chicago Press, 2004.

30 Raymond H. Geselbracht, ed., *The Civil Rights Legacy of Harry S. Truman*, Kirksville, MO: Truman State University Press, 2007, 191.

31 McCoy and Ruetten, *Quest and Response*, 32–33.

32 Story recounted by Raymond Frey, "Truman's Speech to the NAACP, 29 June 1947," in Raymond H. Geselbracht, ed., *The Civil Rights Legacy of Harry S. Truman*, 93.

33 For the quote see Gail Williams O'Brien, *The Color of the Law: Race, Violence, and Justice in the Post–World War II South*, Chapel Hill, NC: University of North Carolina Press, 1999, 48. For an extensive account of the Columbia riot, as it is sometimes referred to, and more detail on the trials, see ibid., 7–55.

34 See Gerald Horne, *Communist Front? The Civil Rights Congress, 1946–1956*, Rutherford, NJ: Fairleigh Dickinson University Press, 1988, 29–31.

35 Anderson, *Eyes off the Prize*, 79–85.

36 Ibid., 88.

37 June 21, 1946 speech. Folder: General Federation of Women's Clubs, Papers of Tom Clark, Harry S. Truman Library.

38 Laura Wexler, *Fire in a Canebrake: The Last Mass Lynchings in America*, 87–88. New York: Scribner, 2003.

39 See Anderson, *Eyes off the Prize*, fn. 11, 61.

40 Harry S. Truman to Lester Granger, September 12, 1946, President's Personal File 2685, Truman Library.

41 Quoted in McCoy and Ruetten, *Quest and Response*, 47–48.

42 For the grand jury quote see Wexler, *Fire in a Canebrake*, 190; for Wexler's conclusion see ibid.

43 Paul Finkelman, "Paul Robeson," in Paul Finkelman, ed., *Encyclopedia of African American History: 1896 to the Present, Vol. IV*, New York: Oxford University Press, 2009, 225–231.

44 McCoy and Ruetten, *Quest and Response*, 48.

45 *Higher Education for American Democracy, Vol. I Establishing the Goals*, Washington, D.C.: GPO, 1947.

46 *Higher Education for American Democracy, Vol. VI Resource Data*, Washington, D.C.: GPO, 1947.

47 *Higher Education for American Democracy, Vol. II Equalizing and Expanding Individual Opportunity*, Washington, D.C.: GPO, 1947, p. 35.

48 Ibid., 29.

49 "Truman Talk on Training," *New York Times*, December 20, 1946.

50 Quoted in Truman K. Gibson, Jr., with Steve Huntley, *Knocking Down Barriers: My Fight for Black America*, Evanston, IL: Northwestern University Press, 2005, 226.

51 *A Program for National Security: Report of the President's Advisory Commission on Universal Training*, 42–43.

52 Sullivan, *Lift Every Voice*, 342.

53 Anna Kasten Nelson, "Anna M. Rosenberg, an 'Honorary Man'," *The Journal of Military History* Vol. 68. No. 1 (January 2004): 135–141.

54 Ibid., 143–144.

55 McCoy and Ruetten, *Quest and Response*, 48–50.

56 Lawson, *To Secure These Rights*, vii.

57 Nash, Philleo. Interview by Jerry Hess, February 21, 1967. Transcript of tape recorded interview. Harry S. Truman Library, 629.

58 Lawson, *To Secure These Rights*, 17–20.

59 Truman, Harry S., *Public Papers of the Presidents, Harry S. Truman, 1947*, 98–99.

60 McCoy and Ruetten, *Quest and Response*, 80.

61 Ibid., 80–81.

62 Quoted in ibid., 82.

63 Harry Truman to Mary Jane Truman, June 28, 1947, folder: Letters to Mrs. John A. Truman and sister Mary Jane Truman January 25, 1946–November 7, 1948, Set # 1, Post Presidential Papers, 1953–1972. Memoirs File, Harry S. Truman Library.

64 For the quotes see Raymond Frey, "Truman's Speech to the NAACP, 29 June 1947," in Raymond H. Geselbracht, ed., *The Civil Rights Legacy of Harry S. Truman*, 96–97.

65 Truman, Harry S., *Public Papers of the Presidents*, Harry S. Truman, 1947, 311–313.

66 Quoted in "Truman's Speech to the NAACP," 98.

67 W. E. B. Du Bois, Introduction to *An Appeal to the World*. Du Bois Papers (MS 312). Special Collections and University Archives, W.E.B. Du Bois Library, University of Massachusetts Amherst, 1947.

68 For the quotes see David Levering Lewis, *W. E. B. Du Bois: The Fight for Equality and the American Century, 1919–1963*, New York: Henry Holt, 1993, 529–530.

69 Truman, Harry S., *Public Papers of the Presidents*, Harry S. Truman, 1947, 480.

70 Lawson, eds., *To Secure These Rights*, 21.

71 *To Secure These Rights*, 6–9.

72 Ibid., ix, 10.

73 Ibid., 35.

74 Ibid., 46.

75 Ibid., 87.

76 Ibid., 99–102.

77 Ibid., 139.

78 Ibid., 148.

79 Ibid., 151–173.

5 Integration of the Military, 1948–1953

1 Kenworthy, E. W. Interview by Jerry Hess, January 26, 1971. Transcript of tape recorded interview. Harry S. Truman Library.
2 Gibson, Truman. Interview by Carol Briley, July 27, 2001. Transcript of tape recorded interview. Harry S. Truman Library.
3 Quoted in McCoy and Ruetten, *Quest and Response*, 92.
4 Quoted in Michael R. Gardner, *Harry Truman and Civil Rights*, 62.
5 Truman, Harry S., *Public Papers of the Presidents: Harry S. Truman,* 121–126.
6 Richard M. Dalfiume, *Desegregation of the U.S. Armed Forces*, 163–164. For the quote see 163.
7 Quoted in ibid., 164.
8 Quoted in ibid., 167.
9 Ibid.
10 Anderson, *Eyes off the Prize*, 153.
11 Ibid., 151.
12 Michael Gardner, *Harry Truman and Civil Rights: Moral Courage and Political Risks*. Carbondale, IL: Southern Illinois Press, 2002, 169–178.
13 Jeanne M. Holm and Judith Bellafaire, eds., *In Defense of a Nation: Servicewomen in World War II*, 149.
14 Patricia Ward Wallace, *Politics of Conscience: A Biography of Margaret Chase Smith*, 70–73. For the quote see 70.
15 Janann Sherman, *No Place for a Woman: A Life of Senator Margaret Chase Smith*, 72.
16 Janann Sherman, "They Either Need These Women or They Do Not: Margaret Chase Smith and the Fight for Regular Status for Women in the Military," *The Journal of Military History*, 54, No. 1 (January 1990): 77.
17 Sherman, *No Place for a Woman*, 72.
18 Nona Brown, "The Armed Forces Find Woman Has a Place," *New York Times*, December 26, 1948, SM14.
19 Quoted in Dalfiume, *Desegregation of the U.S. Armed Forces*, 169.
20 Clark Clifford to Harry Truman, November 19, 1947, Political File, Papers of Clark Clifford, Harry S. Truman Library.
21 Ibid.
22 Gardner, *Harry Truman and Civil Rights*, 91–92. For more on the ADA see Allen Yarnell, *Democrats and Progressives: The 1948 Presidential Election as a Test of Postwar Liberalism*. Berkeley, CA: University of California Press, 1974.
23 Gardner, *Harry Truman and Civil Rights*, 97.
24 Ibid., 99.
25 Democratic Party Platforms: Democratic Party Platform of 1948 www.presidency.ucsb.edu/ws/index.php?pid=29599#ixzz1gjcWsNgE.
26 See *The Yale Law Journal*, Vol. 82, No. 7 (June 1973): 1534.
27 See correspondence in *Equal Rights for Women (1945–1947)* and (1948–53) folders, Official File 120-A, Truman Papers, Harry S. Truman Library.
28 Gardner, *Harry Truman and Civil Rights*, 99–102.
29 For more on Wallace's campaign see Patricia Sullivan, *Days of Hope: Race and Democracy in the New Deal Era*, 249–275.

30 American Presidency Project: Republican Party Platforms. Republican Party Platform of 1948. www.presidency.ucsb.edu/ws/index.php?pid=25836#ixzz1gjzdv1Qs.
31 McCoy and Ruetten, *Quest and Response*, 98.
32 Ibid., 112, 122.
33 Quoted in ibid., 130.
34 Dalfiume, *Desegregation of the U.S. Armed Forces*, 168–171.
35 McCoy and Ruetten, *Quest and Response*, 129.
36 MacGregor, Jr., *Integration of the Armed Forces*, 310–311.
37 Truman, Harry S., *Public Papers of the Presidents: Harry S. Truman, 1948*, 165.
38 MacGregor, Jr., *Integration of the Armed Forces*, 317.
39 Quoted in McCoy and Ruetten, *Quest and Response*, 130–131.
40 MacGregor, Jr., *Integration of the Armed Forces*, 314.
41 Dalfiume, *Desegregation of the U.S. Armed Forces*, 176.
42 Truman, Harry S. *Public Papers of the Presidents, Harry S. Truman, 1948*, 924–925.
43 McCoy and Ruetten, *Quest and Response*, 160.
44 Ibid., 146.
45 See Virgil W. Dean, *An Opportunity Lost: The Truman Administration and the Farm Policy Debate*, 108 and Allen J. Matusow, *Farm Policies and Politics in the Truman Years*, 185.
46 See MacGregor, Jr., *Integration of the Armed Forces*, 315–342.
47 Dalfiume, *Desegregation of the U.S. Armed Forces*, 179–180.
48 Ibid., 180–181.
49 MacGregor, Jr., *Integration of the Armed Forces*, 343.
50 Quoted in ibid., 352; for Davenport, 355–356.
51 Dalfiume, *Desegregation of the U.S. Armed Forces*, 181–182.
52 MacGregor, Jr., *Integration of the Armed Forces*, 355.
53 Ibid., 345.
54 President's Committee on Equality of Treatment and Opportunity in the Armed Forces Progress report, June 7, 1949, President's Secretary's Files, Truman Papers, Harry S. Truman Library.
55 McCoy and Ruetten, *Quest and Response*, 223.
56 Kenneth Royall to Clark Clifford, March 29, 1949, Subject, File, Clifford Papers, Harry S. Truman Library.
57 RG 220, Records of Temporary Committees, Commissions and Boards "Army Program for Racial Equality Approved by Secretary of Defense," Press release, September 30, 1949, Harry S. Truman Library.
58 MacGregor, Jr., *Integration of the Armed Forces*, 368–370.
59 RG 220, Dwight Palmer to Charles Fahy, February 7, 1950, Fahy Committee Members and Staff, Harry S. Truman Library.
60 McCoy and Ruetten, *Quest and Response*, 231.
61 MacGregor, Jr., *Integration of the Armed Forces*, 373–374.
62 Truman, Harry S., *Public Papers of the Presidents of the United States: Harry S. Truman, 1950*, 431–432.
63 MacGregor, Jr., *Integration of the Armed Forces*, 375–376.

64 Dalfiume, *Desegregation of the U.S. Armed Forces*, 200.

65 MacGregor, Jr., *Integration of the Armed Forces*, 406–407.

66 Sherie Mershon and Steven Schlossman, *Foxholes and Color Lines: Desegregating the U.S. Armed Forces*, 202.

67 Jonathan Rosenberg, *How Far the Promised Land? World Affairs and the American Civil Rights Movement from the First World War to Vietnam*, for the quotes, White and Bunche, 187–188; for Randolph, 192–193.

68 Lewis, *W. E. B. Du Bois: The Fight for Equality*, 546–547.

69 Mershon and Schlossman, *Foxholes and Color Lines*, 222.

70 "Bronx Sergeant Gets Honor Medal; Second Negro to Receive the Award," *New York Times*, February 13, 1952, 4 and "Receives His Son's Medal for Heroism," ibid, March 13, 1952, 6.

71 William T. Bowers, William M. Hammond, and George L. MacGarrigle, *Black Soldier White Army: The 24th Infantry Regiment in Korea*, Washington, D.C.: Center of Military History, United States Army, 1996, 255–256.

72 "Receives His Son's Medal for Heroism," *New York Times*, March 13, 1952, 6.

73 Quoted in "Bronx Sergeant Gets Honor Medal", 4.

74 Truman, Harry S., *Public Papers of the Presidents, Harry S. Truman, 1951*, 628.

75 Monahan and Neidel-Greenlee, *A Few Good Women*, 266–267.

76 McCoy and Ruetten, *Quest and Response*, for the quotes see 237–238.

77 Dalfiume, *Desegregation of the U.S. Armed Forces*, 207–208.

78 Ibid., 208–209.

79 Ibid., 209–210.

80 Ibid., 210–211.

81 McCoy and Ruetten, *Quest and Response*, 242.

82 Dalfiume, *Desegregation of the U.S. Armed Forces*, 218–219. For more on Project Clear see Leo Bogart, ed., *Project Clear: Social Research and the Desegregation of the United States Army*, New Brunswick, NJ: Transaction Books, 1992.

83 McCoy and Ruetten, *Quest and Response*, for the army see 248, for the navy, 247.

84 Michael Cullen Green, *Black Yanks in the Pacific Race in the Making of American Military Empire after World War II*. Ithaca, NY: Cornell University Press, 2010, 110.

85 Gardner, *Harry Truman and Civil Rights*, 178–180.

86 Quoted in ibid. 182–183.

87 Ibid., 181.

88 Quoted in ibid., 194

89 Ibid., 183–184.

90 Anderson, *Eyes Off the Prize*, 180.

91 For the quotes see ibid., 186.

92 Ibid., 186.

93 Quoted in ibid., 188.

94 Ibid., 195–199

95 Quoted in ibid., 208–209.

96 Gardner, *Harry Truman and Civil Rights*, 159–160.

97 Quoted in ibid., 161.

98 Truman, Harry S., *Public Papers of the Presidents, Harry S. Truman, 1952–1953*, 798–800.

6 Historians Debate Truman's Civil Rights Record

1 Carol Anderson, "Clutching at Civil Rights Straws: A Reappraisal of the Truman Years and the Struggle for African American Citizenship," in Richard Kirkendall, ed., *Harry's Farewell: Interpreting and Teaching the Truman Presidency*, Columbia: University of Missouri Press, 2004, 99–100; also reprinted in Raymond H. Geselbracht, ed., *The Civil Rights Legacy of Harry S. Truman*, 47.

2 Michael R. Gardner, *Harry Truman and Civil Rights*, 221–222.

3 McCoy and Ruetten, *Quest and Response*, 221.

4 Bernstein, "The Ambiguous Legacy: The Truman Administration and Civil Rights," in *Politics and Policies of the Truman Administration*, Chicago, IL: Quadrangle Books, 1970, 303.

5 Berman, *The Politics of Civil Rights in the Truman Administration*, Columbus: Ohio State University Press, 1970, 240.

6 Harvard Sitkoff, "Harry Truman and the Election of 1948," in Harvard Sitkoff, *Toward Freedom Land: The Long Struggle for Racial Equality in America*, Lexington, KY: University Press of Kentucky, 2010, 190.

7 Geselbracht, *The Civil Rights Legacy of Harry S. Truman*, xiii.

8 MacGregor, Jr., *Integration of the Armed Forces*, 617.

9 For the quotes see Sherrie Merson and Steven Schlossman, *Foxholes and Color Lines*, 312–313.

10 McCullough, *Truman*, 915.

11 Robert H. Ferrell, *Harry S. Truman: A Life*, Columbia: University of Missouri Press, 1994, 292–293, 298–299.

12 Hamby, *Man of the People*, 640.

13 Brenda Gayle Plummer, *Rising Wind: Black Americans and U.S. Foreign Affairs, 1935–1960*, Chapel Hill, NC: University of North Carolina Press, 1996, 183, 187.

14 Penny M. Von Eschen, *Race Against Empire: Black Americans and Anticolonialism, 1937–1957*. Ithaca, NY: Cornell University Press, 1997, 113.

15 Mary L. Dudziak, *Cold War Civil Rights: Race and the Image of American Democracy*. Princeton, NJ: Princeton University Press, 2000, 83.

16 Ibid., 90.

17 Borstelmann, *The Cold War and the Color Line: American Race Relations in the Global Arena*. Cambridge, MA: Harvard University Press, 2001, 60, 82.

18 Gardner, *Harry Truman and Civil Rights*, 222.

19 Anderson, *Eyes Off the Prize*, 2.

20 Ibid., 3.

21 Anderson, "Clutching at Civil Rights Straws," 36.

22 Quoted in ibid., 46.

23 Clayton Knowles, "Truman Believes Reds Lead Sit–ins," *New York Times*, April 19, 1960, p. 21. For Martin Luther King's quotes see "Dr. King Sees Gain by Negro Sit–Ins," *New York Times*, April 18, 1960, p. 21.

24 Iskra, *Women in the United States Armed Forces: A Guide to the Issues*. Denver, CO: Praeger, 2010, 151.

25 Ibid., 8–9, 17.

26 Ibid., 24.

27 Ibid., 40.

28 Quoted in ibid. 63.

29 Ibid., 11.

30 Allan Berube, *Coming Out Under Fire*, 275.

31 Ibid., 276.

32 Ibid., 278.

33 Judith H. Stiehm, "Sexual Orientation and the Military," in John E. Jessup. Ed., *Encyclopedia of the American Military*, Vol. III, New York: Scribner Book Company, 1994, 2067.

Bibliography

Manuscript Collections

Harry S. Truman Library, Independence, Missouri (HSTL):

Clark, Tom, Papers.

Clifford, Clark, Papers.

RG 220 President's Committee on Equality of Treatment and Opportunity in the Armed Services.

Truman, Harry S., Papers.

Official File.

Post-Presidential Papers, 1953–1972.

President's Personal File.

President's Secretary's Files.

Library of Congress

National Association for the Advancement of Colored People, Records, 1842–1999.

Randolph, A. Philip, Papers.

Oral Histories

Gibson, Truman. Interview by Carol Briley, July 27, 2001. Transcript of tape recorded interview. Harry S. Truman Library.

Kenworthy, E. W. Interview by Jerry Hess, January 26, 1971. Transcript of tape recorded interview. Harry S. Truman Library.

Nash, Philleo. Interview by Jerry Hess, February 21, 1967. Transcript of tape recorded interview. Harry S. Truman Library.

Sweeney, Robert. Interview by Carol Briley, December 12, 1977. Transcript of tape recorded interview. Harry S. Truman Library.

General Bibliography

Allison, William Thomas. *Military Justice in Vietnam: The Rule of Law in an American War.* Lawrence, KS: University of Kansas Press, 2006.

American Presidency Project: Democratic Party Platforms: Democratic Party Platform of 1948. www.presidency.ucsb.edu/ws/index.php?pid=29599#ixzz1gjcWsNgE.

American Presidency Project: Republican Party Platforms: Republican Party Platform of 1948. www.presidency.ucsb.edu/ws/index.php?pid=25836#ixzz1gjzdv1Qs.

Anderson, Carol. *Eyes off the Prize: The United Nations and the African American Struggle For Human Rights, 1944–1955.* Cambridge: Cambridge University Press, 2003.

Astor, Gerald. *The Right to Fight: A History of the African Americans in the Military.* New York: DaCapo Press, 2001.

Bates, Beth Tompkins. "A New Crowd Challenges the Agenda of the Old Guard in the NAACP, 1933–1941." *American Historical Review* 102, no. 2 (April 1997): 340–377.

———. *Pullman Porters and the Rise of Protest Politics in Black America, 1925–1945.* Chapel Hill, NC: University of North Carolina Press, 2001.

Bellafaire, Judith A. *The Army Nurse Corps: A Commemoration of World War II.* Washington, D.C.: U.S. Army Center for Military History, 1993.

Berman, William. *The Politics of Civil Rights in the Truman Administration.* Columbus: Ohio State University Press, 1970.

Bernstein, Barton J. *Politics and Policies of the Truman Administration.* Chicago, IL: Quadrangle Books, 1970.

Berube, Allan, *Coming Out Under Fire: The History of Gay Men and Women in World War II, 20th Anniversary Edition.* Chapel Hill, NC: University of North Carolina Press, 2010.

Bogart, Leo, ed. *Project Clear: Social Research and the Desegregation of the United States Army.* New Brunswick, NJ: Transaction Books, 1992.

Booker, Bryan D. *African Americans in the United States Army in World War II.* Jefferson, NC: McFarland & Company, 2008.

Borstelmann, Thomas. *The Cold War and the Color Line: American Race Relations in the Global Arena.* Cambridge, MA: Harvard University Press, 2001.

Bowers, William T., William M. Hammond, and George L. MacGarrigle. *Black Soldier, White Army: The 24th Infantry Regiment in Korea.* Washington, D.C.: Center of Military History, United States Army, 1996.

Bright, Charles D., ed. *Historical Dictionary of the U.S. Air Force.* New York: Greenwood Press, 1992.

"Bronx Sergeant Gets Honor Medal; Second Negro to Receive the Award," *New York Times*, February 13, 1952, p. 4.

Brown, Jerold E., ed. *Historical Dictionary of the U.S. Army.* Westport, CT: Greenwood Press, 2001.

Bugee, Sylvia J., ed. *An Officer and a Lady: The World War II letters of Lt. Col. Betty Bandel, Women's Army Corps.* Lebanon, NH: University Press of New England, 2004.

Congressional Record Proceedings and Debates Appendix. 76th Cong., 3rd session., 1940. Vol. 86, pt. 16.

Congressional Record Proceedings and Debates Appendix. 76th Cong., 3rd session., 1940. Vol. 86, pt. 17.

Conn, Stetson, ed. *United States Army in World War II.* Washington, DC: U.S. Government Printing Office, 1965.

Coulter, Charles E. "*Take Up the Black Man's Burden*": *Kansas City's African American Communities 1865–1939.* Columbia, MO: University of Missouri Press, 2006.

Dalfiume, Richard. *Desegregation of the U.S. Armed Forces: Fighting on Two Fronts, 1939–1953.* Columbia, MO: University of Missouri Press, 1969.

Dean, Virgil W. *An Opportunity Lost: The Truman Administration and the Farm Policy Debate.* Columbia, MO: University of Missouri Press, 2006.

"Dedicate Ground for Hospital," *Sedalia Democrat*, June 16, 1940, p. 1.

Department of Defense. *The Military Heritage of Hispanic Americans in Our Nation's Defense: An Overview.* Washington, D.C.: U.S.G.P.O., 1990.

Dorset, Lyle. *The Pendergast Machine.* New York: Oxford University Press, 1968.

"Dr. King Sees Gain by Negro Sit–Ins," *New York Times*, April 18, 1960, p. 21.

Du Bois, W. E. B., *An Appeal to the World*, Papers (MS 312). Special Collections and University Archives, W. E. B. Du Bois Library, University of Massachusetts, Amherst, 1947.

Du Bois, W. E. B., *Against Racism: Unpublished Essays, Papers, Addresses, 1887–1961*, H. Aptheker, ed. Amherst: University of Massachusetts Press, 1985.

Dudziak, Mary L. "Desegregation as a Cold War Imperative." *Stanford Law Review* 41, no. 1 (November 1988): 61–120.

Dudziak, Mary L. *Cold War Civil Rights: Race and the Image of American Democracy.* Princeton, NJ: Princeton University Press, 2000.

Dudziak, Mary L. "Brown as a Cold War Case." *The Journal of American History* 91, no. 1 (June 2004): 32–42.

Earley, Charity Adams. *One Woman's Army: A Black Officer Remembers the WAC.* College Station, TX: Texas A & M, 1989.

Egerton, John. *Speak Now Against the Day: The Generation Before the Civil Rights Movement in the South.* Chapel Hill, NC: University of North Carolina Press, 1995.

"The Equal Rights Amendment and the Military." *The Yale Law Journal* 82, no. 7 (June 1973): 1533–1557.

Fairchild, Byron and Jonathan Grossman. *The Army and Industrial Manpower.* Washington, D.C.: Office of the Chief of Military History, Department of the Army, 1959.

Feldman, Glenn, ed. *Before Brown: Civil Rights and White Backlash in the Modern South.* Tuscaloosa, AL: University of Alabama Press, 2004.

Feller, Carolyn M. and Constance J. Moore, eds. *Highlights in the History of the Army Nurse Corps.* Washington, DC: U.S. Army Center of Military History, 1996.

Ferrell, Robert H, ed. *Dear Bess: The Letters from Harry to Bess Truman, 1910–1959.* New York: Norton, 1983.

———. *Harry S. Truman: A Life.* Columbia: University of Missouri Press, 1994.

———. *Truman & Pendergast.* Columbia: University of Missouri Press, 1999.

Finkelman, Paul, ed. *Encyclopedia of African American History: 1896 to the Present.* 5 Vols. New York: Oxford University Press, 2009.

Frederickson, Kari. *The Dixiecrat Revolt and the End of the Solid South, 1932–1968.* Chapel Hill, NC: University of North Carolina Press, 2001.

Frymer, Paul. *Black and Blue: African Americans, the Labor Movement, and the Decline of the Democratic Party.* Princeton, NJ: Princeton University Press, 2008.

Gardner, Michael R. *Harry Truman and Civil Rights: Moral Courage and Political Risks.* Carbondale, IL: Southern Illinois Press, 2002.

Gellman, Erik. *Death Blow to Jim Crow: The National Negro Congress and the Rise of Militant Civil Rights.* Chapel Hill, NC: University of North Carolina Press, 2012.

Geselbracht, Raymond H., ed. *The Civil Rights Legacy of Harry S. Truman.* Kirksville, MO: Truman State University Press, 2007.

Gibson, Jr., Truman K. with Steve Huntley. *Knocking Down Barriers: My Fight for Black America.* Evanston, IL: Northwestern University Press, 2005.

Gilmore, Glenda. *Defying Dixie: The Radical Roots of Civil Rights, 1919–1950.* New York: W. W. Norton and Co., 2008.

Glendon, Mary Ann. *A World Made New: Eleanor Roosevelt and the Universal Declaration of Human Rights.* New York: Random House, 2001.

Goldstein, Richard. "Truman Gibson, 93, Dies; Fought Army Segregation," *New York Times*, January 2, 2006, B7.

Green, Anne. *One Woman's War: Letters Home from the Women's Army Corps, 1944–1946.* St. Paul, MN: Minnesota Historical Society Press, 1990.

Green, Michael Cullen. *Black Yanks in the Pacific: Race in the Making of American Military Empire after World War II.* Ithaca, NY: Cornell University Press, 2010.

Greenberg, Jack. *Crusaders in the Courts: How a Dedicated Band of Lawyers Fought for the Civil Rights Revolution.* New York: Basic Books, 1994.

Grothaus, Larry. "Kansas City Blacks, Harry Truman and the Pendergast Machine." *Missouri Historical Review* 69, no. 1 (October 1974): 65–82.

Hamby, Alonzo. *Man of the People: A Life of Harry S. Truman.* New York: Oxford University Press, 1998.

Hartmann, Susan M. *The Homefront and Beyond: American Women in the 1940s.* New York: Twayne Publishers, 1995.

Henderson, Aileen Kilgore. *Stateside Soldier: Life in the Women's Army Corps, 1944–1945.* Chapel Hill, NC: University of South Carolina Press, 2001.

Hohn, Maria and Martin Klimke. *A Breath of Freedom: The Civil Rights Struggle, African American GIs, and Germany.* New York: Palgrave Macmillan, 2010.

Holm, Jeanne M. *Women in the Military: An Unfinished Revolution.* Novato, CA: Presidio Press, 1992.

Holm, Jeanne M. and Judith Bellafaire, eds. *In Defense of a Nation: Servicewomen in World War II.* Washington, DC: Military Women's Press, 1998.

Honey, Michael K. *Southern Labor and Black Civil Rights: Organizing Memphis Workers.* Chicago, IL: University of Illinois Press, 1993.

Horne, Gerald. *Black and Red: W. E. B. Du Bois and the Afro-American Response to the Cold War, 1944–1963.* Albany, NY: State University of New York Press, 1986.

———. *Communist Front? The Civil Rights Congress, 1946–1956.* Rutherford, NJ: Fairleigh Dickinson University Press, 1988.

Iskra, Darlene M. *Women in the United States Armed Forces: A Guide to the Issues.* Denver, CO: Praeger, 2010.

Jackson, Paul. *One of the Boys: Homosexuality in the Military During World War II. 2nd ed.* Montreal: McGill–Queen's University Press, 2010.

Janken, Kenneth Robert. *White: The Biography of Walter White, Mr. NAACP.* New York: The New Press, 2003.

Jefferson, Robert. *Fighting for Hope: African American Troops of the 93rd Infantry Division in World War II and Postwar America.* Baltimore, MD: Johns Hopkins University Press, 2008.

Jessup, John E., ed. *Encyclopedia of the American Military.* 3 vols. New York: Scribner Book Company, 1994.

Johnson, David K. *The Lavender Scare: The Cold War Persecution of Gays and Lesbians in the Federal Government.* Chicago, IL: University of Chicago Press, 2004.

Johnson, M. Glen and Janusz Symonides. *The Universal Declaration of Human Rights: A History of its Creation and Implementation.* Paris: UNESCO Publishing, 1998.

Kaplowitz, Craig A. *LULAC, Mexican Americans, and National Policy.* College Station, TX: Texas A & M University, 2005.

Kinchy, Abby J. "African Americans in the Atomic Age: Postwar Perspectives on Race and the Bomb, 1945–1967." *Technology and Culture* 50, no. 2 (April 2009): 291–315.

Kirby, John B. *Black Americans in the Roosevelt Era: Liberalism and Race.* Knoxville, TN: The University of Tennessee Press, 1980.

Kirkendall, Richard, ed. *Harry's Farewell: Interpreting and Teaching the Truman Presidency.* Columbia: University of Missouri Press, 2004.

Knowles, Clayton. "Truman Believes Reds Lead Sit–ins," *New York Times*, April 19, 1960.

Kremer, Gary. "William J. Thompkins: African American Physician, Politician, and Publisher." *Missouri Historical Review* 101, no. 3 (April 2007): 168–182.

Larsen, Lawrence H. and Nancy J. Hulston. *Pendergast!* Columbia: University of Missouri Press, 1997.

Lawson, Steven F. ed. *To Secure These Rights: The Report of the President's Committee on Civil Rights.* Boston, MA: Bedford St. Martin's, 2004.

—— and Charles Payne. *Debating the Civil Rights Movement, 1945–1968.* 2nd. Ed. New York: Rowman & Littlefield Publishers, 2006.

Layton, Azza Salama. *International Politics and Civil Rights Policies in the United States, 1941–1960.* Cambridge, MA: Cambridge University Press, 2000.

Leadership and the Negro Soldier: Army Service Forces Manual, M5. Washington, D.C.: United States Government Printing Office, 1944.

Lee, Ulysses. *The United States Army in World War II Special Studies: The Employment of Negro Troops.* Washington, DC: Office of the Chief of Military History United States Army, 1966.

Lentz-Smith, Adriane. *Freedom Struggles: African Americans and World War I.* Cambridge, MA: Harvard University Press, 2009.

Lewis, David Levering. *W. E. B. Du Bois: Biography of a Race, 1868–1919.* New York: Henry Holt, 1993.

———. *W. E. B. Du Bois: The Fight for Equality and the American Century, 1919–1963.* New York: Henry Holt, 2000.

Litoff, Judy Barrett, and David C. Smith, eds. *American Women in a World at War: Contemporary Accounts from World War II.* Wilmington, DE: Scholarly Resources, 1996.

Lurie, Jonathan. *Military Justice in America: The U.S. Court of Appeals for the Armed Forces, 1775–1980.* Lawrence, KS: University of Kansas Press, 2001.

MacGregor, Morris J., Jr. *Integration of the Armed Forces, 1940–1965.* Defense Studies Series. Washington DC: Center of Military History, U.S. Army, 1981.

Matusow, Allen J. *Farm Policies and Politics in the Truman Years.* New York: Athenaeum, 1970.

McCluskey, Audrey T. and Elaine M. Smith, eds., *Mary McLeod Bethune: Building a Better World: Essays and Selected Documents.* Bloomington, IN: Indiana University Press, 1999.

McCoy, Donald R., and Richard T. Ruetten. *Quest and Response: Minority Rights and the Truman Administration.* Lawrence, KS: University Press of Kansas, 1973.

McCullough, David. *Truman.* New York: Simon & Schuster, 1992.

McGuire, Phillip, ed. *Taps for a Jim Crow Army: Letters from Black Soldiers in World War II.* Lexington, KY: The University Press of Kentucky, 1983.

———. *He, Too, Spoke for Democracy: Judge Hastie, World War II, and the Black Soldier.* New York: Greenwood Press, 1988.

Mershon, Sherie and Steven Schlossman. *Foxholes and Color Lines: Desegregating the U.S. Armed Forces.* New York: Johns Hopkins University Press, 1998.

Meyer, Leisa D. *Creating GI Jane: Sexuality and Power in Women's Army Corps During World War II.* New York: Columbia University Press, 1998.

Minchin, Timothy J. *The Color of Work: The Struggle for Civil Rights in the Southern Paper Industry, 1945–1980.* Chapel Hill, NC: University of North Carolina Press, 2001.

Monahan, Evelyn and Rosemary Neidel-Greenlee. *A Few Good Women: America's Military Women from World War I to the Wars in Iraq and Afghanistan.* New York: Alfred A. Knopf, 2010.

Moore, Brenda L. *To Serve My Country, To Serve My Race: the Story of the only African American WACS Stationed Overseas During World War II.* New York: New York University Press, 1996.

———. *Serving Our Country: Japanese American Women in the Military During World War II.* Piscataway, NJ: Rutgers University Press, 2003.

Morden, Bettie J. *The Women's Army Corps, 1945–1978.* Washington, D.C.: Center of Military History, U.S. Army, 1990.

Morehouse, Maggi M. *Fighting in the Jim Crow Army: Black Men and Women Remember World War II.* New York: Roman & Littlefield Publishers, 2000.

Moreno, Paul D. *Black Americans and Organized Labor: A New History.* Baton Rouge, LA: Louisiana State University Press, 2006.

Morsink, Johannes. *The Universal Declaration of Human Rights: Origins, Drafting, and Intent*. Philadelphia, PA: University of Pennsylvania Press, 1999.

Motley, Mary Penick, ed. *The Invisible Soldier: The Experience of the Black Soldier, World War II*. Detroit, MI: Wayne State University Press, 1987.

Moye, J. Todd. *Freedom Flyers: The Tuskegee Airmen of World War II*. New York: Oxford University Press, 2010.

Myers, Andrew H. *Black, White, and Olive Drab: Racial Integration at Fort Jackson, South Carolina, and the Civil Rights Movement*. Charlottesville, VA: University of Virginia, 2006.

Nalty, Bernard. *Strength for the Fight: A History of Black Americans in the Armed Forces*. New York: Free Press, 1989.

Nalty, Bernard and Morris J. MacGregor, Jr., eds. *Blacks in the Military: Essential Documents*. Wilmington, DE: Scholarly Resources, 1981.

National Association for the Advancement of Colored People (NAACP) Records, 1842–1999, Manuscript Division, Library of Congress.

National Committee on Segregation in the Nation's Capital. *Segregation in Washington*. Washington DC: Government Printing Office, 1948.

Nelson, Anna Kasten. "Anna M. Rosenberg, an 'Honorary Man'," *The Journal of Military History* 68, No. 1 (January 2004): 133–161.

Nelson, Dennis D. *The Integration of the Negro into the United States Navy, 1776–1947*. Washington, D.C.: Navy Department, 1948.

Nichols, Lee. *Breakthrough on the Color Front*. Pueblo, CO: Passeggiata Press, 1993.

Novotny, Patrick. *This Georgia Rising: Education, Civil Rights, and the Politics of Change in Georgia in the 1940s*. Macon, GA: Mercer University Press, 2007.

O'Brien, Gayle Williams. *The Color of the Law: Race, Violence, and Justice in the Post-World War II South*. Chapel Hill, NC: University of North Carolina Press, 1999.

Orozco, Cynthia E. *No Mexicans, Women, or Dogs Allowed: The Rise of the Mexican American Civil Rights Movement*. Austin, TX: University of Texas Press, 2009.

Osur, Alan M. *Blacks in the Army Air Forces During World War II: The Problems of Race Relations*. New Imprint. Washington, DC: Office of Air Force History, 1986.

———. *Separate and Unequal: Race Relations in the AAF during World War II*. Washington, DC: Air Force History and Museums Program, 2000.

Palmer, Robert R., Bell I. Wiley and William R. Keast. *The Procurement and Training of Ground Combat Troops*. Washington, D.C.: Historical Division, Department of the Army, 1948.

Parker, Christopher. *Fighting for Democracy: Black Veterans and the Struggle Against White Supremacy in the Postwar South*. Princeton, NJ: Princeton University Press, 2009.

Patterson, William L., ed. *We Charge Genocide: The Historic Petition to the United Nations for Relief From a Crime of the United States Government Against the Negro People*. New York: International Publishers, 1970.

Pauly, Garth E. *The Modern Presidency and Civil Rights: Rhetoric on Race from Roosevelt to Nixon*. College Station, TX: Texas A & M University Press, 2001.

Plummer, Brenda Gayle. *Rising Wind: Black Americans and U.S. Foreign Affairs, 1935–1960.* Chapel Hill, NC: University of North Carolina Press, 1996.

———. *Window on Freedom: Race, Civil Rights, and Foreign Affairs, 1945–1988.* Chapel Hill, NC: University of North Carolina Press, 2003.

A Program for National Security: Report of the President's Advisory Commission on Universal Training. Washington, D.C.: US Government Printing Office, 1947.

Putney, Martha. *When the Nation was in Need: Blacks in the Women's Army Corps during World War II.* Metuchen, NJ: Scarecrow Press, 1992.

"Receives His Son's Medal for Heroism," *New York Times*, March 13, 1952, 6.

Rickman, Sarah Byrn. *Nancy Love and the WASP Ferry Pilots of World War II.* Denton, TX: University of North Texas Press, 2008.

Rosales, F. Arturo. *Dictionary of Latino Civil Rights History.* Houston, TX: Arte Publico Press, 2006.

Rosenberg, Jonathan. *How Far the Promised Land? World Affairs and the American Civil Rights Movement from the First World War to Vietnam.* Princeton, NJ: Princeton University Press, 2006.

Schirmer, Sherry Lamb. *A City Divided: The Racial Landscape of Kansas City, 1900–1960.* Columbia, MO: University of Missouri Press, 2002.

Scott, Lawrence, and William M. Womack, Sr., *Double V: The Civil Rights Struggle of the Tuskegee Airmen.* East Lansing, MI: Michigan State University Press, 1992.

Sherman, Janann. "'They Either Need These Women or They Do Not': Margaret Chase Smith and the Fight for Regular Status in the Military." *The Journal of Military History* 54, No. 1 (January 1990): 47–78.

———. *No Place for a Woman: A Life of Senator Margaret Chase Smith.* New Brunswick, NJ: Rutgers University Press, 2000.

Sherry, Michael. *In the Shadow of War: The United States Since the 1930s.* New Haven, CT: Yale University Press, 1995.

Shilts, Randy. *Conduct Unbecoming: Lesbians and Gays in the U.S. Military, Vietnam to the Persian Gulf.* New York: St. Martin's Press, 1993.

Shull, Steven A. *American Civil Rights Policy from Truman to Clinton: The Role of Presidential Leadership.* Armonk, NY: M. E. Sharpe, 1999.

Sitkoff, Harvard. "Harry Truman and the Election of 1948: The Coming of Age of Civil Rights in American Politics." *Journal of Southern History* 37, no. 4 (November 1971): 598–616.

———. *A New Deal for Blacks: The Emergence of Civil Rights as a National Issue, the Depression Decade.* New York: Oxford University Press, 1978.

Sitkoff, Harvard. *Toward Freedom Land: The Long Struggle for Racial Equality in America.* Lexington, KY: University Press of Kentucky, 2010.

Sklaroff, Lauren Rebecca. *Black Culture and the New Deal: The Quest for Civil Rights in the Roosevelt Era.* Chapel Hill, NC: University of North Carolina Press, 2009.

Skrentny, John David. "The Effect of the Cold War on African-American Civil Rights: American and the World Audience, 1945–1968." *Theory and Society* 27 (1998): 237–285.

Sullivan, Patricia. *Days of Hope: Race and Democracy in the New Deal Era.* Chapel Hill, NC: University of North Carolina Press, 1996.

———. *Lift Every Voice: The NAACP and the Making of the Civil Rights Movement*. New York: The New Press, 2009.

Taylor, Jon E. *Truman's Grandview Farm*. Charleston, SC: The History Press, 2011.

To Secure These Rights: The Report of the President's Committee on Civil Rights. Washington, D.C.: U.S. Government Printing Office, 1947.

Treadwell, Mattie E. *The Women's Army Corps*. Washington, DC: Office of the Chief of Military History, 1954.

Truman, Harry S., *Public Papers of the Presidents of the United States: Harry S. Truman, 1945–1953*. 8 vols. Washington, D.C.: GPO, 1964.

"Truman Talk on Training," *New York Times*, December 20, 1946.

Tushnet, Mark. *NAACP'S Legal Strategy Against Segregated Education, 1925–1950*. Chapel Hill, NC: University of North Carolina Press, 1987.

Vargas, Zaragosa. *Labor Rights are Civil Rights: Mexican American Workers in Twentieth Century America*. Princeton, NJ: Princeton University Press, 2005.

Vaughan, Philip H. "The Truman Administration's Fair Deal for Black America." *Missouri Historical Review* 70 (March 1976): 291–305.

Villahermosa, Gilberto N. *Honor and Fidelity: The 65th Infantry in Korea, 1950–1953*. Washington, D.C.: Center of Military History, United States Army, 2009.

von Eschen, Penny. *Race Against Empire: Black Americans and Anticolonialism, 1937–1957*. Ithaca, NY: Cornell University Press, 1997.

Wallace, Patricia Ward. *Politics of Conscience: A Biography of Margaret Chase Smith*. Westport, CT: Praeger, 1995.

Weiss, Nancy. *The National Urban League: 1910–1940*. New York: Oxford University Press, 1974.

———. *Farewell to the Party of Lincoln: Black Politics in the age of FDR*. Princeton, NJ: Princeton University Press, 1983.

Wexler, Laura. *Fire in a Canebrake: The Last Mass Lynching in America*. New York: Scribner, 2003.

White, Walter. *A Man Called White: The Autobiography of Walter White*. New York: Viking Press, 1948.

Wilkins, Roy with Tom Mathews. *Standing Fast: The Autobiography of Roy Wilkins*. New York: Viking Press, 1982.

Williams, Chad L. *Torchbearers of Democracy: African American Soldiers in the World War I Era*. Chapel Hill, NC: University of North Carolina Press, 2010.

Williams, Vera S. *WACS: Women's Army Corps*. Osceola, WI: Motorbooks International, 1997.

Wilson, Sondra Kathryn, ed. *In Search of Democracy: The NAACP Writings of James Weldon Johnson, Walter White, and Roy Wilkins (1920–1977)*. New York: Oxford University Press, 1999.

Witt, Linda, Britta Granrud, Judith Bellafaire, and Mary Jo Binker. *A Defense Weapon Known to Be of Value: Servicewomen of the Korean War Era*. Lebanon, NH: University Press of New England, 2005.

Wynn, Neil A., ed. *The A to Z of the Roosevelt-Truman Era*. Lanham, MD: Scarecrow Press, 2009.

———. *The African American Experience during World War II.* New York: Rowman & Littlefield, 2010.

The Yale Law Journal 82, no. 7 (1973).

Yarnell, Allen. *Democrats and Progressives: The 1948 Presidential Election as a Test of Postwar Liberalism.* Berkeley, CA: University of California Press, 1974.

Yellin, Emily. *Our Mothers' War: American Women at Home.* New York: Free Press, 2005.

Zamora, Emilio. *Claiming Rights and Righting Wrongs in Texas: Mexican Workers and Job Politics During World War II.* College Station, TX: Texas A & M University Press, 2009.

Zangrando, Robert L. *The NAACP Crusade Against Lynching, 1909–1950.* Philadelphia, PA: Temple University Press, 1980.

Zieger, Robert H. *For Jobs and Freedom: Race and Labor in America since 1865.* Lexington, KY: University Press of Kentucky, 2007.

Index

Page numbers in *italic* refer to figures.

You may be interested in these other titles in the Critical Moments in American History series:

The Battle of the Greasy Grass/Little Bighorn: Custer's Last Stand in Memory, History, and Popular Culture
By Debra Buchholtz
ISBN 13: 978-0-415-89559-0 (pbk)
ISBN 13: 978-0-203-11678-1 (ebk)

The Assassination of John F. Kennedy: Political Trauma and American Memory
By Alice L. George
ISBN 13: 978-0-415-89557-6 (pbk)
ISBN 13: 978-0-203-12078-1 (ebk)

The Battles of Kings Mountain and Cowpens: The American Revolution in the Southern Backcountry
By Melissa Walker
ISBN 13: 978-0-415-89561-3 (pbk)
ISBN 13: 978-0-203-08186-0 (ebk)